The
Post-
Bureaucratic
Organization

THE POST-BUREAUCRATIC ORGANIZATION

NEW PERSPECTIVES ON ORGANIZATIONAL CHANGE

CHARLES HECKSCHER
ANNE DONNELLON
  EDITORS

SAGE Publications
International Educational and Professional Publisher
Thousand Oaks   London   New Delhi

For information address:

SAGE Publications, Inc.
2455 Teller Road
Thousand Oaks, California 91320

SAGE Publications Ltd.
6 Bonhill Street
London EC2A 4PU
United Kingdom

SAGE Publications India Pvt. Ltd.
M-32 Market
Greater Kailash I
New Delhi 110 048 India

Printed in the United States of America

Library of Congress Cataloging-in-Publication Data

Main entry under title:

The post-bureaucratic organization: New perspectives on
   organizational change / edited by Charles Heckscher, Anne Donnellon.
        p.   cm.
   Includes bibliographical references and index.
   ISBN 0-8039-5717-3 (cl.) ISBN 0-8039-5718-1 (pb.)
   1. Organizational change. 2. Bureaucracy. I. Heckscher, Charles
C., 1949- . II. Donnellon, Anne M., 1943- .
HD58.8.P675 1994
658.4'06—dc20   94-11732

94 95 96 97 98 10 9 8 7 6 5 4 3 2 1

Sage Production Editor: Astrid Virding

CONTENTS

1 INTRODUCTION

Charles Heckscher

Lynda M. Applegate

This book began from a shared intuition. The authors of this collection, and many others involved in large-scale organization change, share a sense that current transformations in corporations involve a leap rather than a step: that their potential is more far-reaching than anything that has occurred since Alfred Sloan implemented the decentralized bureaucratic structure at General Motors in the 1920s. For 60 years, large companies have been engaged primarily in perfecting bureaucracy, but now they are engaged in breaking it. The implications of this transformation are only beginning to be sketched.

We approached this broad and complex topic through a post-bureaucratic collaboration. The authors began to meet in late 1990 to discuss their general sense that something new was happening in organizations. For most of a year we reviewed cases, working papers, and existing articles to gain more clarity. Then, over the following 6 months, we divided up the territory and wrote chapters, each of which was reviewed and critiqued by the full group.[1] The editors acted more as coordinators of the process than as directors, and basic decisions about what to include emerged from the entire group. Many predicted to us that this way of preparing a book would never work; and so we feel that our success in bringing it this far is some vindication, if only in a very small way, of the concepts we outline here.

The Concept of Structural Change

The search for an alternative to bureaucracy is almost as old as the concept itself. Until recently, however, it was a movement on the fringes—the domain of anarchists, humanists, and various other categories of impractical dreamers.

1

It was not until the early 1960s that the first serious claims began to be made that an alternative system of management was developing in the mainstream. We would trace our intellectual roots most directly to Burns and Stalker's *Management of Innovation* (1961), which delineated an "organic" form of organization: more team-based, more flexible, and less rule-bound than the traditional "mechanical" hierarchy. This has been followed by a trickle of works that have in the past decade begun to turn into a respectable stream. Best-sellers such as Peters and Waterman's *In Search of Excellence* (1982) have given the impression that "organic" features have already crystallized into a new model that is about to sweep the economy.

Yet the truth is that although many companies have joined in the anti-bureaucratic rhetoric, few have actually moved more than a step or two from traditional structures. The members of this group have all experienced the shock of disillusionment that comes from examining companies written up in one of the best-sellers or claiming to follow those prescriptions: All too often the exciting concepts fade into ambiguity (or even charlatanism) under closer investigation. We therefore begin with the hypothesis that a major change is occurring, but that it is only in its infancy. We treat this as a hypothesis to be tested, not a form of organizational salvation to be advocated.

Our starting point is not a theoretical concept but a kind of "bin" of empirical developments that tend in one way or another to undermine the pillars of bureaucracy. Many of these have been around for decades, but they have experienced a growth spurt in the past decade and have moved from the periphery to the mainstream of corporate management. They include the following:

1. Worker participation efforts, such as problem-solving groups on the factory floor; self-managing work teams with responsibility for scheduling, discipline, and quality; cooperative union-management efforts seeking increased quality and productivity.

2. Cross-functional task forces and teams in managerial and professional ranks, breaking across the "walls" of functional organization.

3. Mechanisms of "parallel organization," operating on the basis of multilevel consensus, often functioning side-by-side with traditional bureaucracy.

4. Information technology that facilitates much denser networks of communication than in a traditional bureaucracy.

5. "Organizational development" concepts and practices that seek to build the decision-making capacity of peer groups.

6. The opening of formerly closed organizational boundaries: for example, the formation of partnerships between different companies, the elaboration of networks of relationships with suppliers, and the willingness to lay off managerial employees and, conversely, to bring in "outsiders" when necessary.

7. Sharing of information that was previously held only at the top of organizations.
8. Recognition of the importance of negotiated solutions as opposed to solutions determined from above.
9. New explicit managerial roles: task force leader, change agent, coordinator, boundary-basher.

When Burns and Stalker wrote their book, these characteristics of "organic" systems were limited to a few high-tech companies: Today almost all large corporations are at least testing the concepts in some way.

There is a generic similarity among these developments; they put increased emphasis on relations of influence rather than relations of power. Or, to put it another way, they seek to build agreement among people with diverse knowledge and interests not through reference to a higher "level" but through direct discussion and persuasion. The common feature is the development of teamwork.

The grab-bag of development might, of course, be no more than that: a collection of useful innovations that can be added for particular purposes onto "traditional" structures of organization. If one thinks of organizations as loosely patterned, there is no necessary reason why these efforts should have major repercussions or should end in any more than incremental changes in familiar systems.

But the fact is that the efforts we have sketched, partial and incomplete as they are, do not drop so smoothly into place; they have a "radical" quality about them. They arouse resistance and conflict, and they require major changes in motivation and orientation. They appear to have a "logic" that does not fit easily with the bureaucratic type.

So we are led to the theoretical method of "ideal type" analysis. We start from the premise that organizations have internal structural logics and that sufficient violation of these logics produces characteristic patterns of discontinuous change: disagreements at the level of values, resistance, and conflict.

The classic ideal type is the description of bureaucracy formulated a century ago by Max Weber. Though no real organization may have all the theoretical characteristics of bureaucracy, the concept has proved a valuable reference point in a century of research on the dynamics of large organizations.

For the present, the most important thing about an ideal type is that it makes possible extrapolation from partial trends. If the collection of elements we have gathered above prefigures a new type—a transformation of bureaucracy—then it should be possible to work out the "logic" behind the scattered efforts we have observed.

We know that the new type, if such there be, is in a very early stage of development because we can find no developed exemplars of it. We have been to many of the companies that are cited as models for the future: the Saturn Corporation, DEC, and Apple; innovative parts of GE, IBM, AT&T, Honeywell, Allen-Bradley, and Becton-Dickinson; plants at Volvo, Shell, Cummins Engine, and General Foods. (We include two case descriptions in an appendix to this volume.) All of these turn out, on close inspection, to be exciting but also limited and problematic. There is not a single case that we can agree on as a solid demonstration of the generalizable significance of a nonbureaucratic structure.

But this is not necessarily surprising; the emergence of a structure is always halting and difficult. Bureaucracy, for example, hardly emerged full-blown. It was first developed in a few limited and specialized industries after the Civil War; it was not generalized to a widely applicable model until the 1920s; it became fully "worked out" in its details only during the 1950s. The complexity of the shift, in retrospect, was staggering: new forms of communication, reporting systems, reward systems, career paths, job structures, socialization, and social class dynamics—all these had to be developed to fit the requirements of bureaucratic organization. If we are right about the emergent post-bureaucratic form, it will involve the same level of complexity.

Thus our effort here is still an early one. We hope to build on those who have come before—Burns and Stalker and their descendants—by making use of the wealth of experience that has been gained in the experiments of the past decade. These have been both exciting and sobering: exciting because they seem to reveal enormous potentials for improvements in productivity, quality, and human growth; sobering because they have increasingly revealed the magnitude and difficulty of the task.

We need to make at least two types of analyses. The first is why we need a new organizational model—what is wrong with bureaucracy, and has it really reached the end of its usefulness? The second is what the new form offers in the way of improvement. These are not simple tasks. Bureaucracy, for all its bad repute today, had been an enormously effective form of organization, greatly increasing human capacity to carry out large and complex projects. It will be displaced only by something significantly better.

Why Change? The Nature of the Crisis

The first step in working out the "logic" behind a new organizational model demands that we demonstrate a compelling need for radical organizational transformation. Social adaptation theory convincingly argues that organizations undergo radical transformation when the old organizational model no longer enables a company to cope with the demands of a dramatically different environment. Even in the face of serious discrepancies between the demands of the environment and the capabilities of the organization, many companies first attempt to make small incremental changes while keeping the basic foundations of the organization intact. At some point, however, often when survival is threatened, radical corporate-wide "paradigm breaking" change is required. Critics of bureaucracy, especially from a humanistic viewpoint, have been around for over a century. But our search for a new "ideal type" of organization must be founded on the development of pragmatic and compelling business reasons for transforming the very nature of organizations.

From all accounts, the pace of change for businesses throughout the world during the last decade has indeed been dramatic and disconcerting. In the United States, the 1980s began with both opportunity and danger as deregulation in many key industries (e.g., airlines, banking, communications) and a rapid increase in new technologies created new business opportunities for the innovative entrepreneurs. Looking just at the United States, after a decade of almost no growth during the 1970s, the number of U.S. patent applications filed per year rose by 17% during the first half of the 1980s, and the number of shares traded daily on the New York Stock Exchange increased by more than double. But despite this activity, the standard of living remained flat while consumer debt rose by almost 60% and corporate debt increased from $1 out of every $7 in the 1960s to $1 out of every $2 by the end of the 1980s. At the same time, however, the reality of the loss of U.S. economic dominance in the face of stiff foreign competition caused company after company to embark on major restructurings aimed at decreasing time to market and increasing quality while dramatically decreasing costs. Familiar strategies, rigid hierarchies, and swollen middle management ranks became the targets of major organizational reform. Consider the following statistics, recently reported in the business press:

- Between 1987 and 1991, over 85% of *Fortune* 1,000 firms downsized their white-collar workforce; over 5 million jobs were affected. By January 1992, 22% were still looking for work and 13% had left the labor force. Of those who were reemployed, almost half were earning less than they had before. (Koretz, 1992)
- Approximately 25 million people—1 out of every 5 U.S. workers—was unemployed for some portion of 1991. (Murray & Wessel, 1991)
- In June 1992, just as a flood of students and new graduates entered the workplace, the U.S. labor market lost 117,000 jobs. During the first half of 1992, companies shed an average of 1,500 positions per day. (Greenwald, 1992)
- Nearly 1 million United States managers with salaries of $40,000 or more were laid off in 1991. In 1992, white-collar employees constituted 36%

of the non-employed workers in the United States, compared with 22% during the economic downturn in the early 1980s. (Overman, 1991)

But despite the wrenching change and tough-minded reforms, many firms—including such industry leaders as IBM, Kodak, Xerox and General Motors—have failed to reap the anticipated rewards. In a survey of *Fortune* 500 firms, fewer than 1 in 3 senior managers stated that profits had increased secondary to restructuring (Fisher, 1991). A longitudinal study of firms that had written off 10% or more of their net worth found that 2 years after the restructuring, in over half of the firms the stocks were trading below the market by 12% to 48% (Cascio, 1993).

Although the statistics above report changes undertaken by U.S.companies, this is not just a U.S. phenomena. A study of European companies reported that 90% undertook corporate change initiatives during the first half of the 1980s, with 33% reporting "radical change" (Thomson, Pettigrew, & Rubashow, 1985). And, it has also been reported that Japanese firms are making dramatic changes to their strategies and organizations to meet new economics and industry challenges (Drucker, 1991).

Information technology and changes in the character of the workforce were important forces that played a dual role in the above scenario. In one sense, they helped create the conditions for change, while also helping to manage the complexity and enable the creativity that the change demanded. Naisbitt (1984) traced the important role of technology and changes in the workforce to the creation of a new world order that he called the "information society." He anchored the change in the mid-1950s with key technical and human resource events.

From a technical perspective, he noted the initiation of transatlantic cable service in 1956 and, in 1957, the launching of Sputnik, the first satellite, as key achievements that laid the foundation for rapid, global information exchange. From a human resource perspective, the year 1956 was also significant as the first year that, in the United States, white-collar workers outnumbered blue-collar workers. In the words of Naisbitt (1984), "For the first time in history, most of us worked with information rather than producing goods."

Over the past 30 years, the changes in technology and the workforce have continued to influence our concept of organizations. Today, jet travel allows people to cross the Atlantic in 3 hours or less and communications networks allow information to travel around the world in seconds. Distance and time have lost their importance as major determinants of markets and organization structures. In addition, information has become a major economic good to be exchanged in place of tangible goods and services. In the 1990s, there are a number of examples of "virtual" companies—organizations comprised of many small, independent agents(or firms) that serve as nodes on an information network that enables them to achieve dramatic increases in scope and scale. Examples of these "global web" organizations include Colliers, in the real estate industry, and IVANS, in the insurance industry. These arrangements challenge both our legal and social definitions of an organization.

Just as information technology has radically changed how we view the boundaries between firms, it is also challenging our notion of boundaries within firms. As companies install sophisticated information and communication platforms, which have the potential to link everyone within the firm to a common source of organizational memory and a fully distributed network of relationships, the rigid walls around organizational layers and functions are deteriorating. In addition, personal portable technologies are enabling a new class of mobile worker, and a new class of work—"telework."

Turning to the human resource perspective, we see equally dramatic changes taking place. In the past, the hierarchy provided a clear career path and concrete expectations for workers at all levels in the organization. A fundamental tenet of the bureaucracy was that the organization would reward those who fulfilled their organizational obligations as set forth in written policies, job descriptions, and evaluation forms. This was a commitment that organizations made to individuals to secure their loyalty and cooperation: "We will take care of you if you do what we have asked."

In the 1980s, the commitment was broken in company after company as they attempted to restructure their organization to meet the changing competitive picture. Downsizing and delayering changed the career track for workers that remained, leaving no clear path for advancement within organizations. Low morale and decreased loyalty were commonplace in companies that survived the turbulent 1980s. The rapid increase in the number of temporary workers has also fueled the changing nature of corporate loyalty and commitment. Over half of all new jobs created since 1980 went to contingent workers with a much higher percentage of those being professionals.

Changes in the nature of organizational work placed added demands on the education and skill levels required of workers at all levels in organizations. Very few new jobs are created for those who cannot read, use mathematics, follow complex directions, and demonstrate initiative. Ironically, this comes at a time when literacy within the United States is at an all-time low.

Finally, organizations traditionally drew their employees, especially at management levels, from a homogenous pool of white males. Today, the increasing percentage of female, minority, and older workers is demanding that organizations develop new approaches that foster diversity and reap its benefits.

These changes are placing significant strain not only on organizations but also on society. The majority of the organizational and government labor policies in place today were devised in the 1930s or 1960s in response to the conditions and problems of those decades. Health insurance benefits, pensions, social security, welfare, medicaid/medicare, unemployment insurance, and other employee programs often trace their roots to the New Deal or the Great Society. As times and conditions have changed, the relevance of these programs has been called into question. New initiatives have risen in their place as organizations, and society in general, struggle to meet the needs of an aging population and workforce; to reconcile the conflicting needs of women, work, and family; to integrate minority workers fully into organizations and the economy; to deal with an increasingly transient workforce; and to improve the educational preparation of all workers.

Companies spent significant effort during the 1980s reorganizing to meet the challenges discussed above. But, as the 1980s drew to a close, many were forced to face the grim reality that the 1990s would demand even more radical change. For most, it became clear that despite their efforts to restructure, they were still being asked to respond even more quickly to deliver even higher quality products and services and to cut costs even more dramatically. Technology and changes in the workforce were continuing to demand new organizational initiatives. They had cut layers of management and increased spans of control to the point where many worried that "control" had been lost. They had pushed the hierarchy to the limit, violating many of the major tenets on which it was based. In the process, a new organizational model began to emerge.

Thomas Kuhn's (1970) analysis of scientific revolutions suggests that crisis is a necessary pre-condition to the emergence of a new theory. But when presented with crisis, most people do not immediately reject the existing paradigm. Instead, they attempt to relate the new evidence to their existing theories. They attempt incremental adjustments to the theory that, over time, begin to blur the basic tenets of the paradigm. Practitioners are often the first to lose sight of the details of the old paradigm as the familiar rules for solving problems are called into question. At some point, total reconstruction from new fundamental principles is required. During the transition, however, there is frequently an overlap between the problems that can be solved by the old and new paradigms. But, no matter which paradigm is used, there is a decisive difference in the modes of solution.

This is the point where we now find ourselves. A crisis, largely driven by the conditions discussed in the previous section, has called into question our current organizational paradigm. We believe that scientific thinking in this area is currently in a state of transition that, as Kuhn has emphasized, is being led by practice. As a result, the nature of the empirical evidence rests in the common patterns of solution that organizations have adopted as they attempt to cope with the problems facing each organization.

The Emerging Model: Dimensions of the Debate

Over a year and a half of regular meetings the authors of the following chapters developed agreement on many major elements; but we also uncovered some major debates and disagreements that run through our essays.

1. The first is whether the phenomenon we are trying to describe is a matter of contingency or of evolutionary development. The former view sees the post-bureaucratic form as useful in certain rather specific environments but not in others; the latter sees it as more adaptable than bureaucracy, and therefore *generally* superior to it. The contingency view usually suggests that bureaucracy works better in environments that are relatively simple and stable, whereas "organic" forms are better in conditions of complexity and rapid change. Though the argument is rarely developed explicitly, the implication is that organic forms work worse than bureaucracy in stable situations: for example, that they are more subject to loss of focus or excessive costs. These are weaknesses that are less important in periods of rapid change but that become crucial when the environment settles down.

The developmental view, by contrast, argues that the advantages of team-based systems apply everywhere—that when cost-effectiveness is needed, they can solve that problem just as well as they can the problem of the innovation. Evidence alone is not enough to settle the issue at this point; because post-bureaucratic forms are relatively new, they have not necessarily been able to show their full capacities. Like all the issues we have encountered, this involves the challenging process of extrapolation from existing cases.

2. A second dimension of debate has involved the relation of hierarchy and equality. The current wave of innovation centers on mechanisms of integration among peers—that is, on reducing the role that hierarchical superiors play in managing decisions. The question is, just how far does this reduction go?

All the authors agree that in a general sense, hierarchy is not going to vanish—that there is a role in the foreseeable future for levels of authority. We can also agree that alternatives to the use of authority are increasing. What we have not pinned down is how these two aspects of organization will relate when the current changes reach equilibrium. Thus, on the one hand, David Krackhardt argues that "iron law of oligarchy" will continue in force, though in a different form; on the other, Anne Donnellon and Maureen Scully pursue a more radically egalitarian vision.

3. These issues are intertwined with another dimension of difference: the relevance of human values, including participation and democracy, to the trends we are describing. There is little doubt empirically that these values have motivated many critics of bureaucracy. And today, even the most tough-

minded manager, such as Jack Welch of General Electric, is prone to use value-laden terms such as *empowerment* of employees.

But this introduction of human values into business policies makes many people—including some contributors to this book—uncomfortable. There is a strong current of thought that argues, with Milton Friedman, that "the moral responsibility of business is to make a profit." From this perspective, the sole test of organizational innovations is their contribution to performance, and other criteria only introduce distractions and distortions to our understanding. Even accepting the validity of discussions of the "good," moreover, there have been disagreements about what *is* good. One that surfaced early in our discussions involves the importance in post-bureaucratic systems of formalized processes of decision making and value-discussion, often taking the place of informal relationships. Some saw this process focus as liberating, creating a larger zone for equal dialogue among diverse groups; others saw it as oppressive, a depersonalization of relationships and an invasion of the personal sphere of beliefs.

It is, of course, extremely important to distinguish the values that concern us, and not to let these issues contaminate our interpretations of the evidence. For the most part, our focus will be on business standards of effectiveness. Yet we will raise at times other types of consequences—for employees, for communities, and so on. If the changes are as broad as we believe, they will, like bureaucracy, eventually penetrate to all aspects of the society; it is therefore particularly important to consider the consequences for the social realm.

4. Finally, and inevitably, there were differences about just what fit the category of *post-bureaucratic*. At times, as we discussed it, it seemed that nothing fell into the bin; at others, it seemed that almost everything did. What about a company with a strong emphasis on face-to-face teamwork within an otherwise traditional hierarchy? Or a company that has very flexible systems at the operational level, but a sharp separation between these and processes of strategic decision making? What about "Japanese-style" companies, which show respect for employees through their policies of lifetime employment and strong efforts at consensus-building but which are at the same time very heavily layered and rule-bound? Are these variants of bureaucracy or different modes of post-bureaucracy?

These ambiguities prevented us from settling on a single positive term to describe the phenomenon. For a time we used the term *network organization* but turned away from it as suggesting too radical a sense of free and unconstrained communication. Charles Heckscher's term in Chapter 2—*interactive organization*—came up late in the process and was not discussed by the group.

Those debates and others are reflected throughout the chapters that follow. Some are addressed directly, some by implication. Though we have not tried to unite behind a single detailed model, our extensive discussions have cleared much of the underbrush and make more visible the contours of the underlying terrain.

The Structure of the Book

Books share a limitation of bureaucracies in being linear. There is no way to organize the chapters so as to capture the tone of back-and-forth debate and mutual learning that characterized the discussions underlying them. We have grouped them into four basic units, besides the introduction:

I. Chapter 2, by Charles Heckscher, seeks to define the new structure as an ideal type—extrapolating from the concrete and limited examples of innovation the logic of an "interactive" system that goes beyond them. It outlines the fundamental weaknesses of bureaucracy and sketches a structure that can fulfill the essential functions of organization—the production of binding and effective decisions—without a bureaucratic hierarchy.

II. The second section consists of three chapters that critique fundamental assumptions of the old order and explore alternatives to them:

1. Anne Donnellon and Maureen Scully in Chapter 3 examine the ethic of individual *merit* and its various policy consequences, especially pay for performance. They argue that merit pay is fundamentally based on and reinforces bureaucratic assumptions, despite the veneer of individual empowerment. They also recommend a reward system for a post-bureaucratic order.

2. Benn Konzynski and John Sviokla's focus on advances in information technology in Chapter 4 lead them to a critique of the notion of decision-making *roles*. Going beyond the common image of a human "network," they suggest that humans and computers are increasingly involved in dialogue and interchanges. This radical dissolution of the role of the individual leads them to an image of a corporation as a bundle of decisions rather than of decision makers.

3. Nitin Nohria and Jim Berkley in Chapter 5 similarly undermine the assumptions of *location* and *office*. They propose that with advances in information technology the classical physical requirements for coordinated effort—proximity and documents—are no longer necessary constraints on organizing. They also argue that technology has created an "implosion of bureaucratic specialization into . . . cross-functional, computer-mediated jobs, such that individual members of the organizations may now be considered holographically equivalent to the organization as a whole."

III. Chapter 6—by Charles Heckscher, Russ Eisenstat, and Thomas Rice—stands alone in analyzing the process of change *from* bureaucracy *to* a post-bureaucratic order. It notes the high incidence of "successful failures"—efforts that start promisingly but mysteriously fade away—and seeks to distinguish the kind of intervention that is most likely to overcome resistances and establish itself firmly. It distinguishes this "collaborative" process from other frequently used strategies that fail to break the hold of the old order.

IV. Three chapters follow that raise problems and reasons for skepticism:

1. Jan Klein in Chapter 7 examines a currently widespread practice that seems to reflect post-bureaucratic values: quality management. She suggests that its key tenets—utilizing the knowledge of all employees and eliminating variability through the standardization of work methods—hide a paradox, creating an undesirable opposition between commitment and control. She offers several suggestions for managers who seek to avoid this "false dichotomy."

2. Fred Gordon in Chapter 8 introduces evidence from social psychology about the powerful dynamics of group pressure and conformity; he fears these will overwhelm any group that is not guided by clear leadership and policies. The role of bureaucratic hierarchy in this view is to provide an "outside" control on group dynamics, and he wonders how this can be accomplished without bureaucracy.

3. David Krackhardt in Chapter 9 uses the tools of social network research to identify several significant constraints on the new organizational form. He identifies three "laws" of social systems—focusing on a version of the iron law of oligarchy—and certain properties of emergent organizations that limit a move away from bureaucracy. He concludes, in a direct challenge to Heckscher's thesis in the ideal-type chapter, by proposing a contingency theory of organizational form.

We conclude with two case studies that the group discussed and that illustrate both the strengths and weaknesses of advanced cases today.

1. Allen-Bradley stirred a lively controversy within the group about whether it was a "real" example of the post-bureaucratic form, or whether it remained too hierarchical and constricted.

2. Shell-Sarnia illustrates some important mechanisms of a post-bureaucratic system, including the use of "meta-structures" in its Team Norm Review Board. It is one of the longest-lived and most successful examples, although limited to a single small plant.

It is fitting to end the book with cases, because this is clearly a domain in which practice is outstripping theory. We leave readers to draw their own conclusions about the validity of the basic intuition with which we began—and perhaps to move beyond it by a deeper understanding of current practice.

Note

1. Fred Gordon's chapter was the sole exception: It was a response written after the completion of the rest of the chapters, which seemed worth including even though it had not been through the group review process.

References

Burns, T., & Stalker, G. M. (1961). *The management of innovation.* London: Tavistock.

Cascio, W. (1993). Downsizing: What do we know? What have we learned? *Academy of Management Executive, 7*(1), 95-103.

Drucker, P. F. (1991, October 2). Japan: New strategies for a new reality. *Wall Street Journal,* p. 12.

Fisher, A. (1991, November 18). Morale crisis. *Fortune,* pp. 70-80.

Greenwald, J. (1992, July 20). The great American layoff. *Time,* pp. 64-65.

Koretz, G. (1992, September 28). The white-collar jobless could really rock the vote. *Business Week,* p. 16.

Kuhn, T. (1970). *The structure of scientific revolution.* Chicago, IL: University of Chicago Press.

Murray, A., & Wessel, D. (1991, December 12). Torrent of job cuts shows human toll of recession goes on. *Wall Street Journal,* pp. 1-8.

Naisbitt, J. (1984). *Megatrends.* New York: Warner Books.

Overman, S. (1991, August). The layoff legacy. *HR Magazine,* pp. 29-32.

Peters, T., & Waterman, R. (1982). *In search of excellence.* New York: Harper & Row.

Thomson, A., Pettigrew, A, & Rubashow, N. (1985). British management and strategic change. *European Management Journal, 3*(3), 165-173.

2   DEFINING THE POST-BUREAUCRATIC TYPE

Charles Heckscher

Although almost everyone involved in corporations today "knows" that major organizational changes are under way, it is frustratingly difficult to define these changes or to anticipate their course. One can say that they center on the notion of "teamwork," or lateral coordination; yet it turns out that some highly traditional and bureaucratic organizations have a great deal of teamwork. The variation among efforts is so great, moreover, and the results so hard to judge, that there sometimes seems to be no pattern at all.

In navigating this confused terrain, attempting to assess the probable results of change efforts, we need a map that will answer the fundamental questions: How far will this road take us? Where will it end?

I will argue that the current changes in corporate organizations can best be understood as part of a long-term shift with two basic characteristics. The first is that a type of organization is being invented centered on the use of influence rather than of power. The second is that this type of organization is not merely different from bureaucracy but is an evolutionary development beyond it, generating a *greater* capacity for human accomplishment.

The sequence of the text is as follows:

1. The introductory part tries to clear the ground of two related conceptual problems: first, the nature and use of "ideal type" analysis; and second, the question of how one can use evidence from partial cases to make an argument about a structure which does not yet exist (at least in complete form).

2. The second part explores the limits of bureaucracy, trying to disengage what are *fundamental* problems from those that are merely matters of poor implementation. The fact that there are bad bureaucracies does not imply that

all bureaucracies are bad; nevertheless, I argue, there are some critical problems that are in fact inherent to *all* bureaucracy.

3. The third part explores the emerging post-bureaucratic model.

- It sketches the key elements of the ideal type, starting from the master concept that everyone takes responsibility for the success of the whole rather than for a particular job. Here I suggest a positive term to describe what we are looking for—"interactive" systems—to fill in the definition-by-negation of the term *post-bureaucratic*.
- I distinguish this type from several "deceptive variants" that, although claiming to break the logic of bureaucracy, in fact reinforce it.
- I then look at *existing* approximations of post-bureaucratic systems in realms outside the corporation, because some of these have moved farther than the corporate sphere and may provide clues to the future. The two closest are the professions and science (as an institution); the later in particular has shown a remarkable ability to make clear directional progress without a clear director.
- From these examples I move to perhaps the central problem in innovative forms: the question of whether a nonbureaucratic system can effectively generate binding decisions and maintain enough discipline to function. I argue that it can—though the mechanisms to do it are still being invented. They involve creating legitimacy for decisions through *consensual processes* that involve key stakeholders in defining shared principles. One major element has to be a "meta-process" that decides how key decisions are going to be made—rather than relying on a fixed structure of offices, it must put together the right people and steps for each major case to gain support and legitimacy.
- Finally, I consider the question of whether this is a contingent form, appropriate only for certain sectors, or an evolutionary advance—and end up arguing the latter.

4. The final section reviews what evidence there is about the effectiveness of these systems, arguing that there is already some evidence that they are highly effective, and no good evidence that they are worse than bureaucracy on dimensions such as rapidity of response or ability to make major changes.

Method of Analysis

Concepts: Ideal Types and Developmental Stages

Post-bureaucratic organization is not a real system but an ideal type. An ideal-type description organizes reality by drawing, through the innumerable variations of real life, the boundaries where the terrain changes. These boundaries are in part deduced by logical analysis: They are patterns that "make sense." But they can also be recognized empirically in two ways. The first is by the fact that key elements from different sides of such a boundary mix poorly, producing conflict and resistance. The second is that one can observe *tendencies* to move away from the edges and toward the centers of the types. Thus, for example, if one introduces a few bureaucratic elements into a communal organization, one of two things is likely to happen: The new elements will be rejected as "foreign," or they will so infect the organization that other aspects will change as well, until the whole more closely resembles the bureaucratic model.

The level of excitement, conflict, and unanticipated change in the current restructuring of many corporations is the first indication that we are dealing with a new *type*, marked off from traditional bureaucracy. The conviction increases as we see that the changes "ripple" out to affect institutions far from the source. Career systems, for example, are being severely shaken by the need for flexibility in new systems; this in turn affects residential patterns (when is one secure enough to buy a house?), socialization (what expectations should one have in entering the labor force?), and class relations (how can one anchor one's identifications in an insecure world?).

These elements—socialization, careers, classes, the work ethic, and all the other institutions that interact with changes in industry—have grown over the past century into a coherent pattern with industrial bureaucracy at its core. Schools, neighborhoods, stores, banking practices all reflect in various ways the hierarchies of the corporate world. Thus, corporate bureaucracy today is held in place not only by its internal coherence and power, but also by the external pressures of the social institutions that interact with it.[1] If we are witnessing a change as fundamental as a change of type, then we should see strains in these surrounding institutions as well.

This contention that current changes cross a boundary is my first claim. The second is that the boundary marks a shift to a developmentally more advanced stage of organization.

This is directly counter to the more widely accepted theory of *contingency*. Lawrence and Lorsch (1967) proposed a quarter century ago that "organic" forms are appropriate to situations of high environmental complexity and uncertainty, but not to ones of routine and stability. Thus, in this view, neither form is "better" except by relation to particular environments.

The developmental claim, by contrast, is that one form is indeed "better" in the sense of incorporating the other, and of being able to adapt to a wider range of conditions. Such developmental sequences have been shown to exist in other areas of human action. For example, scientific theories are developmental rather than contingent. Newton's theory effectively accounts for many real-world phenomena and is still in practice used for these purposes; but relativity theory accounts in a coherent way for these phenomena *and* for others that Newton gets wrong. Similarly, Piaget (1932) has demonstrated the existence of stages of human learning: a child of 7 gets certain problems right, but a child of 12 can get both these *and* more complicated things right with a single consistent approach. The latter approach is not just different, or contingent, but *more advanced.*[2]

There have not been such convincing demonstrations of the existence of developmental stages of social organization,[3] but there is little doubt that they do exist. Max Weber's treatment of bureaucracy, for example, showed how effectively this structure *replaced* the communal forms that preceded it; and Alfred Chandler has extended the argument in his analysis of managerial capitalism's triumph over craft and other federative structures.[4] This does not mean that there are no craft organizations left. But it does mean that the bureaucratic form has a greater capacity for mobilizing human energy and cooperation. Though it originated in a few particularly favorable sectors—railroads and heavy industry—it has gradually extended its reach until it has penetrated almost every crevice of the economy.

It is this lesson, I believe, that should be applied to the present circumstances. The fact that organic forms are currently limited in scope does not mean that they necessarily will remain so. If there is reason to believe that they represent a general increase in capacity, then we should expect their extension far more widely than their current domain.

One commonly cited problem in this argument is in showing that post-bureaucratic forms can effectively produce binding decisions. This is something a bureaucracy is extremely good at, whereas there is a sense that participation and consensus-building makes it more difficult to make decisions and to enforce accountability. If this were true, then the new form would *not* be a step beyond the old—it would merely be different. The argument here, however, is that participative systems can be just as "decisive" as bureaucracies, though in a different way.

The Use of Evidence

The discussion of post-bureaucratic organization is complicated by the fact that it doesn't exist. To my knowledge there is no concrete example that truly exemplifies the type—certainly not in business, certainly not on a large scale or for more than a short period. Thus the analysis is more than a matter of culling "best practices" and investigating causes and effects.

The notion of a post-bureaucratic type is drawn from a set of (largely partial and short-lived) examples of organizations that seem deliberately to violate bureaucratic principles. Among the more fully-developed of these are ones that are often referred to in this volume: the Saturn Corporation, GE-Canada, Shell-Sarnia. More piecemeal examples range widely—shop floor worker participation efforts, "quality of worklife" and autonomous teams, cross-functional product development groups, participatory strategic planning processes, and so on. Many people have expressed a sense that these are in a vague way part of the same phenomenon—something to do with teamwork, with lateral coordination, with networks. It is this imprecise sense of a single phenomenon that this essay attempts to sharpen and define more closely.

The essential proposition here is that these mechanisms, which are currently growing up within bureaucracy, can be extrapolated to a full and distinct form of organization with greater capacity than bureaucracy itself. There are several reasons for believing this. First, a few cases seem actually to approach it, especially the "organic" systems reported in Burns and Stalker (1961) and similar research. Second, the range of these mechanisms has greatly widened in recent years, extending deep into old-line industries. Third, some recent change efforts go beyond the scope even of organic systems in trying to formalize organization-wide mechanisms: These include the Saturn's organization design team, composed of 99 employees from all levels of the corporation, which established the basic principles of the company; or Honeywell Commercial Aviation Division's 18-month process of organization-wide discussion of principles for organization change.[5]

The test of the adequacy of the type description cannot, however, be that it accurately describes existing phenomena: It doesn't. Most examples of "participation" and "empowerment," in fact, are merely cases of old wine in new bottles. There is no inconsistency in claiming the birth of a new form and arguing that most who aspire to it are missing the mark.

Testing the claim therefore involves making heavy use of theory to leverage a small amount of data. The model must pass a fourfold assay: (1) it must be *consistent with sociological laws* that have been grounded in other empirical analyses, (2) it must be *fundamentally different from bureaucracy,* (3) it must be *internally consistent* and logical, and (4) it must be *consistent with the available evidence* from the partial and fragmentary examples just sketched.

The Limits of Bureaucracy

It is not easy to take even the first step in this analysis, which is to understand the limitations of the bureaucratic form. Engulfed by the current wave of criticism, we tend to forget its historically demonstrated strengths. Most critics, moreover, make a crucial mistake: They fail to distinguish which aspects of these problems are results of *badly managed* bureaucracy, and which are *inherent* in the model. For if the main issues are of the first type, then the solution is to tighten up the traditional systems—to "clean up" the bureaucracy. If, however, they are of the second type, the solution is a much more complex transformation.

The concept of bureaucracy has been so heavily treated in both popular and academic literature that only the highlights need be sketched. The major concepts articulated by Weber are the same ones still used by most managers in their conscious planning: rationality, accountability, and hierarchy.

For Weber, perhaps the central concept was the differentiation of person from *office*: That is, jobs were defined by the needs of the organization rather than by the people in them. This was one of the most important breaks with prior tradition, when nonbureaucratic tax collectors, for example, had the job as a personal possession and defined it according to their own interests.

Thus the key to bureaucracy is the rational definition of offices. In order to guarantee the functioning of the organization, each piece has to be clearly specified in terms of its duties and methods. The more complete the specification, the more confident the leaders can be that their orders will be interpreted correctly, rather than being distorted by personal interests.

The principal boundary or point of conflict in the early growth of bureaucracy was with "communal" systems dependent on personal relationships; in the business world these included partnerships, federations, and craft networks.[6] Except for isolated niches, bureaucracy won the battle hands down. It was far superior in organizing large numbers of people in a goal-directed effort.

The Red Herring of Badly Managed Bureaucracy

As the triumph of bureaucracy has been consolidated, there have emerged many "failures of the first type"—organizations that are badly managed. It is, for example, common for a successful bureaucracy to become complacent and lose its focus on the mechanisms that got it to its position of dominance. A *good* bureaucracy is not fat: It establishes positions through a careful analysis of tasks to be performed. It is not soft: It has strong control systems that establish goals and reward performance in achieving them. And it is not necessarily inflexible: It can respond rapidly to demands from the top. These principles are built into the classic theories of bureaucratic management and have always been manifest in successful large companies.

When a company succeeds too well, however, and pressure from the environment diminishes, its focus may become dulled. General Motors, under the leadership of Alfred Sloan in the 1920s and 1930s, was a model of a good bureaucracy, tightly managed through clear objectives and measurements. Later, with lack of real competition, it added fat and lost its ability to evaluate. These problems do not require great inventiveness to fix.

But this type of bureaucratic dysfunction is a major source of confusion and distraction. When one evaluates an organization as ineffective, there are two choices: to better enforce the bureaucratic pattern, or to seek another one altogether. Many of the efforts at "de-bureaucratization" are in fact nothing but efforts to get rid of the fat and waste of a badly managed system and return to the pure, clear model.

In order to justify the highly uncertain search for something entirely new, it must be clear that the problems of bureaucracy are more fundamental than this—that they are inherent even in *well-managed* systems.

The Fundamental Problem of Bureaucratic Segmentation

There is such an inherent and fundamental limitation of bureaucracy, one that derives from its very foundation in the specification of offices: That is that *people are responsible only for their own jobs.* The point of the system is that it divides work up into chunks and holds individuals accountable for different pieces. If they move beyond their specific realms, or seek to communicate outside of their appointed channels, they cause trouble: they confuse lines of responsibility and authority. The paradigm of a bureaucrat's attitude—a *good* one as well as a bad one—is, "That's not my job"; and in the traditional organization, anyone who tries to break this bond will be *told,* "That's not your job." Improving bureaucratic management only makes this *more* true. Segmentation of responsibility is vital to the massive effectiveness of the structure.

This segmentation brings with it, however, a set of undesirable consequences.

The Waste of Intelligence

The first is that it systematically limits the use of intelligence by employees: The system uses only a small fraction of the capacity of its members.

The slotting of people into predefined offices would make full sense if, and only if, individuals were so matched to jobs by training and aptitude that the job used all their abilities.[7] But this is logically improbable, and by now it is clear that it is empirically false. Whenever employees, at whatever level, have been involved in decision making beyond the limits of the usual job descriptions, they have proved capable of developing improvements that their superiors could never do alone. This is the source of the success of Quality Circles and other shop floor participation groups: these have their limitations, but they *always* produce gains unforeseen by the industrial engineers whose "office" it is to maximize their effectiveness.

An essential assumption of bureaucracy is that the top managers can get into their heads all the necessary information to make the best possible decisions about the whole system; then the head can delegate pieces of implementation to people who are not so gifted. The top layer has a fundamentally different nature from the rest of the organization: It is the only place where the substantive questions of direction and strategy can be considered. All other levels deal only with implementation. In Weber's terms, this is a locus of charisma in the otherwise rational organization.

The alternative view is that strategy is best developed through a social process of discussion that uses the full intelligence of all. On purely logical grounds, it seems irrefutable that a successful mobilization of multiple intelligence will outdo any individual, no matter how smart. The issue then becomes an empirical one: Can such a system be made to work without falling into chaos?

The Formal-Informal Split

The second consequence of bureaucratic segmentation is a failure effectively to control the "informal" organization. The formal links of the bureaucratic structure are too impoverished to support the real work of organizations; if everyone really followed the rules, if everyone really went through the boss to work out relations with their peers, the system would grind to a halt. Indeed, unions have long demonstrated the effectiveness of the tactic of "working to rule"—following the formal structure of the organization to a T, which is even more devastating than a strike.

Therefore, a whole set of informal systems and relationships is essential if a bureaucracy is to work at all. But these informal systems are "hidden," as it were, from the control systems, comprising the ambiguous realm of "politics." These dynamics often do work in support of the organization, as has been convincingly demonstrated in the case of blue-collar work: The development and application of "working knowledge" even in assembly-line operations is necessary to smooth functioning, and not even the tightest bureaucratic controls can make it unnecessary.[8] At the professional and managerial levels of organizations, where the need for cooperation and the difficulty of control are much higher, the political realm is still more critical.[9]

In other cases, of course, "politics" works against the organization. At the blue-collar level it can become organized rate-setting or "soldiering"; among managers and professionals it can turn into empire-building and private deal-making. Such patterns are remarkably impervious to bureaucratic control. The famous management theorist Frederick Taylor devoted his life to stamping out "soldiering" by taking rational bureaucracy to new levels—trying to specify tasks so exactly, and enforce them so strongly, that the informal organization would be destroyed. He succeeded in driving the rate-setting practices further underground, but he never succeeded in eliminating them:

they remain a major feature of factory work to this day. Efforts to rationalize away white-collar politics have met with no greater success.

The art of "leadership" in a bureaucracy is largely a matter of understanding these subterranean processes—"how things really work around here"—and turn them toward support of collective goals. Nevertheless, this domain—the world of lateral connections beyond a single manager's authority—remains detached from the control systems of bureaucracy. There is little formal attempt to structure informal "politics"; compared to the steady development and learning about bureaucratic structures, this realm remains stunted, with little cumulative learning.

Even in the most favorable cases, under the best leadership, lateral politics are systematically limited: They do not maximally contribute to the functioning of the organization:

1. They are built from personal contacts and are dependent on accidents of friendship and personal trust. Thus they do not necessarily involve those with knowledge relevant to a decision; the political network follows paths defined by other, more personal criteria.

2. They generally function only in homogeneous groups, ones in which the members can easily trust each other because of their similarity; this is the source of exclusive "old-boys' networks." One of the great problems in integrating minority groups is that they disrupt the personal links that make organizational cooperation possible, thus pushing the structure toward more formal and "bureaucratic" systems.

3. The informal networks are built from series of one-to-one relationships; the building of *group* associations outside the hierarchy is viewed as especially threatening. People may view themselves as part of a category— "the programmers," "the old-timers," and so on—but they do not act in a concerted manner. Thus, achieving a coherent team effort across bureaucratic boundaries is extremely difficult.

4. When conflict among different groupings does emerge, as in the case study described by Pettigrew (1973), there are few mechanisms for resolving the dispute. Because the groupings themselves are unacknowledged by the formal organization, there is no way to discuss the differences. The conflict remains a matter of water-cooler conversation rather than open dialogue, and it is dealt with through backroom maneuvering and horse-trading.

5. When there are differences in view between levels of the hierarchy, a vicious cycle of power and resistance is easily set up. Middle managers, for example, often disagree with the dictates of the top: sometimes this is for "good" reasons (they know important things that the top does not) and sometimes for "bad" (they are resisting changes that might disrupt their domains). But in either case, it is difficult to overcome the misunderstanding.

The Crudeness of Organization Change

The third limitation of even the best bureaucracies concerns their pattern of change and adaptation: They do not effectively manage processes over time.

The common claim that bureaucracy is inflexible cannot be entirely accepted: One of the great successes of the structure was that, unlike traditional craft systems, it was able to respond quickly to changing commands from the top. And the differentiation of a strategic level of management, one of Alfred Sloan's major innovations, made it more possible than before to separate long-term issues from the daily pressures of operational management. Yet there remains a clumsiness about the process of change that has become increasingly visible in recent years.

Bureaucracies tend to evolve not smoothly, but in fits and starts: Periods of routine are punctuated by intense periods of revolution from above. This results, again, primarily from the segmented structure: By design, only the top of the organization has a full picture of the whole plan of change. Those lower down see only the pieces that they are "assigned"; they are unable to adapt smoothly to the inevitable shifts in relations to other parts of the organization and have to refer problems for formal resolution to their bosses. This results in a tremendous grinding of the gears.

Another way of putting this is that, as we have seen, management operates primarily through formal structure; change therefore almost always involves "restructuring." And restructuring—the shifting of job responsibilities and offices—is always a highly painful and disruptive process. The possibility of smoother, more gradual evolution is limited by the formalism of the system.[10]

The limitation of vision to the top further means that change in a bureaucracy is entwined with the charisma of top leaders, who necessarily have a very limited time in office to realize their aspirations. Thus the pacing and timing of change is forced into an artificially narrow range of possibilities.

Finally, the rigidity of the segmental structure typically results in a tendency toward inertia and *gradual degeneration over time*, which can only be countered by sudden and dramatic "shaking-up" from above. The reasons for this degeneration are several:

1. Rules tend to accumulate: Whenever a mistake is made, a rule is made to prevent its recurrence; but there is no process for undoing it again.
2. Operational responsibility tends to drift upward for much the same reason: When mistakes are made, higher levels take over direct review of that domain. Then there is no clear point or reason within the bureaucratic logic to push it down again.

3. Rules become "sanctified" rather than a means to an end. In bureaucracy, after all, people are *supposed* to be responsible for the rules but neutral with regard to the whole. The psychological tendency to identify with one's responsibility therefore leads to the emotional attachment to bureaucratic rules rather than to the wider goals.[11]

These dynamics, accumulating slowly, inevitably bring out the worst aspects of bureaucracy and bury the best. Then what happens is a "restructuring": The top levels see the irrationalities and try to re-balance the system. Bureaucracy therefore tends to move in fits and starts, accumulating little dysfunctions until it is reorganized and shaken from top to bottom.

There is a growing sense that effective organization change has its own dynamic, a process that cannot simply follow strategic shifts and that is longer and subtler than can be managed by any single leader. It is generated from the insights of many people trying to improve the whole, and it accumulates, as it were, over long periods. Dramatic moments of "revolutionary" transformation are only a small piece of it, and often are not the most effective way to bring about change.[12] If this is true—and there is much reason to believe it is—the bureaucratic structures are not the most effective ones for managing the process.

The Post-Bureaucratic Model

The Ideal Type

This definition of the weaknesses of bureaucracy brings the desired change into focus. The master concept is *an organization in which everyone takes responsibility for the success of the whole.* If that happens, then the basic notion of regulating relations among people by *separating* them into specific, predefined functions must be abandoned. The problem is to create a system in which people can enter into relations that are determined by problems rather than predetermined by the structure. Thus, organization control must center not on the management of tasks but the management of relationships; in effect, "politics" must be brought into the open.

This suggests a positive name to replace *post-bureaucratic:* Because of the crucial role of back-and-forth dialogue rather than one-way communication or command, I will call it the *interactive* type.[13] The set of mechanisms that drew our attention in the introduction all have to do with achieving effective organized action without the "prop" of a positional framework to predetermine the key relations: they are essentially structures that develop *informed consensus* rather than relying on hierarchy and authority. Examples of such mechanisms in industry include all kinds of consensus-based committees: task forces, product development teams, and problem-solving groups. These involve all those concerned with a given issue in discussion, gathering of information, and development of agreement.

In order to accomplish this basic shift, we can derive—both from theory and from the admittedly incomplete examples—the following conceptual description:

1. In bureaucracies, consensus of a kind is created through acquiescence to authority, rules, or traditions. In the post-bureaucratic form it is created through institutionalized dialogue.[14]

2. Dialogue is defined by the use of influence rather than power: That is, people affect decisions based on their ability to persuade rather than their ability to command.[15] The ability to persuade is based on a number of factors, including knowledge of the issue, commitment to shared goals, and proven past effectiveness. It is not, however, based significantly on official position. Relations of influence can and do form a hierarchy: some people are more persuasive than others. Thus this system is not in any strict sense "egalitarian." But the influence hierarchy is not embedded in permanent offices, and is to a far greater degree than bureaucracy based on the consent of, and the perceptions of, other members of the organization.

3. Influence depends initially on trust—on the belief by all members that others are seeking mutual benefit rather than maximizing personal gain. Without this basic trust, persuasion is impossible, because everyone assumes that others are trying to "put one over" on them. A system stressing influence must have a higher level of internal trust than one based on command and power. The major source of this kind of trust is interdependence: an understanding that the fortunes of all depend on combining the performances of all. Specifically, in a business, it derives from an understanding of the ways in which different parts of the organization contribute to the accomplishment of the overall strategy.

4. Because interdependence around strategy is the key integrator, there is a strong emphasis on organizational *mission*. The trend has been to focus on what the company actually seeks to achieve rather than on universalistic statements of values. It is often hard for an outsider to understand what all the effort is about: Most mission statements seem remarkably innocuous. They say something about improving quality and cutting costs, and something about the kind of business the company is in—rarely anything surprising. But the mission plays a crucial integrating role in an organization that relies less heavily on job definitions and rules. Employees need to understand the key objectives in depth in order to coordinate their actions intelligently "on the fly."

5. In order to link individual contributions to the mission, there is widespread sharing of information about corporate strategy, and an attempt to make conscious the connection between individual jobs and the mission of the whole. This enables individuals to break free of the boundaries of their "defined" jobs and to think creatively and cooperatively about improvements in performance. In the past decade, companies have greatly increased the dissemination of information about systemwide performance, even to blue-collar employees. A decade ago very few companies gave productivity data to blue-collar employees; now it is common. And even at the present day, in my own research, I have found most middle managers struggling to cope with the flood of new information about strategy and mission that they have been asked to absorb. Information technology has greatly facilitated the dissemination of information. Since computer networks tend to be quite open, this information often flows not just from the top down but is criticized and added to from the bottom up. This process increases the *credibility* of the data being shared.

6. The focus on mission must be supplemented by guidelines for action: these, however, take the form of *principles* rather than rules. The difference is that principles are more abstract, expressing the *reasons behind* the rules that are typical of bureaucracy. The use of principles carries a major advantage and a major danger. The advantage is that principles allow for flexibility and intelligent response to changing circumstances: People are asked to think about the reasons for constraints on their actions, rather than rigidly following procedures. The danger is that this flexibility can be intentionally or unintentionally abused, threatening the integration of the system. The dangers are reduced by two mechanisms: the creation of trust, derived especially from a clear understanding of the interdependence among all; and by periodic reviews and discussions of the principles to be sure that they accurately capture what is needed and have not been distorted. Post-bureaucratic organizations spend a great deal of time developing and reviewing principles of action.

7. Because of the fluidity of influence relations by comparison to offices and authority, decision-making processes must be frequently reconstructed; they cannot be directly "read" from an organization chart. The choice of "who to go to" is determined by the nature of the problem, not by the positions of those initially raising it. Thus, processes are needed for *deciding how to decide*—what might be called "meta-decision-making" mechanisms. In a number of companies there are cross-functional and perhaps cross-level committees that sort issues and try to develop appropriate processes for each of them. To choose a single example: At a Shell plant in Canada, issues that cannot be dealt with by individual teams of workers go to a "team norm review board" composed of operators, union officials, and managers; this

committee then establishes a way of resolving the problem—they may, for example, set up a subcommittee, or a series of meetings of the affected groups, or call for additional information from inside or outside, or some combination of these tactics.

8. Though relationships of trust are a critical ingredient in these systems, these are not the warm *gemeinschaft* solidarities of traditional communities, or even of the communal version of bureaucracy. Relationships in such a system are formalized and specialized to a high degree: it is a matter of "knowing who to go to" for a particular problem or issue, rather than a matter of building a stable network of friendship relations. Thus influence relations are wider and more diverse, but also shallower and more specific, than those of traditional "community."[16] Managers in systems moving toward a more interactive form often report a sense of loneliness and isolation, in comparison to the "old days" of communal bureaucracy.[17] Information systems have also facilitated the building of temporary networks. It is now possible in some companies for managers to put out a general message asking for help on a given project, or to collect a list of people who have knowledge and experience in the area: they can maintain contacts with people whom they never meet face to face.

9. In order for a system of influence to function, there must be ways of verifying and publicizing reputations. There must, therefore, be unusually thorough and open processes of association and peer evaluation, so that people get a relatively detailed view of each others' strengths and weaknesses. Perhaps the best example of such systems in industry is in investment banking: in many such firms people work in a wide variety of peer teams and are constantly involved in mutual evaluation.[18]

10. A post-bureaucratic system is relatively open at the boundaries. A critical manifestation of this is career patterns: Unlike the situation in large bureaucracies, there is no expectation that employees will spend their entire careers in one organization. There is far more tolerance for outsiders coming in and for insiders going out. This ingredient of the pattern has recently caused great distress in the closed communities of the corporate management. The competitive pressures of the 1980s have caused widespread managerial layoffs for the first time, and simultaneously the speed of technical innovation has required increased hiring of outsiders. Both these developments have threatened the "family" atmosphere that has fostered unity and cooperation in the past. A second aspect of "openness" is the growth of alliances and joint ventures among different firms. These have been growing explosively in recent years even among firms, such as AT&T or IBM, which have had a long tradition of "going it alone."

11. The problem of equity acquires some new wrinkles. In a bureaucratic system, the main touchstone is always objectivity and equality of treatment:

Thus, there is a constant effort to devise rules for treatment of employees, and to minimize the element of personal judgment. In a post-bureaucratic order there is first of all an effort to reduce rules, and concomitantly an increased pressure to recognize the variety of individual performances. This is a major point of tension in many innovating companies at the moment. It is likely that the solution involves the development of *public standards* of perform-ance, openly discussed and often negotiated with individual employees, against which they will be measured; this is an apparently increasingly common approach to compensation.

12. Time is structured in a distinctly different way from a bureaucracy. In the latter, decisions are made with an expectation of permanence: "This is the right way of doing things." Review processes occur at regular intervals, usually annually in a budgeting process, as a way of checking that things are functioning as they should—but not with the anticipation of making funda-mental changes. Thus, structural change in bureaucracy comes as something of a surprise, as a dramatic "break" in the flow of events. A post-bureaucratic system, by contrast, builds in an expectation of constant change, and it there-fore attaches time frames to its actions. One element in structuring a process is to determine checkpoints for reviewing progress and for making correc-tions, and establishing a time period for reevaluating the basic direction and principles of the effort. These time periods are not necessarily keyed to the annual budget cycle: They may be much shorter or much longer, depending on the nature of the task. This flexibility of time is essential to adaptiveness because the perception of a problem depends on putting it in the right time frame. If one focuses—as most managers do—on the issues that must be dealt with in the next week, one will simply never recognize the existence of issues that have a longer "cycle time"; and of course the reverse is equally true. The ability to manage varying time frames is a major advantage of the post-bureaucratic system.

Deceptive Variants

In the move to "de-bureaucratize" corporations, many things have been tried that fit the vague "feeling" of interactive systems—seeking to move away from rule-boundedness and toward more involvement or participation—but that do not fall into the more specific type just defined. The type can be further delineated by exploring what it is *not*.

Cleaned Bureaucracy

Probably the most common move is not to move away from the principles of bureaucracy at all, but merely to clean it up. This is rarely a conscious strategy: Those who employ it use the language of "empowerment" and "de-bureaucratization." But what they are doing is fundamentally different.

The core of this version of change is increasing the autonomy of the parts of the organization: Its proponents sometimes talk about "making the boxes larger." What this means is that the scope of responsibility of those lower in the organization is widened, so that operational authority is decentralized. Frequently this involves a revival of Sloan's principles of "Management By Objectives": rewarding people according to their success in meeting the goals established for their particular organizational "boxes."

Though this may feel revolutionary to an old bureaucracy encrusted with decades of rules and procedures, and though the trumpets of novelty may sound aloud, it is in actuality nothing but a return to the roots. Weber saw bureaucracy as providing scope for autonomous action by experts; and Sloan and Dupont, as they elaborated industrial structures in the early years of this century, included decentralization of operational responsibility as a basic principle. The fact that these principles have often been violated is a sign of the systematic tendency to degeneration discussed earlier; returning to the starting point does not change this tendency.

Other variants of this "false" version include most "Just-In-Time" production systems and most forms of "Total Quality Management." These consist in essence of putting bureaucratic tools of analysis in the hands of the workers themselves, and giving them the autonomy to apply them. Thus they tighten up, eliminate slack, and reduce layers of hierarchy; but they do nothing to increase dialogue among various parts of the organization or create a system of collective experimentation.[19]

Perhaps the sharpest conceptualization of this approach is Peter Drucker's model of "the new organization." His two central examples are the British Civil Service in India and a symphony orchestra. In each case what you have is a single all-knowing and all-powerful force at the center—the Civil Service administrator; the conductor—holding together a group of otherwise autonomous individuals.[20] This is undoubtedly a version of "empowerment," but it is not an interactive system: Consensual dialogue is absent. And, it should be noted, neither orchestras nor the Civil Service are noted for their ability to evolve gracefully in response to changing environments.

What marks the *interactive* model is dialogue among boxes, not increasing their size. The pull toward autonomy—"Tell me what to do and leave me alone"—is a profoundly bureaucratic instinct that does nothing to improve the *basic* weaknesses discussed above. One can therefore observe in corporations that have pursued such a decentralizing strategy an immediate tendency to recentralize, to put layers back in. Sometimes this is a reaction to mistakes and loss of uniformity; sometimes it is a way of maintaining career opportunities; but either way it is a concession to the logic of the old order.

Over the long run, indeed, the pattern of bureaucratic evolution is an oscillation between centralizing and decentralizing moves; in recent years it appears this oscillation has speeded up in many companies, because *neither* solution deals with the essential problems.[21]

If the mark of an ideal-type divide is, as we have argued, a tendency to move toward the center of the type, this difficulty on the part of many companies in "escaping" from bureaucracy is evidence of its solidity. The call for teamwork and dialogue leads toward a *different* type; but the stress on autonomy is a reinterpretation that strips it of its challenge and brings this dynamic safely back within the old paradigm.

The Closed Community

A different "alternative" to bureaucracy is to develop a strong and unified culture. IBM is—or until its recent troubles, was—often cited as the model for the success of this approach; the claim was that such shared values made tight control by rules less necessary and promoted unity of purpose.

The notion of a strong culture is however not a new one; it developed quite early from the weaknesses of the pure bureaucratic form. As early as the 1920s, leaders of corporations began consciously structuring their organizations as *communities*, stressing values of loyalty and cooperation. And though IBM may be more self-conscious than most, the growth of strong closed communities is widely characteristic of large firms.

Among the signs of this was the growth of policies designed to attach people permanently to particular firms, especially nonportable pensions. More subtly, career success came increasingly to depend on mastering the cultural codes of the company: clothes, patterns of speech, acceptable behavior. It was really this development that William Whyte (1956) caught in *The Organization Man*, when he complained of the growing pressure for internal conformity. He was one of many who described and criticized the importance of surface presentation and image, and the significance of internal rituals and symbols. A number of influential writers, indeed, have used metaphors of family or feudalism to describe the closeness of the corporate community.[22]

All this appears alien to the sober logic of bureaucracy, in which appointment is supposed to depend entirely on rational criteria of technical skill and measurable performance. The communal elements introduce a number of apparently counterproductive factors into the equation. They make it very difficult, for example, to exert effective evaluation and discipline: Even poor performers in such organizations tend to be carried for long periods in order to maintain the "family" relationship, and layoffs are very rare. They restrict the range of strategic flexibility by installing a set of "corporate values" as an anchor for the community. And they create a sense of in-group superiority that can dull responses to the outside world.

Despite these evident dangers, all large corporations with which I am familiar adopted this approach to a significant degree, not just recently but from the early years of the century. General Motors and Dupont were never mere bureaucracies; they greatly stressed loyalty and shared identity. Typical Japanese firms pushed the symbols of unity still further—as in the famed morning calisthenics—and a few U.S. counterparts such as IBM approached the same level. Their success has generated a number of theories touting the virtues of deliberately developed "corporate culture."[23]

The virtue of this model, counterbalancing its vices, is the relatively high level of trust and cooperation that it engenders. In effect, it fills one of the gaps of classic bureaucracy by *organizing* the informal or "irrational" elements of human groups around the good of the whole.

The building of a community overcomes much of the formalism of the bureaucratic order. It gives a common focus to all, in contrast to the narrow job focus of the bureaucrat. Leaders in such organizations commonly establish credibility by working their way up through a range of functions and tasks, helping in this way to break down the "walls" among the more narrowly defined segments. And there is a feeling of "specialness" unifying employees, deliberately reinforced by policies and symbols that distinguish the group from the outside world.

Thus there is a greater ability in such an organization to adapt flexibly through informal cooperation, without the clumsy restructuring of a bureaucratic environment. The peer networks that remain underground in a bureaucracy here are structured by the relation to a shared set of values: "Doing one's job" means, in part, furthering these general aims as well as one's specific job description. Teamwork is potentially more open and more effective. Decentralization of operations becomes easier because lower levels have a clearer sense of what their job is "about" in relation to the whole and do not have to be given as many specific instructions.

These virtues, which have been effectively demonstrated in many Japanese firms, have led some to argue that this model represents the future of organization. It has produced a popular wave of writing and consulting that emphasizes the importance of leadership and the definition of *special* values distinguishing the firm from others.[24]

Despite its strengths, however, the limitations of this form remain grievous:

1. The values that hold the system together, being relatively narrow and specific to the company, can become barriers to needed change. To take two examples:
   - At United Parcel Service, the long-held traditions that managers begin by working on the trucks and that coffee not be allowed at desks have interfered

with the growing need to recruit technicians and engineers. These seemingly petty issues became major disputes because they were so freighted with the symbolism that united employees.[25]

- At AT&T, the traditional values of unconditional quality and of universal service continue, after a decade of deregulation and change efforts, to hold back the company's move into a more competitive environment.

The values of bureaucracy, being extremely abstract and formal, are compatible with a very wide range of organizational practices: the bureaucrat says, in effect, "Tell me what to do and I'll do my best." The closed community increases the amount of lateral cooperation and trust by narrowing these values. This generates a sense of unity at the expense of limiting the range of action.

2. The tendency to close off to the outside—to see oneself as "better" than the environment—reduces flexibility across company boundaries. It is extremely difficult to incorporate lateral hires: indeed, Japanese firms have made it virtually impossible to join above the entry level. And, conversely, it is difficult to get rid of people, since the ethic of "family" unity makes rejection difficult. It is very likely, though I have no real evidence of this, that it also makes more difficult the kind of project partnerships that are becoming an increasingly valuable technique for innovation.

3. The promises of security on which such closed cultures depend introduce major rigidities into the system that only very large companies can tolerate—and nowadays not even them. Even IBM has found itself unable to deal with surpluses by moving people around inside the company; after holding out far longer than most others, it finally was forced to abandon its *de facto* security policies.

4. The closed community is highly dependent on the leader, and especially on the founder. He (occasionally she) not only plays the formal role of establishing direction but becomes the symbolic embodiment of the values of the corporation. Thus one finds, at Toyota or IBM, a tremendous *reverence* for the founder and leader. But when the leader and direct descendants depart—the Watsons (at IBM), the Fords, the Duponts, Toyoda (at Toyota)—a vulnerability is revealed: It is hard for anyone who does not wear the mantle to sustain the burden of such leadership. At IBM John Akers, the first CEO not directly descended from the founder, expressed intense public frustration at the level of complacency he found in the company and the difficulty of waking it to market realities. Toyota, meanwhile—to take another good example of the type—has begun to find that its values conflict with those of young engineers that it needs.[26]

For these reasons this model, which was extremely popular during the "discovery" of Japanese management a decade ago, now appears much less attractive. It is in practice less widely seen as an alternative to bureaucracy; and on theoretical grounds it does not stand up as a model that transcends the old limits.

The Market Model

A third alternative that has gained a great deal of recent attention is again motivated by a desire radically to transform bureaucracy: It seeks to apply the *market* system to organizations. One core of the "Reagan revolution" was the claim that markets are generally better than hierarchies. This view has manifested itself within corporations in an increased use of subcontractors, in the formation of "business units" that must pass market tests, and in the pressure for functional groups such as information systems to "sell" their products to internal "customers."

It is important first to distinguish this type from the "cleaned bureaucracy" discussed above: It is possible to use financial incentives simply as a way of making units more autonomous within the overall hierarchy. Here we are talking of something different: segments of a company in which the goals are not set from above, but are allowed to vary according to lateral contractual negotiations. Here is an example of the difference: A good bureaucratic management might set a goal for maintenance services of 10% cost improvement and reward the department based on its achievement of the goal; but a "market" approach would require maintenance to compete with outside subcontractors, with rewards depending directly on whether others buy their services or not.

The problem with this form is the problem with markets: Economic contracting is not a sufficient mechanism for coordinating activity. Formal organizations are able to set *collective goals* in a way that markets are not; and the ability to pull people together around a goal is crucial to much human accomplishment. That is why bureaucracies developed in the first place and succeeded in taking over large parts of the market domain.[27] It is therefore not possible simply to "reverse field" and go back to a model of individuals in a market.

When you begin to put market mechanisms into a firm, this need for coordination produces a paradoxical result: The setting of goals becomes more opaque and distant. Individuals understand less what is really going on and focus increasingly on their own piece of the action. Thus, internal battles tend to become fiercer—as suggested by this quote from a General Electric manager at a time when "market" mechanisms were being pushed hard:

> GE is a very difficult place for any middle manager to operate. . . . It's very entrepreneurial, and you can get huge amounts of resources if upper management supports you. It's exciting if you're a risk taker. On the other hand, the power base can be taken away from you at any moment. (personal interview, 1989)

When a corporation creates internal markets, in other words, these are very far from being the pure unfettered markets of classical economics: They are heavily structured by higher management, which determines the conditions that will best shape the incentives to contribute to the good of the whole. And the very emphasis on individual contracting reduces the possibility of wider understanding and dialogue.[28]

There is not much solid evidence on the success of this type of reform, because it (like the interactive form) has nowhere been implemented with real thoroughness. Some bits and pieces suggest that it may create unhealthy dynamics: for example, a small group of "superstars" who push their interests at the expense of others; an instability and short-term perspective, and so on.[29] A fuller analysis, however, would be required to put it up against the interactive model: an attempt to sort out whether these problems are short-term errors of implementation or fundamental to the approach.

But the point here is at least to *distinguish* it from the interactive form that is the subject of this essay. The two share one crucial feature: They both arise from an antibureaucratic impulse, an attempt to break down formal rules and constraints. But after that they lead in opposite directions: the market model toward a network of specified contractual ties, and the interactive one toward links of dialogue and trust. The market model moreover preserves the essential ingredient of bureaucracy, which is the separation of members into sharply discrete parts brought together only at the top.

Simple Federation (The Negotiated Order)

One final strand is worth noting: There are those who see the future in terms of simple federations, with essentially no hierarchy. Though these arguments are rarely worked through explicitly, they generally swing toward the *opposite* of bureaucracy rather than the developmentally inclusive model sketched here. It is similar to the market model in attempting to preserve individual freedom in a structure that (it is claimed) will "add up" to benefits for all.[30]

The main problem with pure federation is the same as with the market model: There is no way to develop overall strategy. Action "emerges" out of the interplay of discrete parts—not in this case on a purely contractual basis, but nevertheless a web of negotiated relations. This structure lacks a method of *reflection* on what emerges so that people can evaluate whether it works and understand their relation to the whole.

Such higher-order mechanisms of reflection and the development of *binding* decisions on strategy are central to the interactive model: they are what I have referred to above as "meta-decision-making mechanisms." The interactive model of an organization has a "consciousness"—a way of making the whole explicit, lifting the parts out of their particularistic focus and having discussions about their relation to the whole. It is not an individualistic and lateral type of structure, as is true of both markets and simple federations; it is rather collective and hierarchical. But the key innovation is that hierarchy is legitimated through dialogue.

Analogues: Science and the Professions

Although large business organizations are struggling to discover the first principles of a more interactive form, there exist other institutions that have been wrestling with the problem for centuries. Two in particular have many of the characteristics of the post-bureaucratic order: the professions, and scientific inquiry. These are forms of human organization that have achieved much and survived long without the benefits of a clear bureaucratic focus and hierarchy.

The professions are the older institution. From the perspective of this essay, a key characteristic (frequently cited by scholars of the field)[31] is that they are run on a basis of peer self-government; and what makes this possible is a heavy emphasis on shared socialization. The "true" professions have their own educational systems that build not only a core of knowledge but also a set of ethics and attitudes; a credentialing process enforces this base uniformity.[32]

Although professionalism is often seen as a model for the future, and although the fastest-growing parts of the workforce consistently try to define themselves as professionals, this structure in key respects falls short of the interactive type. First, its mechanisms for identifying reputation are poorly developed: Good professionals are known through the hit-or-miss channels of word of mouth or publicity. It is therefore not particularly difficult for a charlatan lawyer or doctor to flourish. Second, its systems of discipline and concerted action are very weak. This has become increasingly visible in recent years as external pressure for accountability has grown: Professional groups find it extremely difficult to muster agreement for any sort of binding decision, whether it be for punishing the charlatans or establishing enforceable codes of ethics.[33] Indeed, this serious weakness of professionalism may generate skepticism about the whole idea of an interactive organization; it is a thesis of this essay that these limitations are not necessary to the model.[34]

Science is much closer to the mark. It selects and rewards people with great efficiency through formalized peer review in journals. Historically it has not been able to formulate collective goals, but that has changed a good deal in the past few decades. The increasing channeling of funding through centralized sources, especially government, gives a measure of control of priorities; and the use of peer review to allocate those funds prevents that power from falling into a bureaucratic form. Thus, for example, it has proved possible to mobilize a great deal of focused energy around the search for a cure for cancer without adopting a formalistic system of authority that would stifle creativity. This combination of control and flexibility is essentially what managers are seeking as they try to escape the cage of bureaucracy.

Key lessons to be drawn from the analogy to science include the following:

1. As in the professions, a period of shared socialization at a very general level provides a foundation of value consensus that is very crucial to holding the structure together. There is no fundamental disagreement about what is good science: Indeed, a strong *moral* definition is systematically inculcated. But this is not a version of "company culture": It stands *above* particular institutions. Business has lacked this kind of socialization: There has been no generalized core of values and methods that defines a manager. This is a serious weakness in any effort to move beyond rule-based control. Nevertheless, there may have been a giant step in this direction during the 1980s: One aspect of the "rightward" shift in that decade was a tremendous growth in business schools, journals, and magazines, as well as in popular outlets for business ideas (daily newspaper sections and columns, TV shows)—all of which greatly broadened the scope of the shared "language of business."

2. Power is not exercised through offices—that is, decisions about funding are not made by a "science czar." But that does not mean the decisions don't get made. The key to the apparent paradox is the use of peer review, which places different people in control of different decisions at different times, according to their reputations around the problem under consideration (themselves established through very sophisticated mechanisms as mentioned above).[35] The various corporate efforts to build temporary and flexible task forces are moves in the same direction. At the limit, in some investment banks, people form task forces entirely through peer networking, and their evaluations and rewards are based on reports from large numbers—up to several hundred—of peers who have worked with them on team projects.[36]

3. Experimentation is encouraged but also controlled—that is, it is highly valued for people to seek better ways of doing or understanding, but ideas that don't pan out are rather quickly discarded. And not just any idea is open: the scientific fields through their journals define the key problems that need solving, thereby substantially concentrating energy even without the stronger mechanism of centralized funding.

This is hardly an adequate tour of the central institutions of science, but it suffices to give a sense that this is a form of organization that is capable of "businesslike" coordination in addition to its more obvious capabilities in innovation; and further, that it is still evolving in its capacity to combine these two apparently opposite qualities. It avoids bureaucratic authority, but retains the ability to make authoritative decisions.

The Role of Power and Binding Decisions

The most difficult problem in defining the interactive type is in understanding the role of power and authority. The post-bureaucratic type certainly has to do with a reduction or change in the use of power; this could easily be transmuted into a desire to do away with power entirely and rely on pure reason. But this would be a wildly unrealistic direction of thought. Anarchism, the strand of social theory that is most consistent in this regard, has consistently failed to deliver on its theoretical or practical promises. The role of power seems inescapable, and the new type must manage it as well as the old.

We need to distinguish, however, between two basic arguments about the continuing role of power. The first is the argument from *domination*: This claim is that there will always be people who seek to subjugate others, and a system that ignores power will be vulnerable to them. This is in essence a repetition of the case made originally by Hobbes (1651). *Leviathan* is based on a simple logical sequence: *In a state of nature people will try to dominate each other, which will produce general chaos and misery for all; therefore power must be removed from individuals and centralized "above" the warring factions*. This is one of the source arguments for bureaucracy.

The second case for power is a *functional* one, based not on domination of one part by another, but on the need for social groups to make binding decisions.[37] This conception is echoed by managers everywhere: Someone, somehow, has to make decisions that stick. Even if everyone were unselfish and unconcerned with control, there would still need to be a mechanism of power for group action.

These arguments are both as correct now as they have always been: There is neither empirical nor theoretical justification for conceiving of an order without power. The post-bureaucratic organization merely structures it in a different way.

The argument from domination implies that the ability to dominate must be removed from the private realm—that is, members of a group should not be able to control each other for their own interests. That continues to be true. But it does *not* necessarily imply Hobbes' solution—that the ability to dominate must be transferred to a central body. This error produces the antidemocratic result of the *Leviathan*. It was later picked up by Weber with the same consequences: All of Weber's forms of legitimate authority are essentially structures of domination—that is, contexts in which the higher level can command *without giving a justification* (except that "it is so" or "I say so.")

The problem of domination remains strong in the creation of an interactive system. Particularly during the period of transition, there is a high level of vulnerability to private intrigue and bureaucratic power plays: Someone who puts a naive faith in the power of dialogue can easily be chewed up. This transitional problem will be considered more fully in the chapter on transformational process (Chapter 6 of this book).

But once the interactive structure is formed the problem is less serious than it appears: It becomes difficult to use the old forms of power. Consider an analogy: When you set up bureaucratic control, it is always possible for someone to pull out a gun and overthrow the boss. Indeed, this kind of thing (with swords rather than guns) happened a good deal among the early bureaucracies as they grew up within feudal monarchies. However, that is not a major fear of corporate managers today. Once the system is well-established, the use of violence becomes "unthinkable"; the system retains a reservoir of force to deal with possible attack, but it is almost never used.

In the same way the creation of an interactive system requires the protection of a strong bureaucratic leader who can fend off attacks on the old terms but also lead toward the new. Once the structure is established, however, those who play the bureaucratic game find themselves isolated. I have been impressed, for example, by the following experience in one of the more developed examples of post-bureaucracy that I have seen:

> The organizational development function had a great deal of influence, playing much of the "meta-decision-making" role that I have emphasized. One powerful player decided to create and control a new organizational development department, relying especially on the support of a high leader who personally owed him a great deal. A nasty "political" battle erupted, with mutual recriminations and secret accusations.
>
> The head of the whole organization stuck to interactive principles: He instructed the players to generate options, emphasizing only that they consider the requirements of the whole. Over the period of several months, as these discussions proceeded, the person playing power politics was gradually but definitively isolated. His arguments did not stand up to scrutiny; as this became clear his protector backed away, and his other allies were drawn into the public dialogue. The eventual solution improved some of the weaknesses of the old system without granting him his hoped-for power base.

This sort of experience has been repeated frequently enough to suggest that the use of bureaucratic power in an interactive system becomes, in time and with a good change process, *illegitimate* and can be resisted without resorting to a response in kind.

The argument from function is more central: It implies that there must be a way to make decisions that are binding on members of the group. *The central theoretical claim of a post-bureaucratic organization is that it is possible to make binding decisions without relying on offices.* This claim in turn relies on two concepts unfamiliar to bureaucracy: *consensual legitimation* and *process.*

Consensual Legitimation

The bureaucratic type relies on what Weber calls "rational-legal" legitimation: Orders are accepted as valid if they conform to the impersonal rules defining appropriate powers of an office. The *content* of those orders is explicitly not subject to examination by subordinates—as long as it comes through proper channels and in the proper form it is to be obeyed.

Clearly what is going on today in business organizations is a challenge to that definition of legitimacy. Increasingly, it is accepted that orders may come according to the rules and through channels and yet be dumb, counterproductive, and wasteful. And the key point is that this "acceptance" comes not just from rebellious and grumbling subordinates but from the leaders themselves.

These leaders are therefore seeking a definition of conditions for legitimacy that will *work* better. And the various experiments examined in this book share a basic thrust: that legitimate and effective decisions must be justified by the *agreement* (or consent) of those who are affected by them and those who can contribute knowledge to them.

This is a key element that first attracted American management to the Japanese system: The Japanese appeared, especially in their shop-floor relations, to avoid the rigidity of bureaucracy by involving everyone, drawing on ideas, and developing a system that everyone could feel part of. There is considerable dispute about the extent to which this is a true description of the "Japanese model" (see Janice Klein's contribution to this book, Chapter 7); but the issue has already become largely irrelevant. Managers have widely moved toward conceptions of "empowerment" that go a major step beyond that of the Japanese by creating cross-level task forces that operate on the basis of consensus. Though I have not conducted this test, I would venture that a significant minority of managers would now agree with the "post-bureaucratic" definition of legitimate decisions suggested in the previous paragraph.

The conception of consensual legitimacy is, to my knowledge, new to organizational theory, but it is old in other contexts: It is known as democracy. The founders of the American republic, and to a certain extent even the authors of the Magna Carta, appealed to this form of legitimation. In the former case it became institutionalized in the system of government defined in our Constitution—an elaborate system of checks and balances and rights.

That particular form is not the one appropriate to defining consensus within business organizations: It was designed as much to *prevent* government from acting too effectively as to *enable* it to mobilize action. The mechanisms for creating consensus in a business setting, which are very much still being invented, can be grouped under the much-used and -abused term *process*.

Process

What happens in organizations trying to de-bureaucratize (in the sense I have defined) is that decisions are entrusted to "the process": This phrase reappears in dozens of organizations with which I am familiar, including most of those discussed in this book. It is a vague term, often frustratingly so for participants. It is often explained by what it is *not*: "Don't dig into positions, trust the process"; "Don't try to make a rule, use the process."

"The process" can be boiled down to three essential elements: (1) bringing together stakeholders; (2) creating a dialogue; and (3) achieving consensus on a path forward. Each of these is an extremely difficult task, with many elements and also many obscurities. Let me stress just a few key points.

The first is that an effective process accomplishes the key function sketched earlier: It provides a way to make binding decisions without authority invested in (permanent) offices. Rather than referring to a fixed office or position, it brings together those with knowledge and interest in a problem to work out an agreement on action. The outcome is a decision that is seen as legitimate and that in addition is characterized by high trust and understanding among those involved in implementation. This method will vary: It may involve a group, it may involve a sequence of steps, and so on; but whatever it is, it produces decisions more *effectively* binding than those of bureaucracies.

The details of generating binding decisions are the stuff of process consultation. As anyone who has sat in bad meetings can attest, it doesn't happen automatically: It is, for instance, extremely easy in consensual meetings for discussion to wander without getting to a point of decision. Consultants therefore stress the need for *explicit detailing of expected outcomes* in each meeting and build in a good deal of *conscious reflection on process* to quickly identify points of blockage or resistance and develop approaches to overcoming them.

It is also very easy for decisions that do get made to get lost after the meeting. Those who are pushing this domain therefore stress the need to carefully *document* the decisions that are made and to *assign responsibility* (still on a consensual basis) to specific people for carrying out agreed-on steps.

These conceptually simple behaviors are in practice very hard for those who have developed bureaucratic habits. In a good bureaucracy, accountability is generally clear and unambiguous; in an interactive system one has to *remember* consciously to analyze the problem of accountability and reach agreement on how it will be allocated. In a bureaucracy the top official in any meeting brings up the topics he or she wants; now one has to remember to develop an agenda, make sure everyone has input into it, and make explicit the outcomes that are being sought. But taking this extra step of self-awareness one greatly increases the capacity to reach solid agreements.

The second point is that not all decisions need to pass through the "process" for it to be effective. This is a central problem and concern to managers in the early stages: It appears that all time and energy can be sucked into meetings to bring together stakeholders around every issue. In fact, of course, no system can work this way, and failure to resolve this problem creates ineffectiveness.

The resolution is, again, conceptually simple but practically complex. The integration of a post-bureaucratic order requires not that every decision go through a consensus process but that every decision be made *according to principles* that have been developed through such a process. That is, there should be access for stakeholders to the definition of the basic goals and values of each decision area.

In practice, the initial steps involve a large amount of meeting and discussion to establish those basic principles. Furthermore, it is generally difficult to establish the distinction between principles and decisions, so that for a time everyone does want to be part of every decision that affects them. Finally, in a changing order there will continually be decisions that do not clearly fall under principles already agreed-to: This is where the "meta-decision-making structures" described above—structures for "deciding how to decide"—must enter the picture, to establish a new process for making the decision and creating guidelines for the new domain.

The third point is that this "process" incorporates bureaucracy as an option—it is inclusive. The process may (and often does) *set up* pyramidal structures of accountability for particular purposes. In this lies the reconciliation of the pieces separated by contingency theory: Bureaucratic hierarchy does continue as an available structural option, but it is *under the control of* consensual mechanisms. Like Newton's theory, it becomes a pragmatic special case *within* a more encompassing structure of management.[38]

Contingency Versus Transformation

Empirical studies, dating back to Burns and Stalker's (1961) pioneering work, have generally found that "new" forms of organization appear in specific clusters or locations, while the old continue unaffected in others. This has produced a set of "contingency theories" that argue that the new and the old each have specific strengths—that they are, in effect, structures at the same level, with neither being "better" than the other.

The contingency theories themselves take many different forms depending on which phenomena they investigate:

• The usual claim is that rapidly changing or uncertain environments support "organic" forms, whereas bureaucracy works best where the environment is stable. This implies that the new forms may be particularly a phenomenon of developing markets, such as high-tech,[39] and will remain limited in scope.

• A variant is the argument that the two patterns may apply to separate organizational tasks and can therefore be split off in subgroups. For example, some argue that the interactive form is not useful for routine operations but only for relatively limited functions—such as product development teams—in which unstructured invention is paramount. In this case it would remain an organizational segment isolated from the mainstream of daily operations.

• A third version is that the interactive form can be used in routine conditions but not in situations of crisis demanding rapid response. This suggests that they might alternate in time. For example, Norwegian shippers, under the influence of "sociotechnical" consultants, developed a highly participatory structure for normal shipboard duties; but on entering and leaving harbors, the captain once again assumed full control.[40] Note that this view partially contradicts the prior two, since it sees interactive systems as best in *routine* rather than innovative conditions. Nevertheless, all have a surface plausibility!

• Finally, it can be argued that the interactive form is applicable to functions that require cooperation among small face-to-face groups but cannot be extended to larger organizations. In this case the dominant form is likely to be a traditional hierarchy of power, but with teams rather than individuals as the primary unit of accountability. This seems to be empirically the most common pattern today, at least in the industrial sector: Teams have been established for many specific functions, but without significantly altering the larger structure.

The proposition of this chapter is that all these contingency views are wrong. Some of them may be true empirically for the time being, but none of them is a solid truth: All (we are claiming) will fall to the gradual evolution of the interactive form, which is superior overall. It is an argument about *transformation* rather than specific innovation.

There is no direct evidence for this radical view: We cannot now say, as Weber did in his writings on bureaucracy, that the new form has demonstrated overwhelming superiority through its ability to drive out the old. At this point the argument can only be based on two somewhat thinner reeds: first, that the evidence for varieties of contingency is not solid; second, that *theoretically* the post-bureaucratic form is more adaptive than the others.

Let us first consider the various contingency theories. Almost always they make an unfounded empiricist leap: that because the new forms are *found* by the authors of a given study only in certain environments, they *can* only exist in these environments. One needs to be very careful with such extrapolation. Innovation generally does emerge in a limited sector that for essentially arbitrary reasons favors the change; that says nothing about its eventual potential. On this basis one might well have argued in 1650 that market economies could only emerge in cloth-producing areas; or in 1870 that bureaucratic management was appropriate only for railroads. These turned out to be only favorable starting points for a much wider development.

And indeed such a spread of interactive forms is already visible: The essential weakness of contingency theory is that the innovations have extended increasingly beyond their starting points. When Burns and Stalker (1961) wrote *The Management of Innovation*,[41] the structure was apparently found only in a few obscure electronics firms in Scotland. A bit later Lawrence and Lorsch (1967) identified it in a wider variety of firms facing complex environments. But in the meantime a quite different strand of research and practice, deriving from the Tavistock Institute's studies in England, began developing team-based systems in shop-floor production, including many in quite routinized and stable environments. The growth of worker teams in the past 20 years has occurred very largely in industries such as automobiles and steel, often in assembly-line jobs.

For many of these sectors, especially the last, environmental uncertainty has not greatly increased.[42] What has driven these changes is not the need for rapid responsiveness but the discovery that even in these routinized jobs teams can design and allocate their tasks more intelligently than can industrial engineers—if they are provided with information, skills, and authority to resolve issues through discussion. Operators in these systems have demonstrated the ability to make significant improvements in production, even in a stable environment. In brief, they get to use their collective *intelligence* more effectively.

Interactive mechanisms have also been used to great effect in a quite different situation: where outside demands are constant, but where the internal work involves periodic unpredictable crises. This is the case in many continuous-process industries—petrochemicals, for example: chemical workers may spend long hours just watching dials, but when something goes wrong they must work together rapidly and skillfully. The Shell-Sarnia plant referred to earlier has significantly improved output by building effective consensual teams.

Finally, in the past decade one of the most important management developments has been to extend the team concept not to situations of high uncertainty but to those demanding *continuous improvement*. Approaches such as the more extended versions of "Total Quality" shift the paradigm fundamentally: Rather than expecting everyone to do their job until told to do something else, they seek to develop throughout the organization the capacity to inquire, experiment, and change in order to enhance performance. And there is, explicitly, no end to this process—it becomes a part of daily organization. And this is a profoundly unbureaucratic idea.

In the managerial layers, too—though the events here are harder to trace—there has been a steady extension of team systems into conditions that do not easily fit contingency theory. For example, with increasing frequency, leadership groups in assembly plants operate on a consensual basis: Instead of a plant manager who calls in subordinates to tell them what to do, we see extensive strategic planning processes that create a shared vision of the basic direction through a dialogue among equals. These consensual processes are not limited to high-tech or other industries demanding unusual levels of innovation; they are found to my direct knowledge in autos, in paper, in steel, in chemicals, in telecommunications, and in other varied conditions.

In short, though individual contingency theories generally seem plausible, when taken as a whole they are often contradictory and unsupported. One can find clear examples of interactive successes without the hypothesized environmental conditions. Thus the argument that post-bureaucratic structures will be limited to unusually dynamic industries already seems to be being overtaken by events.

One can make a similar point about attempts to *segment* them into the "innovative" parts of given organizations, such as R&D. On the one hand, where that has been done—the classic cases being Bell Labs and Xerox PARC—there have been significant tensions between the operational and research sides that have slowed diffusion of technology; indeed, this problem of diffusion has now become a major concern to management theorists. On the other hand, even the most drab "line" aspects of production have, as mentioned earlier, been drawn into a process of continuous invention and improvement, acting in a miniature way as research labs themselves seeking new ways to do their jobs better.[43] Thus there is no strong case to be made for a segmentation of the two aspects.

Ultimately, the various contingency theories fail a key test: They do not produce an *integrated* organizational theory. When physicists are confronted with an apparently different set of laws at the subatomic level from larger levels, they do not just declare a contingency theory: They struggle to find the principles that unite the two realms. Failure to do so accepts incoherency in theory and also in practice.

The practical result of a contingency approach is a set of mixed types that do not work very well. The bureaucratic hierarchy of power does not mix well with the mechanisms of informed consensus: The relation often seems like that of oil and water. In the organizations that I have observed trying to expand the sphere of teamwork, the teams almost always complain about interference from the authorities—and the authorities fret about the lack of control in the teams. And when teams are constructed from people of unequal position, the distortions introduced by the power imbalance are extremely difficult to overcome.

Does It Work?

Evidence of Performance

Because the concept of *post-bureaucratic organization* is new and sketchy, there has not to my knowledge ever been direct empirical examination of its implementation. The closest we can come is by looking at studies of *participatory* systems—a term that is vague and includes many things that, from our perspective, are very incomplete or even false versions of the type. Still, it is the best we have.

There have been thousands of studies of the productivity effects of participatory organization, the vast majority of which have claimed significant improvements. Few, however, have established even basic credibility. The bulk have been written by, or collected their data from, the very people who implemented the changes; and almost none have had measures of performance independent of self-reporting. It is not particularly convincing when the consultant who has proposed an innovation, or the managers who have tied their careers to it, claim to have seen performance improvement.

There are two studies that I have found more persuasive than most. The first is an internal analysis of the performance of the Shell-Sarnia plant, one of the most advanced exemplars of a post-bureaucratic organization. Corporate researchers who had no stake in the outcome made a major effort to find good comparison plants; and however they sliced it they found the Sarnia organization to be dramatically better than the others on almost all dimensions, from productivity (percentage of machine downtime) to quality to energy utilization.[44]

The second study, by Dan Denison (1990), uses a totally different methodology: It looks at hundreds of companies whose internal cultures have been scored over decades on Rensis Likert's scale, and relates this score to their overall financial performance. The strength of the relations is startling: Firms maintaining a participative culture over many years had corporate performance—

as measured by sales and return on investments—*twice* as good as comparable low-participation firms. Even more impressive, firms that shifted toward greater participation generally showed an upturn in results with a lag of 2 to 5 years (depending on the size of the organization.)[45]

These studies, encouraging but incomplete, are about as much as we can expect at this stage because all the elements in the equation are as yet too vague. We do not have a good way of measuring a post-bureaucratic system and distinguishing good efforts from bad ones; survey studies inevitably mix all kinds of efforts together under a single rubric, which makes the results unreliable. Nor do we have good ways of measuring the outcomes: Financial measures of corporate performance, for example, are certainly affected by employee actions, but they are also affected by many other factors, some of them quite uncontrollable by the organization itself. Attempts to measure more exactly what employees do contribute have been generally frustrating.

A second significant type of evidence indicates that participative systems do not coexist easily with bureaucratic organizations. Several studies have identified the common phenomenon of the "successful failure": the consensus group that appears to fulfill all criteria of accomplishment, from productivity to employee satisfaction, yet vanishes for undefined reasons after a few years. Closer inspection usually reveals that the group was confined to a very narrow scope of action by the surrounding hierarchy; at a certain point the members become discouraged and lose energy. Several independent observers suggest that about 75% of workforce groups—at least when they are not embedded in a larger process of management reform—succumb to this failure.[46]

This is important because it supports the notion of an ideal type: I suggested above that an empirical indicator of such a type is that it does not mix easily with other models. This "oil and water" phenomenon clearly appears in studies of participatory innovation.

Finally, there is strong evidence beyond general impressions that participatory systems have been spreading during the past 30 years, and that the shift has been accelerating. Studies that have tried to estimate the extent of participatory programs have, despite very imperfect methodologies, come up with steadily increasing numbers since the 1970s; the most recent one, based on a 1987 government survey, finds that over 80% of the 1,000 largest employers have implemented some form of real employee involvement (beyond the level of suggestion boxes), affecting about a quarter of all the jobs in these firms.[47]

This pattern over time is extremely suggestive. When one takes a *micro* view, it appears that most participatory efforts fail; but from a *macro* view extending over the last 30 years, it is clear that these systems have spread rather steadily.[48] What has happened, in brief, is that the "failures" have produced not a reversion to bureaucracy but an attempt to go farther. In the 1960s, the first breaks in the Taylorist/bureaucratic paradigm involved adding "vertical responsibility" to individual jobs; as this innovation showed its limits, it led in the 1970s to broader efforts to mobilize employee ideas in discussion groups; a decade later there was a strong growth of teams with authority to shape their own work; and finally, in the late 1980s and early 1990s, there appeared total organizational paradigms that pulled together shop-floor participation with management de-layering and a reduction of rules.

It is this last step that approaches the notion of interactive organization; but the previous ones appear in retrospect as failed partial experiments that pointed the way to a more complete transformation. The refusal on the part of managers to accept failure is one of the strongest pieces of evidence that the problems with the bureaucratic form are *real*, spurring continued efforts to find something better even in the face of resistance and discouragement.

Apparent Problems and Weaknesses

Even with the best current practice, interactive systems face a substantial set of problems and difficulties; most of these have been *reduced* by continuing experimentation, but they are far from being eliminated.

Cost

It is often believed that nonbureaucratic systems are more costly, for two reasons: There is no clear and organized locus for cost control; and there is necessary redundancy built into the need for everyone to understand aspects of the whole, rather than focusing just on their own piece.

Evidence is, again, almost nonexistent. Certainly interactive systems can get "out of control"—the role of professional structures in contributing to the escalation of health care costs is probably an example. However, bureaucracies can equally well become bloated and expensive, as effectively demonstrated by U.S. car companies over the past 30 years.

Conversely, there are interactive systems that are at least as cost-effective as bureaucracies: I refer to volunteer networks, which often accomplish great things on a shoestring. Their defining characteristics appear to be the same as those of cost-effective bureaucracies: External resources are highly constrained, and they have a clear sense of what they are trying to accomplish. Under those conditions, interactive mechanisms may well be as creative in solving the problem of cost as they have shown themselves in solving production and quality problems.

It would certainly be worth studying cost-effective associations to see how they do it. There is no reason why the issue of cost cannot be dealt with by the mechanisms discussed above: a consensual development of principles, then the establishment of systems for implementation and monitoring.

Slowness

It would certainly appear that the development of consensus is slow compared to the potential for swift and decisive action by a bureaucratic leader. Again, however, the obvious is not necessarily true. It should be pointed out, first, that a major argument and motive for *de*-bureaucratizing is to overcome the slowness of bureaucracy—a fine example of the contradictory views currently accepted in this arena!

Some of the most effective military organizations have been run on relatively consensual rather than bureaucratic lines—for example, the German army at the start of World War II and the Chinese Communist army before their victory in 1949 were far less bureaucratic than their opponents.[49] They proved particularly effective in terms of *rapidity of response*. In this respect they suggested that there is truth in the hopes of the de-bureaucratizers: that when people throughout an organization are equipped with knowledge, skills, and authority to cooperate on the fly as needed, they can move much more quickly than if decisions must move up a fixed chain of command.

Of course, the development of this knowledge, skill, and understanding of principles *is* a slow process. The Japanese commonly make the point that their consensual style of decision making slows down the determination of basic strategy but greatly speeds all the implementation decisions that flow from that. Management consultants who specialize in the creation of participatory structures commonly make the same claim—"You need to go slow to go fast," as one group puts it.[50] None of these claims has been well-tested, but at least they indicate that caution is needed in jumping from the slowness of interactive meetings to the assertion that these structures are over all slow in responding to new challenges.

Mediocrity

We have all had the experience that consensus processes tend to wear down bold ideas and to pull everyone toward safe and noncontroversial positions. This is one of the most troubling objections to interactive systems because there is (for once) actual evidence that this common experience carries over to the larger organizational scale. Many independent studies of federational and interactive systems make a similar point: that they may be very nimble tactically, in responding to concrete outside demands, but that they are poor at major strategic "leaps" that require a long-term vision.[51]

The question then is: Is this a *fundamental* weakness of nonbureaucratic systems, or is it merely a failure of implementation that can be overcome? Let me suggest some reasons to think it might be the latter. First, science—an archetypal nonbureaucratic institution—is actually quite good at major leaps. On the contrary, it is when science is bureaucratized, as it was for example in the Soviet Union, that it tends to lose its innovative edge.

The reason science can accomplish major change is twofold: It encourages experimentation, and it has institutions to bring this experimentation to bear on debates about the central issues of the field. The first without the second would produce mere multiplicity. But through journals, conferences, and various forms of refereeing, the scientific community builds from scattered results to focused discussions of key problems. And that in turn produces the occasional "revolution."

There are also instances of business organizations that seem to overcome the problem. They do it much as does science—through a structure of *integrated experimentation*. Managers at 3M and Honda, both known for bold innovation, have a conscious model of scientific progress. They have developed some interesting mechanisms for building the potential for "leaps" into the culture. For example, 3M has an expectation that every division will make 25% of its sales from products that did not exist 5 years earlier. Honda has an elaborate model of "middle-up-down" management in which new practices come from the periphery, deadlines and pressure come from the center, and the middle is responsible for integrating the ideal and the real. Both make heavy use of "skunk works"—small experimental groups who are encouraged to try out novel ideas, which are then examined for their relevance to firm strategy.[52]

Finally, it is again easy to exaggerate the capacity of bureaucracy for making strategic leaps. Those who have watched the struggles of IBM and General Motors over the past 5 years are aware that even determined effort from the top is not sufficient to overcome the resistance of those embedded in routine. On the contrary, some companies have been far more successful in this effort recently by developing interactive methods to a new level: organizing participatory strategic reevaluations that open even the most sacred "ways of doing things" to dialogue and inquiry. This is still rare, but a few instances give some reason for optimism.[53]

Despite some empirical support for the idea, no convincing *theoretical* argument has been made about why post-bureaucratic organizations cannot make major as well as minor shifts. In its absence, and given some counterexamples, it is plausible to reply that the problem has been bad implementation. Post-bureaucratic organizations have tended to be too "loose" at the strategic level, allowing major direction to evolve from the interactions of the various parts. But that is not necessary to the model: It is possible, though more difficult, to design processes of consensual decision making at the strategic level as well as others. That is in effect what scientific journals and conferences are about. In business organizations such processes must aim for more clearly binding decisions; but that, too, as we have argued, is consistent with a post-bureaucratic model.

Faction

This is a variant of the previous argument—a concern that without a stable hierarchy of offices "interest-groups" will take over and make coherent action impossible. We have all, again, observed the danger of this in many settings, not the least of which is the national political arena. The response is in part also a variant of previous points: A post-bureaucratic organization must organize discussion at the level of strategy—that which *unifies* all parts of the system—and it must produce binding decisions through that mechanism.

But one can add another point that gives business organizations an advantage over political parties and other institutions that are highly vulnerable to faction. In businesses there is generally a high level of *interdependence* among the members: It is unusual for someone to be able, like Steven Jobs, to pick up his marbles and go start another company. This fact acts as a natural brake on the centripetal force of faction. There is a strong *interest in unity*, even among strongly hostile groups, which can be leveraged into consensus.

It is in fact my experience, and something that I would propose as a hypothesis, that the degree of interdependence of parts of a system is the strongest determinant of the potential for an interactive order. Interdependence is, of course, not a mere "fact" but also a perception: one can act within an organization to increase the perception and understanding of interdependence—and this is often indeed the best first step in trying to move in this direction. When the fact *and perception* of interdependence are high, the danger of faction is low.

Potential Strengths

The expected strengths of an interactive structure have been implied throughout this chapter, but it is nevertheless worth elaborating a few:

1. The most important strength is that decisions result from a thorough "mixing" of the intelligence found throughout the organization. For that reason one would expect the decisions to be better, especially in the long run.

In the bureaucratic model only the top is expected to use intelligence in the formulation of overall goals, or in relating specific goals to the whole. Others are expected merely to provide information (upward) and to obey orders (downward). They may within their spheres apply intelligence to the solution of problems, but they are not expected to venture further. Indeed, if they do so it throws the whole system into chaos.

This is orderly but highly limiting: It excludes major aspects of intelligence. Shop-floor workers, from their experience in, say, assembling a car, might well develop ideas about better engineering, or design; from their experience as consumers, they might have good thoughts about marketing strategy. In bureaucracy these ideas typically have no place to go; *at best* they may pass as formal suggestions "over the wall" to the relevant department, there almost inevitably to be rejected.

In an interactive model, by contrast, such ideas can initiate a process of *dialogue*. Workers might talk to engineers, and both might talk together with marketers, in a framework of equality and consensus-building. The workers can learn much about engineering limits that might block their ideas, but the engineers can learn—because they cannot ignore—about the perspective that generated the idea. And in such a dialogue the intelligence of all parties is mixed into a brew that is more creative, more inclusive, *richer* than any single intelligence.

We know that bureaucracies tend to become conservative and inward-focused, missing the implications of important changes. The mixing of intelligence is the best mechanism for avoiding this danger.

This is, naturally, a radical simplification. One cannot set up dialogues every time everyone has an idea—no one would get any work done. The mechanisms explored earlier under the concept of "process" are designed to *structure* the dialogue and decision making in a way that efficiently screens out unproductive discussions but encourages productive ones.

2. The second major advantage is more commonly cited: Interactive structures create a framework for greater responsiveness to environmental changes. Because those closest to the work or the customer have the tools to make decisions about change, they do not need to refer things "up the line" and wait for decisions.

The cleaning up of bureaucracy achieves a moderate increase in flexibility by increasing the size of the "boxes" within which individuals work. Interactive structures take this a long way further: If individuals see the need for change that transcends their box, they have the capacity to seek out the others who would be involved and to work out a solution with them. This may be a quick process, involving one or two others, or a long one affecting large parts of the organization—but (if the management of process is effective) it quickly *tailors itself* to the demands of the problem.

3. Closely related to these points is the probability that an interactive structure is better for the creation of evolutionarily new forms. A bureaucracy

is limited by the control systems set at the top; a nonbureaucratic order creates the possibility of recreating the control system.

This argument is drawn largely not from organizational theory, where the concept of evolution has as yet no good operational meaning, but from biology and physics. Scientists in these fields who have tried to understand the process of creation of new forms of organization are essentially still stymied, but they do seem to agree that it does not come from "the top": It emerges from the kind of "mixing" that we have just described. Learning within the brain appears likewise to be a matter of "dialogue" among different parts rather than hierarchically controlled exchanges.[54]

4. It is worth citing again a negative criterion: The superiority of interactive structures does *not* lie in increased satisfaction and commitment by employees. Bureaucratic structures, as indeed tribal or patriarchal or most others, are perfectly capable of achieving these. General Motors employees are traditionally highly loyal to the company and very satisfied with it (which doesn't seem to help the company much). And it is certainly possible for an interactive system to have disgruntled and confused members. *Any* effective system, no matter what its type, will produce good responses from members, and any ineffective one will result in dissatisfaction.[55]

The point in the interactive framework is that the commitment is given a more effective way to manifest itself. Bureaucratic commitment is demonstrated by doing one's job well and upholding the rules; post-bureaucratic commitment is demonstrated by active collaboration with others. The latter produces, or should produce, better organizational outcomes.

I call these strengths "potential," because they have not been fully demonstrated and are at best hard to trace. Though there is evidence, as cited above, that more consensual systems are stronger than more bureaucratic ones, there is much learning to be done before the picture becomes clear.

Conclusion

One reason for pursuing an "ideal-type" analysis is that social action largely works on that basis. Managers are currently pursuing a wave of reforms under the title of "empowerment" not because those reforms have unambiguously demonstrated their success but because they have a *sense* that these changes head in the right direction. If you push managers about the sources of the fundamental decisions they make around de-bureaucratization, they will generally finish by saying something such as, "It feels right." An ideal-type analysis tries to get at the source of the feeling and to clarify its implications.

In exploring the interactive model, I have distinguished it from several "pretenders"—the cleaned bureaucracy, the closed community, the market, and the simple federation—which, it turns out, actually lead in rather different directions. And we have identified one crucial source of confusion that must be the focus of further development. That is the issue of *generating binding decisions*.

Because the shift away from bureaucracy involves a transformation in the use of power, it naturally produces confusion over whether power can be used at all. A common assumption, whether explicit or not, is that people will do the right thing simply because they have agreed to it. This is an example of a proposition that is consistent neither with sociological theory nor with the experience of interactive efforts. On the contrary, decisions must be clearly legitimated and enforced, with accountability for the steps. But the nature of the legitimation changes from a rational-legal to a consensual basis; and the assignment of accountability changes from the definition of permanent offices to the cooperative distribution of tasks.

Let me restate again the claims I have made in this chapter—and especially those I have *not* made. I do not claim that true post-bureaucratic forms exist anywhere at the level of large organizations: They may, but neither I nor my co-authors in this collection are convinced we have actually seen one (and secondhand reports are very unreliable). Nor do I claim that most or even much of the wave of "participation" over the last two decades is really moving in this direction: There is, as I have stressed, a variety of false roads, including the seductive ways of strengthening bureaucracy through the language of empowerment. Nor do I believe that many of the leaders of large corporations would either understand or embrace the model I have sketched.

What I *do* claim is that what is driving all these experiments, whatever their particular forms, is a growing perception of the fundamental inadequacy of bureaucratic organization, its inability to combine innovation with discipline at the levels required by a modern economy. Interactive forms—the participatory systems, task forces, and teams of the corporate world, as well as the self-regulation of professions and sciences—show a greater ability to do so.

The past few decades have produced a tremendous amount of social learning about how to organize such a system—learning that is summarized under many titles, from "sociotechnical systems analysis" to "process consulting" to "mutual-gains bargaining." Each of these is a form of practice that tries to build consensual systems that work. Clearly we are still early on the road to understanding, but enough has been done to see in the distance the outline of the destination.

Notes

1. See, for example, Dimaggio and Powell (1983).
2. Kuhn (1962); Piaget (1932).
When contingency theory exists in physics, it is seen not as a solution but as a problem to be overcome. For example, since the early part of the century quantum physics have been fundamentally different from and untranslatable into the physics of larger scales; there are in effect different laws "contingent on" the scale of observation. But scientists starting with Einstein have labored mightily to overcome this dichotomy and develop a "unified field" theory that would include both—a development that now appears to be close to success.
3. Though Piaget made a persuasive case for social stages in *The Moral Judgment of the Child* (1932). See also Gould (1987).
4. See Chandler (1977, 1981, 1988).
5. On the Honeywell case, see Beer, Eisenstat, and Spector (1990). I am not aware of a good published case yet on Saturn, though Saul Rubinstein, Michael Bennett, and Tom Kochan are working on one.
6. See Chandler (1977, 1981, 1988); Daems (1980); Lazonick (1987); Shorter (1973).
7. In a rather bizarre turn of logic, Elliott Jaques's 1990 defense of bureaucracy comes to just such a conclusion. He argues that different levels of good bureaucracies are marked by different time horizons—the higher up in the organization, the longer the view. Then he argues that there are different types of people who, it so happens, have innate capacities to handle just these different time horizons. The first assertion has a lot of evidence behind it, but the second does not.
8. On the importance of "working knowledge" and informal cooperation among blue-collar workers, see Mathewson (1931); Kaboolian (1991); Kusterer (1978).
9. On informal vs. formal organization, see for example Whyte (1956); Kanter (1977); Rubin (1976); Selznick (1949); Krackhardt (1991); Deinard and Friedman (1990); Blau (1963); Manning (1977); Blankenship (1977), ch. 10; Walton and Hackman (1985); Weir (1973); Alvarez (1991).
10. Henry Mintzberg's (with Raisinghani and Thérêt) study (1976) of change processes notes that "political" shifts, involving this kind of restructuring of offices, brings many efforts to grief.
11. The classic analysis of this dynamic of bureaucratic personality is Merton (1940). See also Veblen (1904).
12. On the inadequacy of the top-down description of planning, see for example Burgelman (1983); Pattee (1973); Golden (1990); Mintzberg and McHugh (1985); Hayes (1986).
13. Others have the term *interactive* in ways related to this—most especially the firm Interaction Associates, which is one of the more advanced consulting groups in this area, and Russ Ackoff (1981), whose concept of "interactive planning" is very consistent with the direction of the chapter.
14. The concept of "dialogue" in this analysis owes much to Habermas's concept of "ideal speech." It is, however, considerably more concrete and less ideal; the types of consensus and discussion found in even the most "advanced" forms of associational organization are far from fully undistorted communication. See Habermas (1991).
15. See Parsons (1969b), ch. 14 and ch. 15.
16. A recent literature originating with Granovetter (1973) has uncovered the importance of "weak ties"—relations that are not communal and exclusive, but open and more shallow—in holding networks together.
17. A number of theorists have in different ways made a distinction between "personal trust"— the traditional friendship or family relationship—and "system trust," which is a depersonalized faith in the functioning of a larger order. (See, e.g., Luhmann, 1979; Silver, 1985; Zucker, 1986; Shapiro, 1987.) I am here adding a third category: a form of one that is *personal*, in the sense

that it is specific to a given individual, and yet *specific* rather than diffuse. A major component of post-bureaucratic organization is a network of relationships based on specific performances and abilities, rather than on friendship: people one can "work with" on particular projects rather than "live with." The closest concept in the literature that I am familiar with is, as mentioned earlier, Granovetter's (1973) notion of "weak ties"—though these are perhaps weaker than I mean!

18. See Eccles and Crane (1987).

19. See Eaton (1992) and Janice Klein's paper in this book for analyses of the weaknesses of the "new production systems."

A recent study by the Rand corporation stresses the problems caused by team systems in high-performing organizations—that they *interfere with* needed communication across departments (see Fuchsberg, 1992).

20. Drucker (1988).

21. A very interesting piece by Maryellen Kelley and Bennett Harrison (1992), which has just come to my attention, develops persuasive empirical support for the argument that much of the current wave of "participation" is merely a way of solidifying bureaucratic patterns.

22. Among those who have noted the similarity between corporate communities and feudal states are Kanter (1977), Whyte (1956), Gouldner (1954), Mills (1951), Margolis (1979), and Jackall (1988).

23. On "corporate culture," see Schein (1985), Main (1981), Ouchi (1981), Deal and Kennedy (1982), Frost (1985), and Davis (1984).

24. See Note 18.

25. Sonnenfeld and Lazo (1988).

26. Dupont, which is also dealing with its first non-"family" CEO, is having similar trouble in breaking its bureaucracy.

Re Toyota, see Taylor (1990).

Wilson (1989, pp. 101ff.) notes similar weaknesses in public bureaucracies that are too strongly focused on a sense of "mission" and shared values.

27. For a famous discussion of the limits of market mechanism, see Williamson (especially 1975 and 1985).

28. A piece by Forrester (1965) is fascinating in this regard: It combines advocacy of a market model with a just-barely-subterranean centralist technocratic elitism. It is clear, though not explicit, that in the systems he is proposing the market is a mechanism of control *within* a sharply hierarchical system.

29. Eccles and White (1988).

30. Richard Munch (1986) provides an incisive analysis of the attractions of the "negotiated order" approach for American social theory.

Among those who more or less explicitly suggest a simple federational model of the "new structure" are Thompson (1973), Orton and Weick (1990), Weick (1977), Sabel (1987 and 1991), Powell (1990), and Nohria (1987).

A fine analysis of the inadequacy of simple federation can be found in Schoonhoven and Jelinek (1990).

31. Key works on professionalism include Merton (1949); Hagstrom (1965); Goode (1957); Strauss, Schatzman, Ehrlich, Bucher, and Sabshin (1963); Parsons (1968); Haskell (1984); Gerpott and Domsch (1985); Jackson (1970); Durkheim (1957); and Torstendahl and Burrage (1990).

32. It is, of course, true that there is a "dark" side to credentialing: It is a mechanism for asserting and maintaining power by excluding outsiders, as well as one for maintaining standards. Some authors, such as Friedson (1980) and Waters (1989), stress the former aspect, but it is only one side of reality. See Haskell's (1984) essay for an excellent overview of the question.

33. See Friedson and Rhea (1963) for a subtle discussion of the problems of control in a professional organization.

34. The craft model, which is sometimes suggested as a good image (see especially Braverman, 1974, and Piore 1982), is even more primitive than professionalism in these regards. Its degree of peer self-governance is made possible chiefly by an emphasis on tradition; it has great difficulty with change, with self-analysis, and with learning from experience. It is this inability to adapt that made it so vulnerable to the growth of the bureaucratic type. By contrast professionalism, through the formalization of its educational processes, has built in at least one major, though slow, technique of managed change.

35. See Zuckerman and Merton (1981) for a discussion of the referee system in this regard.

36. See Eccles and Crane (1987, 1988).

37. See Parsons (1969a).

38. The analysis by Huber (1984) similarly stresses the importance of decision technology (what I am calling "process") and decision-process management (what I am calling "meta-decision-making structures.")

39. See Lawrence and Lorsch (1967); and Burns and Stalker (1961).

40. Bradach and Eccles (1989), among others, make this sort of argument: that "new structures" coexist with or alternate with bureaucracy.

41. Burns and Stalker (1961).

42. An entire "technology" of team-based production has developed around the basic model of shop-floor problem-solving teams. So centered has it been in traditional production that there has been a difficult struggle to extend it to situations of rapid change and flexibility. See Lawler (1990); also Pava (1979).

43. Honda has perhaps gone farthest in seeing itself as a giant research company. See Nonoka (1988) and Maccoby (1991).

44. I am prevented by confidentiality agreements from revealing the details of this study or exact numbers, but it was a far more rigorous examination than most published reports.

45. Denison (1990).

For other attempts to do more than usually careful research in this area, see Levine and Tyson (1990); Levine and Kruse (1991); and Katz, Kochan, and Keefe (1987). The first two of these find generally positive relations of participation to productivity; the last finds a negative relationship in one company. But the authors suggest on the basis of qualitative information that what is happening here is that they are simply investigating a *bad* team system: sloppily implemented, dogged by labor-management conflict, unable to overcome resistance from middle management. This is an instance of the difficulty of sorting out clear categories for broad research in the field.

I should also repeat the caveat that *all* of the studies referred to use definitions of "participation" that overlap with but are not the same as full post-bureaucratic organization.

46. On the phenomenon of "successful failure" see Lytle (1975); U.S. Department of Labor (1985); Goodfellow (1981); Goodman (1980).

47. Levine and Kruse (1991). For other evidence that supports the view of increasing spread of participation, see, e.g., Denison (1990), Goodman (1980), Usilaner and Leitch (1989), O'Dell (1987), Kochan (1984), New York Stock Exchange (1982), and Walton and Schlesinger (1978).

48. Studies documenting the spread of participatory programs include: Levine and Kruse (1991); O'Dell (1987); New York Stock Exchange (1982); Walton and Schlesinger (1978); Goodman (1980); and Goodmeasure, Inc. (1985).

49. On the Germans, see Wilson (1989).

50. Interaction Associates, Cambridge, MA.

51. See, for example, Ibarra (1991); Mintzberg and McHugh (1985); Lawrence, and Johnston (1988); Goold and Campbell (1987); Lorsch (1984); Munch (1986); Weick (1982); Wilson and Corbett (1983).

52. Pascale (1984); Nonoka (1988).

53. See, for example, the Honeywell CAvD case in Beer, Eisenstat, and Spector (1990).

54. On the problem of evolution, see in general Pattee (1973), especially Pattee's own essay. On the implications of brain research for organization theory, see Beer (1981) and Dennett (1991).

55. A large stream of studies of job satisfaction and commitment in the 1960s and 1970s dried up because it essentially failed to show that those variables were related to any organizational outcome variables.

References

Ackoff, R. L. (1981). *Creating the corporate future: Plan or be planned for*. New York: Wiley.

Alvarez, J. L. A. (1991). *The international diffusion and institutionalization of the new entrepreneurship movement: A study in the sociology of organizational knowledge*. Cambridge, MA: Ph.D. dissertation in Organizational Behavior.

Beer, M., Eisenstat, R. A., & Spector, B. (1990). *The critical path to corporate renewal*. Boston, MA: Harvard Business School Press.

Beer, S. (1981). *Brain of the firm* (2nd ed.). Chichester: Wiley.

Blankenship, R. L. (Ed.). (1977). *Colleagues in organization: The social construction of professional work*. New York: Wiley.

Blau, P. M. (1963). *The dynamics of bureaucracy*. Chicago, IL: University of Chicago Press.

Blinder, A. S. (Ed.). (1990). *Paying for productivity: A look at the evidence*. Washington, DC: The Brookings Institution.

Bradach, J. L., & Eccles, R. G. (1989). Markets vs. hierarchies: From ideal types to plural forms. *Annual Review of Sociology 15*, 97-118.

Braverman, H. (1974). *Labor & monopoly capitalism: The degradation of work in the twentieth century*. New York: Monthly Review Press.

Burgelman, R. A. (1983). A process model of internal corporate venturing in the diversified major firm. *Adminstrative Science Quarterly, 28*, 223-224.

Burns, T., & Stalker, G. M. (1961). *The management of innovation*. London: Tavistock.

Chandler, A. D., Jr. (1977). *The visible hand: The managerial revolution in American business*. Cambridge, MA: Harvard University Press.

Chandler, A., & Daems, H. (Eds.). (1980). *Managerial hierarchies: Comparative perspectives on the rise of modern industrial enterprise*. Cambridge, MA: Harvard University Press.

Chandler, A. D., Jr. (1981). Historical determinants of managerial hierarchies: A response to Perrow. In A. H. Van de Ven & W. F. Joyce (Eds.), *Perspectives on organization design and behavior*. New York: Wiley. [Reprinted in Chandler (1988)]

Chandler, A. D., Jr. (1988). *The essential Alfred Chandler: Essays toward a historical theory of big business*. Boston: Harvard Business School Press.

Daems, H. (1980). The rise of the modern industrial enterprise: A new perspective. In A. D. Chandler & H. Daems (Eds.), *Managerial hierarchies: Comparative perspectives on the rite of modern industrial enterprises* (pp. 203-223). Cambridge, MA: Harvard University Press.

Davis, L. E., Cherns, A. B., & Associates. (1975). *The quality of working life*. New York: The Free Press.

Davis, S. M. (1984). *Managing corporate culture*. Cambridge, MA: Ballinger.

Deal, T. E., & Kennedy, A. A. (1982). *Corporate cultures: The rites and rituals of corporate life*. Reading, MA: Addison-Wesley.

Deinard, C., & Friedman, R. (1990). Black caucus groups at Xerox Corporation (A) and (B). Boston, MA: Harvard Business School.

Denison, D. R. (1990). *Corporate culture and organizational effectiveness.* New York: Wiley.

Dennett, D. C. (1991). *Consciousness explained.* Boston: Little, Brown.

Dimaggio, P. J. & Powell, W. W. (1983, April). The iron cage revisited: Institutional isomorphism and collective rationality in organizational fields. *American Sociological Review 48,*(2), 147-160.

Drucker, P. (1988, January-February). The coming of the new organization. *Harvard Business Review, 88*(1), 45-53.

Durkheim, E. (1957). *Professional ethics & civic morals* (C. Brookfiled, Trans.). London: Routledge & Kegan Paul.

Eaton, A. E. (1992). *New production techniques, employee involvement, and unions.* Mimeo, draft: Rutgers University.

Eccles, R. G., & Crane, D. B. (1987, Fall). Managing through networks in investment banking. *California Management Review, 30,*(1), 176-195.

Eccles, R. G., & Crane, D. B. (1988). *Doing deals: investment banks at work.* Boston: Harvard Business School Press.

Eccles, R. G., & White, H. C. (1988, Supplement). Price and authority in inter-profit center transactions. *American Journal of Sociology, 94,* 517-551.

Forrester, J. W. (1965, Fall). A new corporate design. *Industrial Management Review, 7*(1), 5-17.

Freidson, E. (1963). *The hospital in modern society.* Glencoe, IL: The Free Press.

Friedson, E. (1980). *Patients' views of medical practice.* New York: Russell Sage Foundation.

Friedson, E., & Rhea, B. (1963). Processes of control in a company of equals. *Social Problems, 11,* 119-131.

Frost, P. J. (Ed). (1985). *Organizational culture.* Beverly Hills, CA: Sage.

Fuchsberg, G. (1992, October 1). "Total quality" is termed only partial success. *Wall Street Journal,* p. B1+.

Gerpott, T. J., & Domsch, M. (1985). The concept of professionalism and the management of salaried technical professionals: A cross-national perspective. *Human Resources Management, 24*(2), 207-226.

Golden, O. (1990). Innovation in public sector human services programs: The implications of innovation by "groping along." *Journal of Policy Analysis and Management 9,*(2), 219-248.

Goode, W. J. (1957, April). Community within a community: The professions. *American Sociological Review, 22,* 194-200. (Reprinted in Minar and Greer [1969], pp. 152-162)

Goodfellow, M. (1981). *Quality control circle programs: What works and what doesn't.* Mimeo. Chicago, IL: University Research Center.

Goodman, P. S. (1980, August). Realities of improving the quality of work life: Quality of Work Life projects in the 1980s. *Labor Law Journal, 31*(8), 487-494.

Goodmeasure, Inc. (1985). *The changing American workplace: Work alternatives in 80s.* New York: American Management Association.

Goold, M. (1991, Winter). Strategic control in the decentralized firm. *Sloan Management Review,* pp. 69-81.

Gould, M. (1987). *Revolution in the development of capitalism: The coming of the English revolution.* Berkeley, CA: University of California Press.

Gould, M., & Campbell, A. (1987). Many best ways to make strategy. *Harvard Business Review, 65*(6), 70-76.

Gouldner, A. W. (1954). *Patterns of industrial bureaucracy: A case study of modern factory administration.* New York: The Free Press.

Granovetter, M. S. (1973). The strength of weak ties. *American Journal of Sociology, 78*(6), 1360-1380.

Habermas, J. (1991). *Communication and the evolution of society.* Translated and with an introduction by Thomas McCarthy. Cambridge, UK: Polity Press.

Hagstrom, W. O. (1965). *The scientific community.* Carbondale, IL: Southern Illinois University Press.

Haskell, T. L. (Ed.). (1984). *The authority of Experts: Studies in history and theory.* Bloomington, IN: Indiana University Press.

Hayes, R. H. (1986, April 20). Why strategic planning goes awry. *New York Times.*

Hobes, T. (1651/1992). *Leviathan.* New York. Viking.

Huber, G. P. (1984, August). The nature and design of post-industrial organizations. *Management Science, 30*(8), 928-951.

Ibarra, H. (1991, May). *Structural alignments, individual strategies, and managerial action: Elements toward a network theory of getting things done.* Mimeo, draft. Harvard Business School.

Jackall, R. (1988). *Moral mazes: The world of corporate managers.* New York: Oxford University Press.

Jackson, J. A. (Ed.). (1970). *Professions & professionalization.* Cambridge, UK: Cambridge University Press.

Janowitz, M. D., Suttles, G. D., & Zald, M. N. (Eds.). (1985). *The challenge of social control.* Norwood, NJ: Ablex.

Jaques, E. (1990, January-February). In praise of hierarchy. *Harvard Business Review,* pp. 127-33.

Kaboolian, L. (1991). *How is effort determined?* Mimeo. Harvard Kennedy School of Government, Cambridge.

Kanter, R. M. (1977). *Men and women of the corporation.* New York: Basic Books.

Katz, H. C., Kochan, T. A., & Keefe, J. H. (1987). Effects of industrial relations on productivity: Evidence from the automobile industry. *Brookings Papers on Economic Activity.* Washington, DC: Brookings Institution.

Kelley, M. R., & Harrison, B. (1992). Unions, technology, and labor-management cooperation. In L. Mishel & P. B. Voos (Eds.), *Unions and economic competitiveness* (pp. 247-286). New York: M. E. Sharpe.

Kochan, T. (1984, December). *Recent changes in management of industrial relations* mimeo draft. Boston: MIT.

Krackhardt, D. (1991, February). *Does informal structure make a difference? The relationship between social networks and bank branch performance.* Mimeo. Harvard University.

Kuhn, T. S. (1962). *The structure of scientific revolutions.* Chicago, IL: University of Chicago Press.

Kusterer, K. C. (1978). *Know-how on the job: The important working knowledge of 'unskilled' workers.* Boulder, CO: Westview Press.

Lawler, E. E., III. (1990, Autumn). The new plant revolution revisited. *Organizational Dynamics,* pp. 5-14.

Lawrence, P. R., & Johnston, R. (1988). *Are organizational partnerships displacing large corporate dinosaurs?* Mimeo, draft. Harvard Business School.

Lawrence, P. R., & Lorsch, J. W. (1967). *Organization and environment.* Boston, MA: Harvard Business School.

Lazonick, W. (1987). *Organization capability and technological change in comparative perspective.* Mimeo, draft.

Levine, D., & Kruse, D. (1991, March). Employee involvement efforts: Incidence, correlates, and effects. Draft. School of Business Administration, University of California, Berkeley.

Levine, D. I., & Tyson, L. D. (1990). Participation, productivity, and the firm's environment. In A. S. Blinder (Ed.), *Paying for productivity: A look at the evidence* (pp. 183- 237). Washington, DC: The Bookings Institution.

Lorsch, J. W. (1984, Autumn). The other side of excellence. *Chief Executive, 29,* 47-49.

Luhmann, N. (1979). *Trust and power.* New York: Wiley (Orig. German eds. in 1973 and 1975.)

Lynd, A., & Lynd, S. (Eds.). (1973). *Rank & file: Personal histories by working-class organizers.* Boston, MA: Beacon Press.

Lytle, W. O. (1975). A smart camel may refuse that last straw: Case study of obstacles to job and organization design in a new manufacturing operation. In Davis et al. (Eds.), *The quality of working life* (pp. 110-137). New York: The Free Press.

Maccoby, M. (1991, September-October). Move from hierarchy to heterarchy. *Research Technology Management, 34,*(5), 46-47.

Main, J. (1981). Westinghouse's cultural revolution. *Fortune.*

Manning, P. K. (1977). Rules, colleagues, and situationally justified actions. In R. L. Blankenship (Ed.), *Colleagues in organization: The social construction of professional work* (ch. 10). New York: Wiley.

Margolis, D. R. (1979). *The managers: Corporate life in America.* New York: Morrow.

Mathewson, S. B. (1931). *Restriction of output among unorganized workers.* New York: Viking.

Merton, R. K. (1940). Bureaucratic structure and personality. *Social Forces, 17,* 560-568.

Merton, R. K. (1949). *Social theory and social structure.* New York: The Free Press. (1968 expanded edition.)

Mills, C. W. (1951). *White collar: The American middle classes.* London: Oxford University Press.

Minar, D. W., & Greer, S. (Eds.). (1969). *The concept of community.* Chicago: Aldine.

Mintzberg, H., & McHugh, A. (1985). Strategy formation in an adhocracy. *Administrative Science Quarterly, 30,* 160-197.

Mintzberg, H., Raisinghani, D., & Théorêt, A. (1976, June). The structure of "unstructured" decision processes. *Administrative Science Quarterly, 21,* 246-275.

Mishel, L., & Voos, P. B. (1992). *Unions and economic competitiveness.* Armonk, NY: M.E. Sharpe.

Munch, R. (1986). The American creed in sociological theory: Exchange, negotiated order, accommodated individualism, and contingency. *Sociological Theory, 4,* 41-60.

New York Stock Exchange Office of Economic Research. (1982). *People & productivity: A challenge to corporate America.* New York: New York Stock Exchange.

Nohria, N. (1987). *Institutional innovations in high technology clusters: The 128 Venture Group in the route 128 region.* Mimeo, draft, Harvard Business School, Boston.

Nonoka, I. (1988, Spring). Toward middle-up-down management: Accelerating information creation. *Sloan Management Review,* pp. 9-18.

O'Dell, C. (1987). *People, performance, and pay.* American Productivity Center.

Orton, J. D., & Weick, K. E. (1990). Loosely coupled systems: A reconceptualization. *Academy of Management Review, 15*(2), 203-223.

Ouchi, W. G. (1981). *Theory Z: How American business can meet the Japanese challenge.* Reading, MA: Addison-Wesley.

Parsons, T. (1968). Professions. In D. L. Sills (Ed.), *International encyclopedia of the social sciences* (vol. 12, pp. 536-547). New York: Crowell Collier and Macmillan.

Parsons, T. (1969a). On the concept of political power. In T. Parsons, *Politics and social structure* (ch. 14). New York: The Free Press.

Parsons, T. (1969b). *Politics and social structure.* New York: The Free Press.

Pascale, R. T. (1984). Perspectives on strategy: The real story in Honda's success. *California Management Review, 26*(3), 47-72.

Pattee, H. H. (1973). *Hierarchy theory: The challenge of complex systems.* New York: George Braziller.

Pava, C. (1979). *State of the art in American autonomous work group design.* Boston: Busch Center, Managerial and Behavioral Science Center.

Pettigrew, A. M. (1973) *The politics of organizational decision-making.* London: Tavistock.

Piaget, J. (1932). *The moral judgment of the child.* New York: Harcourt Brace.

Piore, M. J. (1982, March-April). American labor and the industrial crisis. *Challenge,* pp. 5-11.

Powell, W. W. (1990). Neither market nor hierarchy: Network forms of organization. *Research in Organizational Behavior, 12,* 295-336.

Rubin, L. B. (1976). *Worlds of pain: Life in the working-class family.* New York: Basic Books.

Sabel, C. F., Herrigel, G., Kazis, R., & Deeg, R. (1987, April). How to keep mature industries innovative. *Technology Review,* pp. 26-35.

Sabel, C. (1991). Moebius-strip organizations and open labor markets: Some consequences of the reintegration of conception and execution in a volatile economy. In J. Coleman & P. Bourdieu (Eds.), *Social theory for a changing society.* Boulder, CO: Westview Press.

Schein, E. H. (1985). *Organizational culture and leadership.* San Francisco, CA: Jossey-Bass.

Schoonhoven, C. B., & Jelinek, M. (1990). Dynamic tension in innovative, high technology firms: Managing rapid technological change through organizational structure. In M. A. Von Glinow & S. A. Mohrman (Eds.), *Managing complexity in high technology organizations.* New York: Oxford University Press.

Selznick, P. (1949). *TVA and the grass roots: A study in the sociology of formal organizations.* Berkeley, CA: University of California Press.

Shapiro, S. P. (1987, November). The social control of impersonal trust. *American Journal of Sociology 93*(3), 623-658.

Shorter, E. (1973). The history of work in the West: An overview. In E. Shorter (Ed.), *Work and community in the West* (ch. 1). New York: Harper & Row.

Silver, A. (1985). "Trust" in social and political theory. In Suttles, G. D. & Zald, M. N. (Eds.), *The challenge of social control* (ch. 4). Norwood, NJ: Ablex.

Sonnenfeld, J. A., & Lazo, M. (1988). *United Parcel Service* (case #9-488-016). Boston: Harvard Business School.

Strauss, A., Schatzman, L., Ehrlich, D., Bucher, R., & Sabshin, M. (1963). The hospital and its negotiated order. In E. Freidson (Ed.), *Patient's views of medical practice* (pp. 147-169). New York: Russell Sage Foundation.

Taylor, A. III. (1990, November 19). Why Toyota keeps getting better and better and better. *Fortune,* pp. 66-79.

Thompson, J. D. (1973, July/August). Society's frontiers for organizing activities. *Public Administration Review, 33-34,* 327-335.

Torstendahl, R., & Burrage, M. (1990). *The formation of professions: Knowledge, state and strategy.* London: Sage. (Reviewed in *CS,* May 1991, p. 389.)

U.S. Department of Labor. (1985). *Quality of work life: AT&T and CWA examine the process after three years.* Washington, DC: U.S. Department of Labor, Bureau of Labor-Management Relations.

Usilaner, B., & Leitch, J. (1989, June). Miles to go or . . . unity at last. *Journal for Quality and Participation,* pp. 60-67.

Veblen, T. (1904). *The theory of business enterprise.* New York: Scribner's.

Von Glinow, M. A., & Mohrman, S. A. (1990). *Managing complexity in high technology organizations.* New York: Oxford University Press.

Walton, R. E., & Hackman, J. R. (1985, July). *Implications of management strategy for groups in organizations.* Harvard Business School working paper.

Walton, R., & Schlesinger, L. (1978, July-August). Plant-level innovations: After a decade of experience. *Harvard Business Review,* pp. 88-98.

Waters, M. (1989, March). Collegiality, bureaucratization, and professionalization: A Weberian analysis. *American Journal of Sociology, 94*(5), 945-972.

Weick, K. E. (1977, Autumn). Organization design: Organizations as self-designing systems. *Organizational Dynamics,* pp. 31-46.

Weick, K. E. (1982, June). Administering education in loosely-coupled schools. *Phi Delta Kappa, 63,* 673-676.

Weir, S. (1973). The informal work group. In A. Lynd & S. Lynd (Eds.), *Rank & file: Personal histories by working-class organizers* (pp. 177-200). Boston, MA: Beacon Press.

Whyte, W. H., Jr. (1956). *The organization man.* New York: Simon & Schuster.

Williamson, O. E. (1975). *Markets and hierarchies: Analysis and antitrust implications.* New York: The Free Press.

Williamson, O. E. (1985). *Economic institutions of capitalism.* New York: The Free Press.

Wilson, B. L., & Corbett, H. D. (1983). Organization and change: The effects of school linkages on the quantity of implementation. *Educational Administration Quarterly, 19*(4), 85-104.

Wilson, J. Q. (1989). *Bureaucracy: What government agencies do and why they do it.* New York: Basic Books.

Zucker, L. G. (1986). Production of trust: Institutional sources of economic structure, 1840-1920. *Research in Organizational Behavior, 8,* 53-111.

Zuckerman, H., & Merton, R. K. (1981). Patterns of evaluation in science: Institutionalization, structure and functions of the referee system. *Minerva, 9*(1), 66-100.

3 TEAMS, PERFORMANCE, AND REWARDS

Will the Post-Bureaucratic Organization Be a Post-Meritocratic Organization?

Anne Donnellon
Maureen Scully

The post-bureaucratic organization envisioned in this book blurs the lines—vertical and horizontal—that demarcate areas of individual expertise, authority, and accountability. Such flexible organizational forms have long been championed from a humanistic perspective (e.g., Burrell & Morgan, 1979; Ferguson, 1984; Thayer, 1981), because they typically allow for greater participation in decision making. Flexible forms are currently gaining enthusiasm for a reason less idealistic but perhaps more compelling from a business perspective: the recognition that increasing competitive pressures and inexorable technological acceleration require sacrificing some of bureaucracy's predictability and control to the hope of achieving better and faster integration of expertise. Meeting these new challenges requires a form of collaboration that does not halt or founder on the limits of assigned authority or role but rather is based on the willing contribution of whatever is necessary to get the job done. The common shorthand for such collaboration is *team work*.[1] In this chapter, we will add our voices to others' throughout industry

AUTHORS' NOTE: This paper has been a team effort between the authors. We thank Russell Eisenstadt, Charles Hecksher, Janice Klein, and Joshua Margolis for helpful comments and thank members of the post-bureaucracy group at Harvard's Graduate School of Business for provocative discussions.

and academia in the United States who propound the importance of teams as an integral feature of the post-bureaucratic organization. We argue that the integration of teams will require a new approach to the division of labor and, perhaps even more challenging to deeply held cultural norms, a new approach to rewards. We are not the first to argue that teams cannot simply be grafted onto existing work and reward structures. The difference in our approach is that we propose fixes that do not simply fix the meritocracy, for example, by assuring individual team members of meritocratic treatment or turning merit-based competition between individuals into merit contests between teams. Instead, we propose that meritocracy is so intrinsically associated with an individualistic, non-cooperative, bureaucratic approach to work that it must be abandoned in the process of moving beyond bureaucracy.

Team work is widely touted as a necessary and achievable component of the post-bureaucratic organization. Recent empirical work, however, has found that the transition to teams is slow and painful and the outcomes far less impressive than is commonly thought (Donnellon, 1992). It appears that managers have not recognized how profoundly different team work is from the bureaucratic model of work and how much the organization must change for teams to flourish. It is only gradually being understood that certain bureaucratic features like a narrow division of labor and the vertical ordering of titles and authority are not hospitable to team work. Too little attention has been paid to the needed changes to the organizational reward structure (cf., Deming, 1986; Kanter, 1987; Lawler, 1990), although virtually everyone agrees, on reflection, that performance appraisal and compensation must change for teams to work.

The structure of rewards is built on the foundation of the bureaucratic division of labor: increasing rewards are tied to specific roles that are supposed, in the formal model of bureaucracy, to be of increasing difficulty and increasing value to the organization. When we begin to shake that foundation, the reward structure should, theoretically, become precarious. A new division of labor ought to occasion a new distribution of rewards. However, attempts to change rewards are likely to meet with resistance, not just because the division of labor has been rationalized within organizations but also because merit-based opportunity is seen as fair and desirable in the broader culture of the United States. From Weber's (1946a) earliest description of bureaucracy through contemporary work as diverse as theories of internal labor markets and theories of procedural justice, it is assumed that the rationality of bureaucracies buffers them from arbitrariness and caprice and makes them appear more legitimate. The possibility that bureaucracies do—and now should and must—stray from a purely rational division of labor may not come as a surprise to academics or practitioners and should only make it easier to adopt teams that cut across traditionally defined roles. However, it is not popular to admit that organizations do—and now should and must— stray from their rational, merit-based logic in the realm of rewards, particularly if this logic has been used to legitimate decisions about who occupies the positions of greatest authority and rewards. The discussion about departures from meritocracy raises difficult issues about how much organizations— both bureaucratic and post-bureaucratic—have been and will be fair in their distribution of tasks, authority, and rewards. Thus, we see that debates about legitimacy, not just debates about the division of labor and technical efficiency, place obstacles on the path to team work and the realization of post-bureaucratic potential.

In this chapter, we will explore how the introduction of team work raises questions about merit-based rewards, which draws our attention back to the traditional bases of organizational legitimacy and why they might be tenacious. We consider why the reward structure may be the most difficult aspect of an organization to change in the pursuit of post-bureaucratic organizing. Although it may be easy enough to imagine people moving fluidly among tasks without hierarchy's guidewires, it is more difficult to envision the distribution of rewards in a fluid, nonhierarchical manner. Alternatives to the current reward structure are difficult to apprehend, but we hope in this chapter to raise issues that will motivate the search. We examine some practices that have been posed as alternatives—such as flatter hierarchies and pay-for-performance—but ask whether these may just constitute meritocracy in another guise and pose the same problems for teams. We may not offer unimpeachable answers to the questions we pose, but we believe these questions must be addressed with new attention and vigor, if the post-bureaucratic organization is to realize its potential.

The Traditional Logic of Bureaucracy

The classic statement about the form of bureaucracy is found in Weber's (1946a) famous essay. Taken alone, this essay does not address the ideology and culture that pervades and supports bureaucracy. Considered along with Weber's *The Protestant Ethic and the Spirit of Capitalism* (1976) and the rest of Weber's considerable *oeuvre,* it advances the argument that certain historic beliefs—the desirability of working hard for ultimate return and the revealed superiority of those who are in society's highest positions—had a crucial, mutually reinforcing relationship with the structures and functioning of a rational bureaucracy. This section reviews these persistent cultural ideas, which we label here as part of *meritocratic ideology.* We then discuss the concept of the rational individual who inhabits the bureaucracy and finally review three features of the bureaucracy on which its rationality and legitimacy hinge but that must change in the move to the post-bureaucratic organization. Our discussion of the ideological underpinnings of bureaucracy is crucial to understanding how the structures of bureaucracy must change, and when they do, the almost obsessive attention to merit—to who gets what and who deserves more—may have to be not merely refined into new forms of pay-for-performance but jettisoned altogether.

Meritocratic Ideology

The term *meritocracy* is a satirical invention of Young (1958) in his fable of the unexpected divisive consequences of a truly merit-based future society. The term has since been applied, somewhat more soberly, to late capitalist systems of status attainment and reward allocation, usually to distinguish them favorably from class-based or aristocratic systems, where birth or family determine outcomes, and to praise these systems for elevating the most talented and deserving (e.g., Bell, 1976). A meritocracy sorts individuals into positions on the basis of their merits. The principles of a meritocratic social order that Daniels (1978) defines are: (1) the selection of individuals for positions on the basis of well-defined merits, (2) the means, such as equality of opportunity, for individuals to develop and display their merits, and (3) a system of attaching rewards to positions.

Scholars have addressed all three of these aspects of a meritocracy. First, different types of merit are defined. In broad strokes, "inputs" such as ability and effort and "outputs" such as performance or contribution are variously regarded as appropriate bases of merit. Second, there have been many attempts (e.g., Jencks et al., 1979) to examine whether equality of opportunity exists, specifically by looking at whether forms of merit (such as SAT scores) determine who gets ahead in the United States rather than forms of privilege (such as family income). The ongoing political significance of this debate is that political conservatives generally argue that merit does count, hence correctives like affirmative action and redistribution are not warranted, while political liberals generally argue that merit is the touted but not actual basis of advancement, hence correctives are warranted. Third, organizational researchers have explored how rewards get attached to positions and how individuals move among positions, garnering the reward associated with the position, rather than with their contribution at any given moment (Baron, 1984). It is in response to this institutionalization of rewards for positions that Kanter (1987) writes that rewards should no longer attach to "status" but to "contribution," essentially an argument for a return to a "truer" form of meritocracy, which we address further on.

The Rational Individual in the Bureaucracy

Weber's sociological work does not directly pose a theory of the psychology of the inhabitants of a successful bureaucracy. However, this model assumes that individuals are willing and able to defer gratification and work hard now in the expectation of rewards later, specifically monetary rewards in a bureaucracy. For bureaucracy to be efficient, such individuals must be motivated by the prospect of a career in which they climb an organizational ladder.

More recent psychological work on motivation, such as expectancy theory (Lawler, 1973; Vroom, 1964), elaborates a similar portrait of individuals who work hard if they feel their effort produces a realizable performance that , in turn, produces a valued reward. According to equity theory (e.g., Adams, 1965), individuals are more satisfied if the ratio of their inputs to rewards is the same as the ratios of others. Individuals in organizations make social comparisons in determining if their rewards are fair (e.g., Martin, 1981; Wood, 1989). The individual appears as a rational calculator, extrinsically motivated and constantly concerned about using power to win a relatively larger share.

Along with the cultural and psychological concomitants of bureaucracy, three structural features of the bureaucratic model combine to generate the efficiency, coordination, incentives, and legitimacy required to maximize outcomes in the industrial era. These are reviewed below: individual performance of tasks, managerial assessment of performance, and hierarchical allocation of rewards.

Individual Performance of Tasks

Part of the logic of bureaucracy is its claim to technical efficiency through the division of labor into subtasks (Weber, 1946a). Roles are discrete to allow boundedly rational employees to focus on a subtask, so as to achieve mastery. The perception of control over, and accountability for, one's performance of a specific subtask creates the incentive to work hard and thus reap the rewards linked to the subtask. Roles are related hierarchically, it is argued, to facilitate employees' learning of ever more complicated tasks and to assist top managers in processing only the important information that is passed upward (March & Simon, 1958). Each individual has a bounded place in the means-ends chain of tasks.

Managerial Assessment of Performance

For bureaucracy to deliver on its promise of technical efficiency, it required people to pursue careers within organizations, as Weber (1946a) outlined and as has been elaborated in the literature on internal labor markets (e.g., Doeringer & Piore, 1971; Osterman, 1984). In these accounts, employees acquire firm-specific skills to ply as they ascend a ladder of increasingly demanding positions. More experienced employees train and evaluate employees below them, with the understanding that, in training their replacements, they too can move up the ladder. Since the job ladder is supposed to reflect a gradient of fewer to more skills, those in higher positions are thought to be best able both to assign tasks and to evaluate the performance of tasks by those below them. This additional monitoring of task performance is typically justified—or critiqued as a mechanism for increasing managerial control. Bureaucracy is believed to work well because its rules are "impersonal," that is, "like" individuals are treated "alike." Meritocracy is a very common system of rules for assessing performance (Lawler, 1973; Murphy & Cleveland, 1991) and is addressed in this chapter; seniority-based rules are another alternative.

Hierarchical Allocation of Rewards

Part of the inducement to remain with the firm and work hard is the promise of ascending to higher positions, to which greater rewards are attached. Each employee is supposed to feel accountable for the successful execution of the tasks within his or her role as the means of earning fair compensation in the near term and promotion in the longer term, both supposedly assigned by an objective and rational authority. Merit, rather than favoritism, is supposed to provide the basis for reward and promotion. Merit-based rewards are supposed to assure that employees are fairly treated and feel motivated to work hard and that organizations identify and promote the most productive talent.

The Persistence of Bureaucracy

Of course, this description of bureaucracy, even when first penned by Weber, is posed as an ideal-typical description. In fact, work in large complex organizations has rarely lent itself to such independence of action in discrete roles. Adjustments could be made in times when there was sufficient organizational slack, through informal mechanisms that reintegrated arbitrarily differentiated responsibilities (Heckscher, 1988). Even if the reintegration was not perfect or timely, the relative lack of competitive pressure allowed the prevailing formal design of work to survive and dominate with little question.

Becoming Post-Bureaucratic

Until the mid 1970s, the bureaucratic form of business organization met and far exceeded expectations of profitability. Stable markets, steady technological advancement, and mass production with its economies of scale created an environment of constrained and predictable competition. In such an environment, bureaucracy's advantages in efficiency, control, and career incentives produced high profits. However, by the late 1970s, momentous changes on several fronts were destabilizing this environment, throwing its strategic and organizational assumptions into question.

The success of Japanese companies in the American marketplace attracted attention to product quality and development time as new competitive advantages. Both issues illuminated the collaborative efforts prevalent within Japanese organizations. Though U.S. firms adopted quality circles, they were slow to recognize the need for more significant organizational initiatives to meet the increasing competitive pressure. The Japanese were simply the most prominent international competitors in a field battling for global markets. At home and abroad, with new technology generating new products and more sophisticated processes for making them, the barriers to entry were tumbling in many industries. The major U.S. firms that had dominated the world for decades were learning that other companies could generate new ideas faster, manufacture them better and cheaper, improve them continuously, and gradually push their way into sizable market shares. The advantages of efficiency and control, achieved through bureaucracy, were no longer paying off.

In fact, with simultaneous improvement in product quality, development time, and costs as the new competitive standard, bureaucracy became the problem. With each passing year, it becomes clearer that to meet such demands, organizations need to be both effective and efficient, to inspire commitment and initiative from their employees while maintaining a significant degree of control over and coordination of the enterprise, and to motivate this commitment in a manner that keeps costs in check. Furthermore, we have come to recognize that the organizational design features that gave bureaucracy its power in an earlier era are now hobbling the effort to meet these post-bureaucratic requirements.

In this section, we consider how the three features of bureaucracy discussed above—individual performance of tasks, managerial assessment of performance, and hierarchical allocation of rewards—need to change for organizations to become post-bureaucratic and reap the rewards of team work. We explain the several practical and political problems associated with each feature, discuss several popular solutions that have been proffered, and assess them, identifying the possible negative consequences of each solution. We focus our discussion on how aspects of bureaucracy must change to accommodate team work, because, as discussed above, team work is emerging as an agreed on and integral feature of the post-bureaucratic organization. Table 3.1 summarizes the main points of our discussion.

Moving Beyond Individual Performance of Tasks

As organizations adopt both efficiency and effectiveness as strategic goals, many of their critical tasks (e.g., product development and order fulfillment) now require knowledge and experience that do not reside in one person but are distributed among people, making them interdependent. Furthermore, this interdependence takes on the reciprocal quality (Thompson, 1967) that renders the tasks impossible to accomplish except by a group or team. Thus, the predictable synergistic outcomes that may arise when members from different parts of the organization get together to work on a problem have become more of a necessity than a luxury and teams are the common solution.

The primary practical concern about moving away from individual performance of tasks is the ubiquitous assumption that lack of individual accountability will create a disincentive for individual contributions to teams. Of course, this consequence is entirely possible; however, its correspondence with bureaucracy's implicit model of motivation should subject this assumption to the same kind of reexamination to which bureaucracy itself has been subject. It is quite possible that to elicit necessary contributions to teams, the removal of disincentives would prove far more productive than the introduction of incentives. Research on professional teams (Donnellon, 1992) finds that team members very frequently described a tension between wanting to devote time to team tasks but feeling they had to fulfill their functional responsibilities first, because those were the essence of their jobs.

An additional complication of the bureaucratic feature of individual task performance created by reciprocal tasks and the team approach is that for many professional and managerial employees, their job descriptions include both team assignments and individual tasks. To ensure that individuals continue to perform these tasks, the common solution is to preserve individual performance assessments and rewards. One possible negative consequence of this solution is that, even if individuals were personally motivated to contribute to the team despite the lack of individual accountability for team outcomes, their individual accountability for other nonteam tasks could discourage the diversion of attention and energy to team tasks.

One obvious solution to this problem that many companies are experimenting with is the assessment of individual contribution to teams, which is added to the other assessments of individual performance. This scheme has great intuitive appeal because it fits neatly with the bureaucratic assumption

TABLE 3.1 Assessing Solutions to Bureaucratic Problems

Post-Bureaucratic Requirements	Inhibiting Features of Bureaucracy	Problems With These Features	Popular Solutions	Possible Negative Consequences
Efficiency *and* Effectiveness	Individual Performance of Tasks	Most critical tasks now are reciprocally interdependent Inhibits flexible and fluid participation	Assign most critical tasks to teams Adapt individual assessment and reward system Assess individual "team skills" as part of assessment of individual responsibilities	Lack of individual accountability for team work encourages lack of contribution to team Individual accountability for other work discourages contribution to team Individuals act strategically to maximize the visibility of their contribution Integrative team spirit threatened Team task not optimally performed
Coordination *and* Commitment	Managerial Assessment of Individual Performance	Arbitrary due to lack of observed data (on teams) Arbitrary due to interdependence of tasks Political; not useful in enhancing performance	Have team members assess each other Assess team members' contribution to team performance Assess team performance	Recognized individual accountability for other work and to manager may discourage team contribution and make this meaningless in terms of improving team performance Outcome measures too distant; hard to control and give incentives on annual basis With fluid team participation, distribution of rewards may be too difficult and wide

71

TABLE 3.1 Continued

Post-Bureaucratic Requirements	Inhibiting Features of Bureaucracy	Problems With These Features	Popular Solutions	Possible Negative Consequences
Incentives *and* Cost Control	Hierarchical Allocation of Rewards	Preserves attachment to hierarchy and individual performance assessment; creates a disincentive for team work May be a disincentive to many in organization May not be cost-effective	Flatten the hierarchy Pay for contribution/skills	Does not eliminate attachment to hierarchy and individual accountability Retains problems of individual performance assessment described above May lead to friction over total range of pay within and across levels

that people only do what they are held individually accountable for doing. However, there are several negative possibilities attached to this solution.

Such reviews require going back and trying to discern whose individual contribution yielded which portion of the final results. This is not only impractical but counterproductive to the integrative spirit of team work. The old reward scheme—in which skill, knowledge, and effort are resident in and traceable to singular individuals—cannot be used. If individuals in a team think that such an algorithm is to be applied, then they might withhold information from one another or use other strategies to assure that their individual contribution stands out, at the expense of optimal team performance and synergistic outcomes. Solutions that alter the individual basis of performance and reward are likely to encounter even bigger obstacles of the political and ideological variety. These are taken up in a subsequent section.

Moving Beyond Managerial Assessment of Performance

The increasing complexity and interdependence in tasks as organizations adjust to new competitive pressures have also made the bureaucratic feature of managerial assessment of individual performance problematic. Because the critical organizational tasks now create more interdependence, attempts to define individual areas of responsibility for assessment are inherently arbitrary. Furthermore, the assessment of individual performance on teams will seem somewhat arbitrary because of the lack of actual observations of the individual behavior on the team. An additional problem with managerial assessment of individual performance, which would persist in the post-bureaucracy, has long been suspected by employees and detailed by researchers (e.g., Jackall, 1988; Longenecker & Gioia, 1988; Murphy & Cleveland, 1991): the process is inherently political and therefore unrelated to performance enhancement.

The manager's assessment role has typically involved ranking a group of employees and distributing performance ratings and raises to them (Dornbusch & Scott, 1975; Murphy & Cleveland, 1991). To give excellent employees a higher raise and still meet a targeted average raise, some employees are inevitably forced into the lower tail of the distribution. Firms' formal espousals that merit criteria guide performance ratings are supposed to placate those employees not chosen for the best ratings or promotions, but Scully (1993) finds that these employees are less likely to believe a firm's assertions about the role of merit. Although some people who get low ratings might be expected to increase their efforts in the next period to insure "fair" and favorable assessment in the next review, others are just as likely to reduce their contributions in order to achieve a tolerable balance between effort and reward (Lawler, 1973). A manager giving performance evaluations in a firm that espouses meritocracy may find himself or herself in the awkward position of generating more feelings of disappointment and grievance than satisfaction and fairness.

Assessing the psychological dynamics of competition, Kohn (1986) argues that a system that encourages competition among individuals so that an individual can gain self-esteem by winning will ironically result in a desperate need to win that deflates the self-esteem of most people. Experimental manipulations show that a competitive, individualistic distribution system correlates not only with lower self-esteem among participants but also with lower satisfaction ratings and performance (Gumpert, Gordon, Welch, Offringa, & Katz, 1992). In a study of performance-based rating systems in high technology firms, Zenger (1992) found that those engineers most likely to depart were not just the extremely low performers but also those moderately highly rated performers who might be disappointed at falling short of the highest ratings.

To cope with these numerous tensions, while striving to ensure high group performance and to manage his or her own interdependencies, the manager has few options beyond assessing performance in a politically expedient way. For example, sometimes managers just rotate who gets the best performance evaluation, and their groups are complicit in this turn-taking. However, although such political approaches do serve to keep the peace and save face, as Murphy and Cleveland (1991) have concluded from the literature, there is no empirical evidence that performance assessments enhance performance.

A possible solution to managerial performance assessment is that the team members in a post-bureaucratic setting, not a manager, should assess one another's contribution to the performance. This solution has several benefits. It places assessment in the hands of those people who actually observe a person's contribution to the team performance. Therefore, it may be based on more concrete and less political criteria. And since the measurement would reflect multiple raters, it would probably be more reliable.

However, when teams are crossfunctional—which is increasing in popularity—team members tend to experience tension, which has a negative effect on their team contribution and is likely to make accurate assessment of one another impossible. The tension is a function of contradictory messages from the organization. On the one hand, they are told the team is to be held accountable for the team task. But on the other hand, their performance evaluations continue to be conducted on an individual basis by the functional manager. The persistence of a functional hierarchy in organizations with teams means that team members derive most of their professional identities from the function, and their function is where their hopes of future promotion lie. Team members recognize one another's torn loyalties and, at best, they empathize with their colleagues and do only the most perfunctory assessment. At worst, the understanding of others' dual loyalties causes them either to reduce their own contributions to match others' or to create a climate of defensiveness and ill will in the team by criticizing others' deficiencies of contribution. In all these cases, team performance is not enhanced.

The popular solution to the interdependence challenge to managerial assessment of performance is to resort to the assessment of individual contributions to teams. This practice is critiqued above, in terms of its implicit encouragement of strategic behavior on the part of individuals. The obvious alternative to these problems and to the concern that managerial assessment is political and irrelevant to performance is to assess the performance of the team as a whole. Research indicates that this alternative is not common and suggests that the reason for that is managerial concern with two potential negative consequences (Donnellon, 1992). The first is that, because team outcome measures may not be available on an annual basis, managers feel they would be unable to provide adequate incentives and sense of control needed to influence performance. Second, for those people who believe that the primary purpose of individual performance assessment is to provide a fair basis for the distribution of rewards, team rewards are too great and uncertain a departure. Groups that work closely together may default to a more egalitarian division of rewards if differentiation is uncomfortable and embarrassing for people who interact frequently (Pfeffer & Langton, 1988). Yet at the same time, if is often suggested that team rewards that are divided in an egalitarian fashion are not fair. In addition, the possibility that team members move fluidly among teams complicates the issue of assigning bonuses to "Team A," a team that may be defined by a set of tasks, not a stable roster of members.

Moving Beyond the Hierarchical Allocation of Rewards

As discussed earlier, the bureaucratic model of organization is based on a hierarchical distribution of knowledge, responsibility, and reward. The model is based on the assumption that the hierarchical allocation of reward provides people with an incentive to develop their knowledge base and to work hard in expectation of moving up to higher levels of responsibility and reward. The evolution of bureaucracy brought a tight coupling of narrow definitions of jobs with narrow bands of income, as a means of balancing the incentive of the career ladder with the control of incentive costs.

In the post-bureaucratic era, with its requirements for knowledge contributions on the part of all employees and for control of costs, this feature creates three problems. First, the persistence of a hierarchical allocation of rewards preserves the attachment to hierarchy and to individual performance assessment as the requisite vehicle for moving up the hierarchy. As explained earlier, these two aspects of bureaucracy create serious obstacles to effective team work. Second, given the narrow bands and depending on the permeability of the boundaries between them, such a distribution of rewards based on hierarchy could act as a disincentive for most people to contribute their knowledge and ideas. The attendant mental calculations might include such ruminations as, "They get paid the big bucks to think of a solution, so I'll just keep my thoughts to myself." Third, the post-bureaucratic emphasis on market orientation and customer satisfaction depends on valuable knowledge contributions from *all* employees. A hierarchical and top-heavy distribution of rewards conveys the message that contributions from those at the top are disproportionately valuable. Such a reward structure is likely to be costly both in terms of the cynicism and lowered morale it can breed among employees and in terms of the rents diverted to the top. Wage gaps on the order of 85:1 are seen in the United States and are discussed with greater frequency and concern in the business press (e.g., Crystal, 1992).

The flattening of hierarchies, by removing layers of middle management, is often mentioned in the same breath as team work as a solution to the problems of hierarchical bureaucracy. In practice, however, the flattening of hierarchies, without attention to more fundamental questions about reward structures, may simply result in two distant levels with nothing in the middle. The wage gap may not close.

Lower-level production employees have no more job ladder above them once the first-line supervisory positions are eliminated. Instead, they are urged to focus on job rotation. The highest positions in the company are unattainable, but because these highest positions are still there, job rotation feels like a consolation prize. One feature of a meritocracy was that any employee was supposed to be able to rise from the mail room to the board room, but now the ladder has been kicked aside. The highest positions still exist, and still command a higher wage. The merit contest becomes a contest within levels—production workers compete for raises with other production workers and executives compete for raises with other executives. Within levels, small differences between people who work closely together are magnified. Between levels, the vast difference is sometimes questioned by external critics, but appeals to the greater difficulty of executive work are used by organizations to justify this difference, essentially still an appeal to different merits.

The flatter hierarchy, painted here in stark colors on purpose to squelch some of the enthusiasm for this "solution," retains some of the worst features of meritocracy, such as vast pay differences for work that is only traditionally and habitually assumed to be vastly different in its value to the company. This system loses some of the best features of meritocracy, such as opportunities for advancement that at least formally attempt to bridge the lowest and highest levels. It reduces some of the incentive for contribution, and it does not eliminate the attachment to hierarchy and individualistic competition within levels.

Assigning rewards to individuals for their contribution, irrespective of their position, is another popularly advocated "solution" for moving beyond the hierarchical allocation of rewards. Kanter (1987) advocates reviewing and tightening the relationship of pay and performance. Variants of this solution go by the names "pay-for-contribution," "pay-for-performance," and "pay-for-skills." This type of solution, on the one hand, retains some elements of bureaucracy and, on the other hand, poses some deep challenges to bureaucracy. Both of these aspects are discussed below.

These solutions, as their monikers suggest, remain tied to pay as the carrot for effort and some classic type of merit (contribution, performance, or skills) as the yardstick. They also retain an individualism that is counter to the spirit of teams. As the hierarchy of jobs is disappearing, a set of skills or objectives to master is defined for each individual, who can climb his or her own skills hierarchy. Pay-for-contribution, as outlined by Kanter (1987), is supposed to allow the contribution of many kinds of skills from many quarters. But in practice, it is likely that the set of skills defined for an individual's mastery remains close to an expanded listing of what the original job title was in the functional hierarchy. It is true that this list of skills might include team facilitation skills. But team skills are thereby still measured as individual, rather than collective, attributes or accomplishments. An individual, when ready, might go to an interpersonal dynamics course to be certified for this skill, but the team as a whole is not learning skills together. The demonstration of contribution or skills may be produced at the expense of team goals; for example, a marketer (demonstrating skill at market segmentation) may insist on additional market research that will cost the team time. Tracking the attainment of these skills still requires a means of measurement. A manager is likely to continue to be the one to measure the skill or performance level. The departure from status and politics that these schemes promise may not be delivered. At the same time, the pay-for-contribution type of solution poses some challenges to the bureaucratic logic that may hold clues to post-bureaucratic alternatives. If adopted in the spirit intended, pay-for-contribution opens the possibility that, in some time periods, a production worker might deserve to be paid more for a contribution than a vice president. Kanter (1987) argues that this decoupling of status and reward may pose the biggest obstacle to the adoption of such schemes by executives.

Rather than accepting this political resistance as an insurmountable obstacle and looking for minor, practical, likely-to-be-adopted fixes for reward systems in the post-bureaucratic organization, we want to push harder on the issue of how reward systems might be truly changed, tackling their ideological, cultural, and psychological underpinnings. New ways of thinking about rewards should not be simply one step removed from the status quo but should be a broad leap away. As such, the concrete details may not be clear, but giving some attention to the vision may push new solutions. Because many people have been socialized to, and have developed, vested interests in meritocratic differentiation of pay, it is easy to look at solutions and say things such as, "That will never work," "It will never get passed by those in power," or "Things will fall apart if we try that." But interests can be pushed in new directions by a new vision, as Weber (1946b, p. 280), the chronicler not only of bureaucracy but of cultural and institutional shifts, has written:

> Not ideas, but material and ideal interests, directly govern [people's] conduct. Yet very frequently the 'world images' that have been created by "ideas" have, like switchmen, determined the tracks along which action has been pushed by the dynamic of interest.

The shift to post-bureaucratic organizations creates a time of rupture and discontinuity, which can be an opportunity for examining assumptions and asking some bolder questions about reward systems. As some examples: if everyone in the post-bureaucratic organization is a flexible, multiskilled member trying to make an organization work, why should some people be given vastly higher incomes than others? Why try to come up with ever better logics and procedures for pay differentiation? Why not scrap the notion of pay differences and focus on the intrinsically challenging work to be done (without closing the discussion by leaping to objections such as, "But people will shirk")? Why not make job rotation a real benefit, not a consolation prize, by situating it in a more egalitarian context? Pay differentiation may simply create differences in lifestyles and life chances that are difficult to justify and that cause tensions among people who are supposed to work together as equally invested organizational members. It may thwart more contribution than it induces.

In the next section, an alternative approach to becoming post-bureaucratic is considered. This approach pushes us to think about why the abandonment of meritocracy—pursued with a modest, flexible, humanistic, and team-spirited demeanor—may be precisely the key to post-bureaucratic success.

An Alternative Approach to Becoming Post-Bureaucratic

The discussion in this chapter so far points out how the common approach to becoming post-bureaucratic appears to have two incompatible tendencies. First, it involves *major* revisions in the division of labor, such as the performance of tasks by teams, cross-training and the blurring of job and functional boundaries, flexibility in updating assignments and tasks, synergistic contributions of effort, and a more advisory or coach role for managers. Second, so far, it involves only *minor* changes in how evaluation and rewards are handled. Team work is such a different mode of working, but it is coupled with old, familiar ideas about performance, evaluation, and rewards, which result in trying to ascertain individual contributions to a team or simply raising the merit contest one level, from competing individuals to competing teams.

In this final section, we propose what some *major* changes to performance evaluation and rewards might look like, to match the radical but necessary departures of the post-bureaucratic mode of working. That is, given that some mix of team work and individual work is crucial to meeting the post-bureaucratic requirements for effectiveness and efficiency, we take up the question of how to motivate the requisite commitment and contribution by all organizational members.

Table 3.2 shows an alternative approach to performance and reward in the post-bureaucracy, summarizes some likely objections, and summarizes our reply. The following discussion expands on these themes.

Rely on Intrinsic Motivation (and Have an Income Floor)

Imagine an organization in which everyone earned an income that provided adequately for food, shelter, and a mix of necessities and some luxuries. Thus taken care of, they could clear their minds to do the best job possible, to willingly contribute whatever was necessary to get the job done, without constant worry about livelihood. Furthermore, if pay no longer symbolized personal worthiness, then people might also spend less time running mental batch jobs on equity comparisons.

Only if one takes a dim view of human nature does the necessity of tying pay to work seem crucial. The bureaucratic distribution of pay relies on two caricatures of individual psychology, addressed above. One is the person at the bottom, who might shirk, who might contribute only in small increments and then only if given small incremental increases in pay, and to whom pay is therefore meted out in small doses. The other is the person at the top, who stereotypically is wooed by the company with money, is lured away from other competitor companies with money, and has supposedly been induced to undergo demanding training and put in long hours by the promise of more money. This section addresses the problem of shirking and motivation. The next section addresses the problem of recognizing top performers.

Economists have tended to worry that employees will shirk if pay is not made contingent on effort and contribution. It is possible to take a different view of motivation than the one assumed, rather than demonstrated, in the hierarchical model. Recent research (e.g., Bazerman, Loewenstein, & White,

TABLE 3.2 Teams, Performance, and Rewards in the Post-Bureaucracy: Getting to Post-Meritocracy

Alternative	Likely Critiques	Our Reply
Rely on intrinsic motivation (and have an income floor)	People will shirk	Too dim a view of human nature; people rise to situation
	Too expensive	More focus on task; likelier to enhance work quality and performance
		Losing good people is more expensive; income ceiling contains costs on other end
Celebrate excellence (and have an income ceiling)	Will demoralize the "stars"	Teams do not need stars; they require many kinds of excellence & contribution
		Dim view of really talented people as reluctant to contribute without big prizes
	Will not motivate individuals to make necessary but risky decisions	Individual risk-taking is loosely correlated to organizational gain now; teams can learn processes for sharing risky decisions
Keep the concept of merit out of the language and culture	Merit creates higher standards and achievement	Merit creates invidious competition, which demotivates many and can lead to less than full potential performance
	Merit insures fairness and objectivity	By creating the promise of fairness and objectivity, but not fulfilling it, merit systems do more harm than good
	Merit is part of the American dream and national culture	Post-bureaucratic team work and reward-sharing should help more people live fuller lives

1992; Gumpert, Gordon, Welch, Offringa, & Katz, 1992) offers encouraging evidence that there is at least an abstract preference for distributive justice that could be influenced into tolerance for a more egalitarian distribution system.

The model of job enrichment advanced by Hackman and Oldham (1980) is quite consistent with this post-bureaucratic vision of motivation. Arguing that tasks can be designed so as to enhance the intrinsic motivation of the work itself, they found that several core dimensions of tasks influenced the psychological states associated with high motivation, performance, and job satisfaction. The core dimensions, some of which are strikingly similar to features now heralded as essential to using teams well and competitively, include: skill variety, task integrity, task significance, autonomy, and feedback.

The job enrichment literature was sometimes criticized (e.g., Nord, 1974) because it remained stuck, as teams often do today, in the bureaucratic mold. These critics argued that "interesting work" and the appearance of greater participation might just be ways of coopting employees' commitment, without really granting greater autonomy or involvement. In addition, job enrichment was criticized as an attempt to distract employees' attention away from pay raises, which was seen as particularly unfair to employees paid at or just above the minimum wage, for whom even small marginal raises significantly influence well-being. As bureaucracy breaks down, better conditions may be created for the success of job enrichment in the non-cooptive spirit originally intended. However, if reward systems do not change, then conditions may remain inhospitable. If employees have to compete for each small pay increase, their relative performance ranking will probably continue to be as salient a concern as the enrichment of their work.

Donnellon's (1992) data suggest that higher-paid professionals focus far more on the work itself than on its extrinsic rewards. Salary and compensation were virtually never mentioned by the more than 200 people interviewed, and even when they talked about promotions, it was generally in the language of "opportunity" rather than "reward," connoting that their primary interest was in doing more challenging work (or possibly in gaining more autonomy, rather than gaining materially). It may be that professionals are paid at a level where they are freed from focusing on small marginal increases in income (the value of money being logarithmic) and can focus instead on the inherent interest in their work. This is not to say that these professionals were not concerned about their careers. It does suggest that reliance on intrinsic motivation—a more positive view of human nature—set in a context of greater pay equality and multiple forms of skill and contribution may be the recipe for the success of the post-bureaucratic model. Team members may be drawn to their team primarily by the attraction of doing interesting work in concert.

Though this notion is rarely discussed in current debates about the appropriate basis of pay systems, the idea is not new, nor without corroboration. Long ago, Chester Barnard decried the formalization of organization that "separated the efforts of individuals at work from any sense of contribution or place in the creation of the final product" (Scott, 1992, p. 128). Barnard's theory of cooperation, as explicated by Scott (1992), recognized the salience of nonmaterial inducements in motivating contribution. Moreover, Barnard argued that the inculcation of nonmaterial motives was superior to the rationalization of opportunity, because the latter "was insufficient to bring forth from people a full measure of cooperation" (Scott, 1992, p. 130). Recent research on creative work (Hennessey, Amabile, & Martinage, 1989) suggests that intrinsic motivation is enhanced by a combination of intrinsically rewarding work and extrinsic rewards.

Suppose we actually accepted the age-old notion that organizational performance is dependent on the constant interaction of people working interdependently, long understood by those who live and move in the real, informal structure of the organization. If we accept Hackman and Oldham's (1980) model of enriched work, then we could let go of the ideals of individual accountability and reward, because they serve neither to enhance the task performance nor the motivation. Then we could design tasks to enhance their motivational potential, giving teams', responsibility for significant tasks as well as the autonomy to determine how these should be accomplished.

Performance evaluation has a feedback and learning function as well as a rating and sorting function. The latter function often swamps the former; we become so concerned with evaluation that we fail to recognize its negative effects on the outcome that it is supposed to produce—performance. If organizations could be less concerned about dividing income and legitimating inequality, then the rating and sorting function of evaluation would be less important. The learning and feedback function could be given more focus and should at the same time prove to be the superior route to higher quality and higher performance.

The alternative to a meritocracy may be a more equal distribution of income, together with a focus on skill development. The real benefit from work for individuals would be challenge, stimulation, and growth. The benefit for organizations would be the willing contribution of initiative and innovation. It is possible that such a system would prove at least as cost-effective as the best pay-for-performance system.

Celebrate Excellence
(and Have an Income Ceiling)

Egalitarianism, in the bureaucratic way of thinking, is argued to be demoralizing to "star" performers. Bureaucracies were designed to identify and advance high achievers. The pyramidal shape of most bureaucracies allows fewer and fewer people to move to successively higher levels. The roughly bell-shaped distribution of performance ratings also allows only a few people to be rated "excellent" and become candidates for promotion. The relative scarcity of both promotions and excellent ratings makes them valued rewards for star performers (Jackall, 1988). To the extent that the post-bureaucratic organization moves away from pyramidal hierarchies and competitive performance evaluations, it removes these long-standing means of recognizing star performers (although it is just as likely that bureaucracies socially constructed the notion of "stars" in the first place, rather than simply rewarding naturally existing "stars").

A common critique of a social system that does not allow star performers to stand out is that there will be a crisis of motivation, particularly from those talented employees whose contributions are most needed. Indeed, Kohn (1986) worries that, in our current competitive way of thinking, giving everyone an excellent rating or an excellent salary would not be construed to mean that everyone is contributing worthy talents but would only be a source of disappointment for those who do not feel recognized as the "winners."

One response to this common concern is elaborated above: the post-bureaucratic organization needs the willing contribution of effort and talent from all quarters, not just from a few excellent people. Expertise could become a particular form of contribution, rather than a basis for status. In fact, since tasks now create such interdependency among individual experts, teams require not stars but excellence in all of their experts.

A second response is to question the view of human nature that is implicitly evoked by arguments that star performers will be demoralized and will slack off if there is a ceiling on how far they can get ahead of everyone else. Again, this view of "stars," like the view of shirkers critiqued above, might reflect too dim a view of human nature. Economists and functionalist sociologists have argued that the most important jobs should have the highest wage attached to them, to reflect their greater functional importance to society and in order to induce the most talented members of society to undertake demanding training and to apply themselves to these jobs. Perhaps this argument views the most talented members of society as people who would be petulant or act out of pure self-interest unless given extra rewards (particularly extra rewards for what may simply be inherited talents that merit praise and recognition but not a better standard of living than those born less talented [Sher, 1979]).

In fact, two alternative logics for how rewards should be distributed would not give the highest rewards to stars. First, there is the opposite notion that the most dangerous and grueling jobs, often low-skilled jobs, should command the highest wage premiums as recompense for taking care of society's most unsafe and unpleasant work (Walzer, 1983). Second, there is some evidence that, in the United States, people prefer that rewards be based on effort rather than ability (Coleman & Rainwater, 1978). Effort can be contributed by anyone at any level and does not imply an underlying distribution with few star exerters.

There is debate at workplaces and in varied academic literatures over whether ability, effort, final productivity, amount of improvement, or numerous other measures are the most appropriate indicators of merit. Rather than trying to adjudicate among multiple rationales for wage differentiation, a wage ceiling—to prevent any group from securing a wage that is too out of line—and greater egalitarianism might allow organizations to shift attention from thinking about the wage a job commands to thinking about the content and expertise of the job. In the post-bureaucratic organization, undertaking training and performing challenging work may not be kinds of effort that have to be induced. Instead, they may be rewards in themselves.

Another predictable critique of an income ceiling is the argument that it would eliminate the incentive for managers to make the risky strategic decisions that organizations require. The claim typically put forward here is that, unless individuals feel they stand to gain a great deal personally, they will be unwilling to take the risks that could yield high organizational gain. Our response again appeals to the argument that high individual gain does not automatically reflect or translate into high organizational outcomes. This argument and supporting evidence is summarized, ironically, by proponents of a solution quite different from ours—tightening the pay and performance link and allowing wide reward differentials (Baker, Jensen, & Murphy, 1988).

Our response also appeals to small group theory and practice: teams can be used to make strategic decisions in the post-bureaucracy. As part of a team, individuals may be more inclined to take risks than they are on their own, while at the same time, the pressure for group consensus creates a natural forum for debate, compromise, and limits. If the phenomenon of groupthink can be avoided (Janis, 1972), teams provide the ideal forum for "controlled risk-taking." Indeed, in Donnellon's (1992) research on product development teams, the organization that coined the phrase "controlled risk-taking" to label their goals for teams subsequently realized such benefits.

Two logistical concerns follow from the idea of granting teams the autonomy to make decisions. The first is how to coordinate among teams and the second is what the role of former managers—general and functional—will be in a more egalitarian, team-based organization. We propose a linkage between these concerns.

The organization could have a team of senior, experienced "manager advisors" whose task is to advise teams on strategic opportunities. These managers might also serve as the coordinators of a federation of teams that makes final decisions on strategic direction and resource allocation to teams. Functional managers could then be brokers of functional expertise, rather than controllers of resources. They might become "producing managers" (Lorsch & Mathias, 1987), continuing to contribute their specific expertise to teams while they also perform the occasional coordinating or developmental work required in the organization. Such changes would mitigate the perceptions of vertically ordered challenge and contribution that are used to justify hierarchically graded rewards. They would also reduce the benefits that narrow divisions of labor have provided to functional managers, thus removing a daunting barrier to cross-functional team work.

The post-bureaucratic organization makes it possible for many people to be deemed excellent, and certainly the ongoing recognition and celebration of excellence should continue to be important. Rewards less scarce than annual promotions and fantastic executive salaries can be used and come to be valued.

Many readers may think an income ceiling "sounds too idealistic" or "sounds like communism," just when the demise of communism is being heralded in so many quarters. We hope that such labels do not prompt immediate dismissal of new ideas about dividing labor and livelihood. We have tried to argue for the advantages of post-meritocratic job flexibility and pay equality as intrinsic requirements of post-bureaucracy, which might help address some potential obstacles. We try to stand *inside* the post-bureaucratic system and assess its logic. We do not stand *outside* the system and pose idealistic alternatives for their own sake.

Keep the Concept of Merit
Out of the Language and Culture

This solution may be the best hope of the post-bureaucratic organization, not just to create a vision of a better place in which to live and work but to achieve its very efficiency aims. The backdrop to the bureaucratic organization has been a national culture imbued with the language and ideal of meritocracy. When people question whether meritocracy prevails, it is usually with an eye to making a situation more meritocratic, to assuring that merit is fairly measured and commensurately rewarded, as in the case of affirmative action programs and some corporate efforts at "rescoping" jobs and redesigning performance evaluation criteria and forms.

The usual solution to problems with merit systems, advanced in the human resources literature (e.g., Ilgen & Feldman, 1983) has been to try to improve the process and take subjectivity out of evaluations, for example, through managerial journal keeping, to make evaluations more truly meritocratic. However, there may be no way to obtain unbiased merit ratings, and, even if there were, they might not neatly fall onto a nearly normal distribution and point to a "star" in the right tail. Deming (1986) has warned against merit-based rating systems and illustrated that apparent differences among individuals may be produced not by differences in merit but by the range of errors inherent in the work system.

The more important point is that, even if perfect merit ratings were possible, a pure meritocracy may be inherently invidious and undesirable as a way to order social life. Making an organization more meritocratic may involve staying too close to the bureaucratic model. Meritocracy and bureaucracy have tenacious links. The romance of meritocracy created problems for bureaucracies and may even more profoundly impede progress toward the post-bureaucratic goals of team work, speed, learning, and flexibility. It may be necessary to move the discussion to an issue that is not commonly raised: questioning meritocracy itself (cf., Kohn, 1986; Scully, 1992).

Ironically, however, the dismantling of merit systems might leave many employees alarmed, in spite of how heatedly their numerous shortcomings and political strategems have been denounced around the water cooler. Merit systems represent the intention to live up to a claim to rational fairness. Their elimination would leave open the possibility of arbitrariness, even from the perspective of those who were skeptical about meritocratic claims in the first place. Weber (1946a) praised bureaucracies for their rational fairness and impersonality in the distribution of status and rewards. In small, start-up companies, where everyone pitches in and no one bothers with titles, there have been instances where employees, rather than reveling in this nearly post-bureaucratic state of affairs, have pushed for greater bureaucratization. For all its red tape, bureaucracy seems to promise equal treatment and protection from favoritism.

The post-bureaucratic organization may not be free to evolve slowly as a loosely organized network that initially favors only a few lucky members of the better teams but may need to change quickly to demonstrate that fair treatment and secure livelihoods are part of its foundation. Such quick change to a new form will be difficult, particularly because it involves a new psychological and cultural orientation. Indeed, some of the changes we advocate go beyond the scope of what a single organization can achieve, particularly if there are first-mover disadvantages to adopting more egalitarian pay structures. Organizational boundaries may have to blur in a way that allows more concerted efforts to change reward structures. Organizational scholarship may have to recover a focus on how organizations both respond to and fuel social norms about inequality. "Recent scholarship generally seems to have lost sight of the fact that—at least within sociology, economics, and political science— much of the classical interest in understanding organizations and inequality was in divining their implications for the social and political order" (Baron & Cook, 1992, p. 196).

Over time, the discourse of meritocracy—its language and its embodiment in social and political institutions—produces a world view in which there are low-paid peons, high-paid stars, and scores of contenders in the middle competing with each other in a lottery for very few rewarding positions. Organizations become designed accordingly. Some see this engine of competition as good: make individuals work hard and the sum of their efforts will generate productivity. But this chapter and this book are about an organization

that is not the sum of its atomistic parts but a forum in which eager contributors are trained and encouraged to work collectively. Such organizations
might help mitigate the tenacity of meritocratic thinking in society at large.
A post-bureaucratic organization may require a kind of trust in what is best
in human nature and also send a signal that trust, cooperation, and sharing
are not ideals too abstract for a social order.

Conclusion

In this chapter, we have considered how several features of the bureaucratic model of organization limit the potential for the flexible, post-bureaucratic organization, and for its hallmark, team work. We have argued that
team work is inhibited by more than the much cited narrow division of labor,
vertical ordering of titles and authority, and strong identity of functional areas.
We focused on three foundational features of bureaucracy—individual accountability, managerial evaluation, and hierarchically graded rewards—that
must change in the move to the team-based, post-bureaucratic organization.
These three features are undergirded by a meritocratic reward structure,
which upholds and legitimates bureaucracy.

We have argued that, to change the dysfunctional features of bureaucracy,
the reward structure must change concomitantly. Indeed, the overlooked
need to change the reward system may pose the greatest obstacle to the
development of a team-based post-bureaucratic organization. More strongly
put, simply changing the division of labor will not suffice to realize the
promises of the post-bureaucratic organization. The reward structure must
be changed to bolster post-bureaucracy. Some of the minor changes tried so
far have lingering problems, which we elaborated.

Following our analysis (summarized in Table 3.1), we derived an alternative post-meritocratic approach (summarized in Table 3.2) to performance
and rewards that might enhance the prospects of the team-based, post-
bureaucratic organization. Our alternative constitutes a major change, and
like most major departures, it is difficult to envision the specific content of
the change and likelihood of implementation. We considered the sources of
resistance to changing the reward structure, both from those who feel
empowered by meritocracy and those who hope to be protected from meritocracy. The alternative focuses on how intrinsic motivation will be achieved
when individuals can move beyond mundane concerns about each small
pay raise. And excellence can still be recognized and celebrated, but within
parameters that make sense when we value multiple kinds of contributions.
These ideas may well meet with resistance. Paradoxically, the flexibility,
trust, and fast adaptation that are supposed to be *results of* post-bureaucracy

may indeed be required *in advance* to move effectively and creatively toward post-bureaucracy and radically new reward systems. It is worth putting forward new ideas—such as the complete departure from meritocratic thinking—in the spirit of contribution that the post-bureaucratic organization encourages.

Note

1. In this chapter, we use the phrase "team work" to refer to the kind of tasks that require teams to accomplish. This concrete and operational sense of these words is to be distinguished from the abstract and highly valued outcome that the single word *teamwork* connotes.

References

Adams, J. C. (1965). Inequity in social exchange. In L. Berkowitz (Ed.), *Advances in experimental social psychology, Vol. 2* (pp. 267-299). New York: Academic Press.

Baker, G. P., Jensen, M. C., & Murphy, K. J. (1988). Compensation and incentives: Practice vs. theory. *The Journal of Finance, 42,* 593-616.

Baron, J. N. (1984). Organizational perspectives on stratification. *Annual Review of Sociology, 10,* 37-69.

Baron, J. N., & Cook, K. S. (1992). Process and outcome: Perspectives on the distribution of rewards in organizations. *Administrative Science Quarterly, 37,* 191-197.

Bazerman, M. H., Loewenstein, G. F., & White, S. B. (1992). Reversals of preference in allocation decisions: Judging an alternative versus choosing among alternatives. *Administrative Science Quarterly, 37,* 220-240.

Bell, D. (1976). *The coming of post-industrial society: A venture in social forecasting.* New York: Basic Books.

Burrell, G., & Morgan, G. (1979). *Sociological paradigms and organizational analysis.* London: Heinemann.

Coleman, R. P., & Rainwater, L. (1978). *Social standing in America: New dimensions of class.* New York: Basic Books.

Crystal, G. (1992). *In search of excess: The overcompensation of American executives.* New York: Norton.

Daniels, N. (1978). Merit and meritocracy. *Philosophy and Public Affairs, 3,* 206-223.

Deming, W. E. (1986). *Out of the crisis.* Cambridge, MA: MIT Center for Advanced Engineering Study.

Doeringer, P. B., & Piore, M. J. (1971). *Internal labor markets and manpower analysis.* Lexington, MA: Heath.

Donnellon, A. (1992). *The meaning of team work.* Book manuscript.

Dornbusch, S., & Scott, W. R. (1975). *Evaluation and the exercise of authority.* San Francisco, CA: Jossey-Bass.

Ferguson, K. (1984). *The feminist case against bureaucracy.* Philadelphia, PA: Temple University Press.

Gumpert, P., Gordon, F. M., Welch, K. R., Offringa, G., & Katz, N. (1992). *Toward a Rawlsean system of distributive justice: Effects of reward distribution on performance, behavior and psychological orientation.* Working Paper. Boston, MA: Boston Institute for Psychotherapy.

Hackman, J. R., & Oldham, G. R. (1980). *Work redesign.* Reading, MA: Addison-Wesley.

Hecksher, C. (1988). *Loyalty.* Working paper. Harvard Graduate School of Business.

Hennessey, B., Amabile, T., & Martinage, M. (1989). Immunizing children against the negative effects of rewards. *Contemporary Educational Psychology, 14,* 212-227.

Ilgen, D. R., & Feldman, J. M. (1983). Performance appraisal: A process focus. In L. L. Cummings & B. M. Staw (Eds.), *Research in organizational behavior, Vol. 5.* Greenwich, CT: JAI Press.

Jackall, R. (1988). *Moral mazes: The world of corporate managers.* New York: Oxford University Press.

Janis, I. L. (1972). *Victims of groupthink.* Boston, MA: Houghton Mifflin.

Jencks, C., Bartlett, S., Corcoran, M., Crouse, J., Eaglesfield, D., Jackson, G., McClelland, K., Mueser, P., Olneck, M., Schwartz, J., Ward, S., & Williams, J. (1979). *Who gets ahead? The determinants of economic success in America.* New York: Basic Books.

Kanter, R. M. (1987, January). From status to contribution: Some organizational implications of the changing basis for pay. *Personnel,* pp. 12-37.

Kohn, A. (1986). *No contest: The case against competition (Why we lose in our race to win).* Boston, MA: Houghton Mifflin.

Lawler, E. (1973). *Motivation in work organizations.* Monterey, CA: Brooks/Cole.

Lawler, E. (1990). *Strategic pay: Aligning organizational strategies and pay systems.* San Francisco, CA: Jossey-Bass.

Longenecker, C. O., & Gioia, D. A. (1988, Winter). Neglected at the top—Executives talk about executive appraisal. *Sloan Management Review,* pp. 41-47.

Lorsch, J., & Mathias, J. (1987, July-August). When professionals have to manager. *Harvard Business Review,* pp. 78-83.

March, J., & Simon, H. (1958). *Organizations.* New York: Wiley.

Martin, J. (1981). Relative deprivation: A theory of distributive injustice for an era of shrinking resources. In L. L. Cummings & B. M. Staw (Eds.), *Research in organizational behavior. Vol. 3* (pp. 53-107). Greenwich, CT: JAI Press.

Murphy, K. R., & Cleveland, J. N. (1991). *Performance appraisal: An organizational perspective.* Boston, MA: Allyn & Bacon.

Nord, W. (1974). The failure of current applied behavioral science—A Marxian perspective. *The Journal of Applied Behavioral Science, 10(4):* 557-578.

Osterman, P. (1984). Introduction. In P. Osterman (Ed.), *Internal labor markets.* Cambridge, MA: MIT Press.

Pfeffer, J., & Langton, N. (1988). Wage inequality and the organization of work: The case of academic departments. *Administrative Science Quarterly, 33,* 588-606.

Scott, W. (1992). *Barnard and the guardians of the American administrative state.* Lawrence, KS: University of Kansas Press.

Scully, M. (1992). *Organs and organizations: Can objections to merit-based distribution of organs be used to inform objections to merit-based distribution of jobs and incomes?* Unpublished manuscript. Sloan School of Management, MIT.

Scully, M. (1993). *The imperfect legitimation of inequality in internal labor markets.* Working Paper #3520-93. Sloan School of Management, MIT.

Sher, G. (1979). Effort, ability and personal desert. *Philosophy and Public Affairs, 8,* 361-376.

Thayer, F. C. (1981). *An end to hierarchy and competition: Administration in a post-affluent world.* 2nd ed. New York: Viewpoints.

Thompson, J. D. (1967). *Organizations in action.* New York: McGraw-Hill.

Vroom, V. H. (1964). *Work and motivation.* New York: Wiley.

Walzer, M. (1983). *Spheres of justice: A defense of pluralism and equality.* New York: Basic Books.

Weber, M. (1946a). Bureaucracy. In H. H. Gerth & C. W. Mills (Eds.), *From Max Weber: Essays in sociology*. New York: Oxford University Press.

Weber, M. (1946b). The social psychology of the world religions. In H. H. Gerth & C. W. Mills (Eds.), *From Max Weber: Essays in sociology*. New York: Oxford University Press.

Weber, M. (1976). *The Protestant ethic and the spirit of capitalism*. New York: Scribner's.

Wood, J. V. (1989). Theory and research concerning social comparisons of personal attributes. *Psychological Bulletin, 106*, 231-248.

Young, M. (1958). *The rise of the meritocracy*. New York: Penguin.

Zenger, T. (1992). Why do employers only reward extreme performance? Examining the relationships among performance, pay, and turnover. *Administrative Science Quarterly, 37*, 198-219.

4 COGNITIVE REAPPORTIONMENT

Rethinking the Location of Judgment in Managerial Decision Making

Benn R. Konsynski
John J. Sviokla

Information technology is one of mankind's most malleable inventions. Unlike bridges, rockets, printing presses, or cars, information technology is vastly plastic and rarely constrained by physics, chemistry, or physical limitations. When managing such a tangible device, the soundness of design concepts and management principles is paramount. Many a manager has hoped for an intelligent, dynamic, and adjusting information system, just to find that the possibilities of the technology were eroded by current patterns, behaviors, and expectations of the technology—based on old design paradigms.

In this chapter, we put forth the idea of *cognitive reapportionment,* a concept that draws on ideas from organization design, decision support systems, and model management. In cognitive reapportionment, we suggest the idea that the organization can be conceived of as *bundles* of decisions[1] and that these bundles can be allocated across humans, systems, or combinations of humans and systems. Also, we suggest that the allocation of these cognitive[2] responsibilities can be dynamic—taking into account the user, the system status, and the decision environment.

In the business environment of tomorrow, pressures will continue to grow for skills needed to capture, filter, use, and convey useful information and knowledge more precisely and more quickly. Organizations need the right mixture of human and machine-based intelligence available to respond to the volatile business environment. Volume, volatility, velocity, and veracity (the four *V*s) of information in the emerging business environment demand skills that have historically eluded the organization of the past that had depended on people to perform all interpretation of policy and values of the firm.

Given the huge and ever-growing invested base of information technology (IT) in which many decision policies are tacitly enacted, managers need a way to understand these assets. Looking forward, organizations are under extensive pressures to monitor and distill external data, leverage internal expertise in decision making, and modify and update current systems. In such a demanding information environment, managers need to begin to off-load cognitive responsibilities onto systems. Thus, this concept should have applicability for existing as well as future management of systems within organizations.

This is not an information age that raises this challenge. Rather it is a knowledge age that extends beyond the management of facts and truths. Skills, understanding, expertise, and experience are reflected in the capabilities required in this emerging era. The continuous change of the firm in response to the increasing dynamics in the marketplace is an accepted reality. Productive use of the skills and capabilities of humans and systems is no longer a desired condition, it is essential for effective market and management performance.

Managing becomes designing. We can expect that as the capabilities increase to relocate judgment and decision making, the manager's role will change from coordination and development of the portfolio of people talent to one of continuous organizational design. It is true that the "organization" we refer to is a local, temporary arrangement of human and system *cognitors*.[3] This has been ever true, but never more important a general management role as local autonomy, less rigorous job descriptions, increasing reporting responsibilities, and other pressures bear on teams and business units.

Cognitive Reapportionment Defined

Cognition deals with acts of thinking that are associated with judgment and decision making. At the core of the cognitive reapportionment concept is the idea that cognitive responsibilities can be allocated to a human or humans, or to a system or systems. Most early automation efforts focused on taking thinking responsibilities from individual workers and putting them into information systems. The creation of the massive policy transaction systems that formed the back office of most life insurance companies saw tremendous substitution of computing power for human clerical work. Much of the early history of computerization was logged in accounting and finance—the factories of financial services. This automation was also largely static—that is, the dialogue between the system and the human cognitor was static. Regardless of the skill of the person interacting with the system, the machine always performed the same repertoire of cognitive acts.

This automation-driven approach to the allocation of cognitive responsibilities is the predominant design paradigm in operation today. Despite the creation of flexible user interfaces, presentation capabilities, and advanced decision logics, there is still an overriding focus on gathering human cognitive responsibilities and placing them in the system. We suggest that this narrow view of cognitive reapportionment constrains the capabilities of systems, because system designers often limit themselves to those systems that can be "fully automated." Moreover, and perhaps more important, it creates a uniform system that does not sense its user or its decision environment. Any dynamic allocation of cognitive responsibilities must come from the user, or systems builder.

Emerging in some other domains, we already see dynamic allocation of cognitive responsibilities. There are, in the automation of decision processes, also examples in which the cognitive reapportionment has shifted from the machine back to the human being. In a range of avionics systems, the pilot is permitted to take over control and coordination responsibilities that will permit him or her to perform special maneuvers. In other words, depending on conditions, the pilot or the supporting avionic systems are both capable of performing critical decision tasks. Yet, there are situations in which only one of the actors should be allowed to make the decisions—say critical trim controls at high speed for the avionics, and ejection decisions for the pilot. In a design paradigm driven by cognitive reapportionment, the design that provides the best set of decision outcomes wins out. In the avionics system, the trim controls are often left with the information system, but the ejection decisions with the pilot.

Thus, in certain situations the expert may be more interested in taking on cognitive responsibilities that might otherwise be handled by the system. In this sort of environment, the human being acts as a co-cognitor—we have the computer as colleague. As computer support environments are more able to support this form of situational movement of decision capabilities from systems to humans, we will become more accustomed to sharing decision-making responsibilities in these human/system dialogues. Moreover, more of these human/system dialogues and more of their important details will be available for manipulation and design.

In cognitive reapportionment there is a conscious design decision focused on the dynamic allocation of thinking responsibilities. The best analogy is the idea of delegation from superior to subordinate. When a superior delegates a decision, he or she gives up direct decision control, but reserves the right to re-take control. In cognitive reapportionment, the design consciously takes into account the ability to allocate decisions to people and/or systems with the ability to dynamically share, or even take back, control.

This is not an anthropomorphic view of technology. Rather it is the recognition that acts of cognition can be allocated to humans and systems alike. The range of capabilities in information technologies has increased to a point where the general manager may freely delegate tasks that were considered squarely in the domain of human cognitive capabilities in the past.

There will clearly be a class of decision situations that are more suited to human cognitors (many involving intuition, aesthetics, and leaps of belief) and those better suited to the high performance characteristics of the system environment (speed, total enumeration, and massive data consideration). At the same time, the range of cognitive acts that are suitable for allocation to both humans and systems is growing.

It is important to note that cognitive reapportionment is not a one-way street—human cognitive acts assigned to system cognitors. In fact, the two-way street is open for traffic. Many of the more interesting allocations of cognitive responsibilities will involve dynamic allocation of responsibilities among human and system cognitors.

Before providing more specific examples of the cognitive reapportionment concept at the individual, group, and organization level, we feel it is useful to address some of the intellectual roots of the idea.

The Rise of the Human/System Dialogue in Management and Organization

The core of the cognitive reapportionment concept can be traced to the very roots of the computer science field. Early in the history of computer science, one large, and influential faction applied computers to human thought with the goal of simulating as much of the known processes and thinking abilities of human beings as possible. When Turing created the concepts of the universal Turing machine, and the digital computer was actually created, theorists, such as Newell, Shaw, and Simons (1963), reasoned that one could create any kind of intelligent action. The spirit of their work was apparent even by the names of their early projects, such as "General Problem Solver." The hope was to create a complete range of intelligent behavior (Sviokla 1986a, 1986b). In fact, a theme that recurs throughout the history of computer science theory and engineering has been the goal, or refutation of the goal, of creating "thinking machines." (See McCorduck, 1979, for a spirited history of the field and its personalities.)

In the commercial world, the application of information technologies has provided a significant number of opportunities and challenges. Zuboff

(1988) has noted that one of the primary differences between information technology and all previous technologies is that in the process of automating, information technology provides new information about the task being automated. For example, when a robot welds a weld, the exact temperature is known with much more precision than when a human welder does the job.

Over time, many businesses have used this information and applied models to structure tasks and allocated any rote or prescribed decisions to be carried out without human intervention. Starting in the late 1960s, there was a movement to create a set of decision-support tools that helped the decision maker come to a better decision within an organizational context. The work of early researchers such as Keen and Scott-Morton (1978), Sprague and Carlson (1982), and others, described the creation of systems to help individuals come to more effective decisions. The themes that come out of this early work echoed the predictions of Gorry and Scott-Morton (1971), in which they felt that the use of decision-support systems would center on semi-structured managerial work. In such tasks the concept was to automate "beside" not "through" the individual. The idea had thus emerged to have the computer as colleague.

More recently there has been an acknowledgment of an encompassing view of systems that includes both the individual and the tool that the individual is using. Jaikumar and Bohn (1988a, 1988b) denote intelligent systems as a combination of person and system. They posit a continuum of knowledge (containing eight stages) that begins with recognition of the occurrence of data associated with a task through to complete algorithmic knowledge and control of the task. Jaikumar and Bohn argue that those tasks that are at "highest level of knowledge" can be completely automated. The tasks in the middle— between art and science—need a balance of human and system support.

In the expert-systems realm there is also a recognition of this combination of system and person. Luconi, Malone, and Scott-Morton (1985) note a continuum of systems from data processing systems through decision-support systems, through expert support systems to expert systems. The critical difference is that in expert systems, the flexible problem-solving strategies are embedded in the system and not under the direct control of the users, whereas the flexible problem-solving strategies are under the control of the user of an expert-support system. Fjeldstad and Konsynski (1986) deal with reapportionment of cognitive responsibilities in decision-support systems dialogues more directly. Using examples from the world of operating systems and group decision support, they note that information systems designers now have the ability to "re-examine the proper apportionment of cognitive responsibilities in the human systems dialogue." Similar threads of thought have been examined by people concerned with model management and dialogue management (Dolk & Konsynski, 1986; Elam & Konsynski, 1988; Kuo & Konsynski, 1988).

Overall, a design perspective is emerging that suggests managers have an option to decide what kinds of policies and procedures should be delegated to the system and which types of policies and procedures should be delegated to the person interacting with the system. An important development in this stream of thought is the idea that this kind of allocation can be dynamic and fitted to match the changing business and environmental needs.

To summarize, the argument so far has been to suggest that the manager needs new design concepts to effectively manage today's systems and to design tomorrow's. The concept of cognitive reapportionment articulates the concept that tasks can be viewed as a set of cognitive acts that can be "allocated" across combinations of human and machine systems. The design should encourage the idea that the dialogue with these systems can be dynamic, so that they can adjust to new decision situations and users. In addition, we argued that a central theme in computer science has been the design of systems to emulate cognitive acts.

We feel what has been missing in the intellectual tradition to date is full realization of the implications of the allocation of cognitive responsibilities on tasks and the management of tasks. Moreover, changes enabled by cognitive reapportionment are occurring at a number of levels: individual, organizational, and interorganizational. The following section provides examples of each.

Changing Individual, Organizational, and Interorganizational Activity

At American Express, 80%-85% of all credit requests are authorized by an algorithm in the credit authorization software. A group of about 400 credit authorizers in four major centers situated in strategic locations in the United States, deal with the remaining 15%-20%. In making this decision, a credit card authorizer examines as many as 13 different databases of client information, such as payment history, charges outstanding, and vendor history. This transaction optimally should occur while the merchant and client are still on the phone—a window of approximately 30 seconds to 3 minutes.

American Express decided to use the knowledge of its best authorizers to create an expert system to help all of its authorizers. The system reallocated some of the cognition of the credit card authorizers and put it into a support system. In the process, the credit card authorization expert system improved the productivity of the credit card authorizers. On average, it took 20% less time to scan data and start from a suggested decision than it did to examine the 13 databases and make judgments from experience alone. The system aided in intelligent search and inference about credit but still left the final decision to the individual. Management also reported that the quality of decisions improved as knowledge of what makes a good or bad credit risk became more readily available.

Cognitive Reapportionment at the Organization Level

Our organization designers of today perceive that people are in control of all decision activities in the enterprise. Indeed, for the most part, they define the enterprise in terms of the people that make up the employment of the firm. The reality in terms of essential nature of the firm is somewhat different. Although decision processes are, for the most part, defined by people and delivered (decisions made) by people, the growing opportunity for individual assessment of business situations and "independent" action by systems is an emerging reality.

The examples used in this chapter thus far have dealt with support of a single individual. There are also examples of controlling and administering the cognitive processes across different functions within the organization. Gleason Manufacturing has accomplished substantial penetration of CAD into their engineering department. The firm directly feeds CAD drawings into the manufacturing process, standardizing the primitives (e.g., the basic building blocks) of the dialogue between the engineering and manufacturing departments. These primitives can be configured in many different ways, allowing significant complexity in the final design, but all within the grammar of solutions embedded in the tool.

In the creation of the B2 Stealth Bomber, Northrop went directly from the electronic description of the system to manufacturing without the creation of an aerodynamic half- or quarter-scale prototype for wind tunnel testing. The engineers were so confident in their ability to model the system and have that model be consistent across all the disciplines necessary to create the plant that they went straight from information description to creation of the tangible product. By sharing the same cognitive tool across different functions, many of the translation functions that used to occur when an engineer needed to have a design translated from mechanical drawings into design and production processes are subsumed in the tool. The cognition associated with moving the design from function to function as it went through the process from engineering and product concept to manufacture and service is thus shifted to the machine.

In these two examples, creation and use of a common cognitive platform for design allowed a completely new manner of coordination. This type of coordination delivered faster turnaround in a critical business process. It also enabled a higher level of integration of physical processes, based on a higher level of integration of cognitive processes.

Cognitive Reapportionment
at the Interorganization Level

In the context of interorganizational systems, a clear example is provided by TelCot, which employed an interorganizational system in the trading of cotton futures. In 1988, there were millions of cotton transactions in the United States representing over $250 million worth of cotton traded. Policy and coordination issues that typically occur within an individual purchasing department or trading area begin to be reflected in policy embedded in the software of the TelCot trading system. Policies around exchange in the market-place create rules and regulations and thinking behavior about the actual transactions outside and across organizations.

Early interorganizational systems were based around the telephone or clerical systems. In these systems, such as simple order entry, the linkages provided simple communications or shared data. The emerging paradigm is one in which there is a rich set of policy and procedures that can be enacted by the channel system, the policy document itself, or a combination of both. In effect, the functions of the agent have been embedded in the systems themselves, allowing these systems to perform transactions faster than hu-manly possible and across time and geography constraints that were other-wise infeasible.

Thus we see that there are examples of cognitive reapportionment in a variety of organizational settings across three levels of concern: individual, organizational, and interorganizational. These systems are often designed to create decision effectiveness or organizational efficiency, and there are potential opportunities and challenges that they present.

Implications of Cognitive Reapportionment
for the General Manager

The management implications of these sorts of examples are many. First, different *economics* come into play as different thinking processes are put into machines. For example, in the American Express and Gleason situations the incremental cost of another credit decision or engineering design and manufacturing layout decreases radically. There is a high fixed cost up front to create the tool but the incremental decision and cognition incurs very little cost. From an organizational standpoint, this means that the decision capacity for the subset of decisions that can be put directly onto the machine is vastly improved. American Express and Gleason have virtually unlimited capacity to handle new transactions as long as they meet the specifications designed into the system.

Second, a more efficient and controlled *diffusion* of knowledge is possible. For example, once the credit card authorization system is in place, the ability to put new credit decisions into the process can happen almost overnight in a step function manner. One could close the books on January 9th and on January 10th come up with a whole new set of credit policies. Formerly, it would have been necessary to create a new set of training procedures and rely on a gradual reception and education of the credit authorization audience. With a knowledge-based system, one can diffuse that knowledge directly to the decision in point.

Third, the use of such *source* systems raises many issues. For example, who should have authority to create the policy that is embedded in the software? By default, policy is often determined by technical experts who have a very weak or tenuous understanding of the business context. The general manager, however, typically has very little understanding of the technical context. Often in the development of electronic data interchange, for example, the technical system designers (analysts/programmers) make critical business policy decisions without consulting the affected managers (marketing, sales, order processing, and so forth).

A fourth issue for managers is that *monitoring* these systems is critical. Given the ability to influence and control the cognitive dialogue of an individual in a machine, one has to be very careful that the right decisions are being made.

Thus, if one notes the increasing capabilities of the emerging business platforms for decision-making, one sees increasing areas for redesign of business decision making processes. If one views the organization as a nexus of decision, not just decision makers, many opportunities come into view to allocate to human, system, or both, the decision making capabilities. The ability to provide dynamic allocation also becomes available. As we have mentioned above, these capabilities are available both at the level of the individual decision maker and at the level of the organization or even across organizations. This has implications for organization structure and management policy. One way to examine the implications on these two central concerns is to characterize these potential "cognitors" by suggesting the types of roles they can serve in the organization.

As future managers, we need to (1) recognize current growth in knowledge scope that involves captured expertise and skills in addition to "information," (2) explore the new forms of decision opportunities that are changing the capabilities of active thinkers, and (3) challenge the social paradigm that will not allow us to embrace an idea of trust and delegation. We must make these considerations, as general managers, in order to move to the next level of organizational dynamics.

Emerging IT Role
in Apportionment of Cognition

The apportionment concept can be further explicated and examined by showing the flexibility of the roles that are possible to enact. We have seen the emergence of information technology systems capable of functioning as active analytic tools (guiding analysis and decision making) and as agents, active monitors, simulators, distillers, amplifiers, interpreters, and excavators. Many of these concepts have been raised as individual applications of advances. We attempt a brief synthesis of these to show that what they have in common is that they each contain kernels of cognitive reapportionment (see accompanying table).

Old Roles	
Clerk	Recording transactions, filing results
Analytic tool, passive	Extensive numeric analysis modeling under direction of user
New Roles	
Analytic tool, active	Actively guiding, analyzing, commenting on decision processes and analyses
Active monitors	Greater scale, specificity, complexity, timeliness than previous monitoring
Simulators	Efficient, effective surrogates for physical reality
Distillers	Refine information to usable form
Amplifiers	Allow the individual to cross roles, time
Interpreters	Show, interpret meaning of symbolic or information technology enabled systems
Excavators	Mine existing logic and software for business policy for interpretation and reimplementation

An explanation of these emerging roles seems indicated. In the area of active analysis, there are a number of systems that attempt to come to conclusions and extensively test and exhaustively enumerate all relevant decision criteria. Expert systems that aid in the pricing of hazardous waste disposal incorporate a number of interacting models that make assumptions about the soil, access to the site, method of cleanup, and timing. Together the models guide the analysis to a full assessment of the possible cost of cleaning up a hazardous waste site. The models, built by companies under contract to the Environmental Protection Agency, are based on experience with the cleanup of hundreds of Navy yard sites and constitute one of the most comprehensive examples of this type of data and commercial information.

In the area of agents, a number of systems are embedding policy and logic that can create transactions for the systems owner or user. For example, embedded in electronic data exchange transactions between Gillette and K-Mart are policy actions such as shipping, pricing, and packing.

As active monitors, some new information technology systems are taking the concept of variance analysis, as practiced by general managers, to new heights of sophistication and emphasis. Frito-Lay, for example, recently created a management system that allows hundreds of general managers within divisions to access operational data on a daily basis. Individual and shared reports that monitor performance to date by volume, profitability, share, and so forth can be set to generate an alert when established parameters are exceeded. The system differs significantly from traditional paper-and-pencil monthly reports in timeliness, volume, and sophistication of the monitoring, and it enables more diffuse and controlled access to data and consistent monitoring.

A particularly exciting area is the realm of simulation. In every business, more and more of the value chain is being absorbed into information technology in the form of models. The airlines, one of the earliest and most sophisticated users of simulation technology, have reached new heights of simulation authenticity. With some new versions of commercial simulators, the first real flight a pilot makes in a commercial plane is with passengers on board!

A number of powerful economic factors drove simulation in the airline arena: it is cheaper and safer to crash simulators than real airplanes. Also, more decision capabilities can be tested, in a shorter period of time, in a simulator than in a plane because of the time it takes to reach altitudes and locations for certain maneuvers.

The same economic logic that drove the creation of flight simulators is now driving the creation of complex models of interaction of physical, biological, and/or logical systems. In chemical, pharmaceutical, auto, even financial firms, sophisticated models and workstations crunch extensive "simulations" of different technologies that allow discreet examination of behaviors (e.g., stress on a piston, return on a synthetic security) of the device before it ever becomes a commercial reality.

In the information technology that is providing tools that serve as "distillers," we are beginning to see sophisticated uses of information systems to provide "information refineries" (Clippinger & Konsynski, 1989). In this role, the information technology takes embedded policy, in the form of a profile of information that a user might want, as a base point from which to filter and distill newspapers, articles, stock information, and so forth. This concept is expanding to include many different types of internal and external information sources and should provide at least one technological crutch for the information overload created by the information technology available to organizations.

Information technologies that function as amplifiers allow individuals to assume new roles by changing assumptions about the sequencing of events and range of skills. The most poignant example today may be in modern music, where it is common to have a single artist perform multiple instruments, multiple voices, and multiple roles. Much of this capability accompanied the advent of recording technology, but until digital synthesizers and mixers became widely available, the quality of the integrations and modifications of instruments and tracks was not sufficiently controllable and did not deliver high enough quality to encourage musicians to use it. This has changed; the role of information technology as amplifier of talent and process is just beginning.

Turning to the last two roles of excavator and interpreter, we find information technology being turned on itself to aid commercial/management processes. For example, as auto companies have embedded more and more information technology in their cars to provide improved functions and features, as well as micro-control of the processes of controlled propulsion, the car has become a "black-box" to the mechanic. More and more of the critical functions of the car must be elucidated by the use of a diagnostic device. Computer-analyzed tune-ups are becoming a necessity.

In a similar vein, companies are turning to information technologies to "excavate" the business logic embedded in existing software systems. Bachman Information systems, endorsed by IBM, is leading the charge of information systems software houses that are creating tools to help systems professionals "reverse engineer" the logic that exists in large, embedded information systems applications. Such systems are often too complex to remove or replace, and the need to update begins with excavation.

These options create new challenges in terms of adoption and maintenance of the knowledge system and location of cognitive responsibilities. Well managed, they can contribute to the knowledge-base of the firm, and thereby influence organizational capabilities and competitive position. This is especially of concern for the general manager today, because there have been significant innovations in the nature of the information infrastructure that supports the business process. With exemplars of the types of decision-making capabilities briefly covered above, we can now become more explicit in describing the cognitive reapportionment concept and its importance in the design of organizations.

Cognitive Reapportionment and Organization Design

New organizational forms, born of increasingly complex, fast-paced, and volatile competitive situations, are emerging—the concepts of networks (Eccles

& Crane, 1988); dynamic networks (Childs, 1987); value-added partnerships (Johnson & Lawrence, 1988), even the "Coming of the New Organization" as Drucker (1988) put it. Certainly to analyze the rich set of insights trying to explain what some are calling the "post-bureaucratic" organization is a book-length topic, which will not be attempted here.

Of principal interest is the idea that there is an emerging set of research and theory that suggests and shows that these new forms are intertwined with the management of information technology (Applegate, Cash, & Mills, 1988; Huber 1984, 1990; Walton, 1989; Zuboff, 1988). Returning to our theme of cognitive reapportionment, these researchers have, for the most part, either tacitly or explicitly assumed that humans are the only cognitors in the systems and, moreover, that information technology is primarily a passive agent, executing known procedures in a static manner.

In practice, which often leads theory, we find examples (as shown above) of organizations consciously relocating and designing the control and trans-action of decision processes and allocating these between and among information technology systems and humans. The more thoughtful practitioners are consciously embedding and influencing firm-specific and industrywide policy through the design and implementation of new business platforms internally and externally. Through these means they create information-technology-based complements and substitutes to human-based decision systems.

Thus we see that the very primitives or organizations design in these new age organizations are not just humans and systems as separate entities, but humans *plus* systems, and systems *plus* systems as interacting entities. Now, if there were a natural separation and allocation of cognitive responsibilities at the individual, organizational, and interorganizational levels among humans and systems, there would be no need to manage the process. The "correct" allocations would occur, would be standard across organizations, and would provide a useful but managerially uninteresting part of the organizational infrastructure.

However, as we saw above, organizations are using information technology to consciously capture scarce expertise (e.g., American Express), change coordination mechanisms (e.g., Gleason) and even reach outside the organization (e.g., K-Mart). Thus, like the technology itself, the evolution and role of the technology are plastic and can be managed to a more or less effective end state.

From another perspective, it would be sensible to ignore the cognitive reapportionment concept, and the innovations in business platform, if the technology were homogeneous and universally available. The telephone provides an example of a technology that is part of the infrastructure, and not many firms find useful advantage from their use of the phone system. It would also be practical to ignore these systems if they only dealt with ancillary

TABLE 4.1 Critical Issues for the General Manager

1. Need to accept that there are human and non-human decision makers.

2. Decisions are and will be allocated to "teams" of human and non-human decision makers.

3. Those that "think" about a situation (scan, interpret, analyze, etc.) versus those that additionally make judgment and have authority to execute.

4. New approaches to management control allow us to move decision-making outside the organization, or into areas where in the past we felt we had less control (insurance companies permitting more underwriting by direct writers, or even independent agents).

5. Skills in decision making and skills in monitor and control of decision making activities are changing the ways we can think about organization design.

6. The *who, when, where,* and with *what* authority are changing in the review of the possible with respect to business processes.

7. Some might say that because the "systems" are taught/or told what they should consider they are merely an extension of their "programmers/specifiers." They might say this is different from people decision makers. This is wrong as people are also trained/told how to interpret and decide.

8. Organizations of the past centered around decisions allocated to specific roles or even individuals. Today we seek a broader decision capability that allows one, or several, of a larger set of decision makers to make decisions.

9. Important that a trail of decisions be made, documenting who made what decision, when, with what knowledge, and what authority (and with what reasoning).

business processes, such as facilities maintenance. However, as shown above, these systems are non-neutral in their adoption and effects.

Therefore, the manager (see Table 4.1) and management researcher need to understand the current application and potential implications of the use of systems to allocate and reallocate cognitive responsibilities at the individual, organizational, and interorganizational levels.

Conclusion

Cognitive reapportionment is a design form than provides a redefinition of possibilities that permit the revisitation of forms that have existed in the past. The consequence is that certain historic organizational forms are made feasible as human/system metaphors in today's and tomorrow's environments. The metaphors of the past communicate many of the underlying philosophies that drive organizational structures, management control processes, and market action.

The philosophies that operated in the citadels of ages past underlay many of the patterns of judgment and behavior that we witness in the strict hierarchies of today's monolithic organizations. Clearly, the emerging trends toward arrangements involving loosely coupled organizations and strong cross-organizational alliances suggest the city-state arrangements of old that reflect a confederation of autonomous but cooperating entities.

New product-oriented organizational structures allow us to consider organizational experimentation that was not feasible in older, "functionally oriented" organizations. The new information technology allows us to establish the proper control environments that permit the kind of controlled experimentation needed to challenge policies on organization structure, management control, cultural change, market relationships, and operating philosophies.

Historically, managers have designed business organizations under the assumption that *people* are the key actors around which we base organization design decisions, especially those associated with assignment of decision-making responsibilities. This situation is changing as emerging information technologies permit us to consider the actual judgment and decision making in the technology environment with the technological options. Such opportunities will allow managers to rethink their processes for development and adaptation of their organizations.

In today's environment, pressures grow for the skills needed to filter, use, and convey useful information and knowledge more precisely and more quickly. It is important that management has the right mixture of human and machine-based intelligence available to respond to the volatile business environment. The volume, volatility, velocity, and veracity (four Vs) of information demand skills that have historically eluded the organization of the past that relied on the effective scanning of the environment by people ill-trained to address the new demands of the current information intensive culture.

In this chapter we have suggested that through the use of new technologies and better understanding of task domains, general managers have the option to begin to choose where knowledge is processes and what kinds of knowledge should go into machines and what kinds of knowledge should stay in the heads of individuals in the organization. The implications of these opportunities are extensive. There are new organizational possibilities. There are new relationships available to customers and suppliers. There is also a new and different dependence on information technology in the management of products and services.

Implications are clearly both wonderful and repulsive. The challenges to the ways that we have thought about roles and responsibilities of general management and information technology are significant. It only remains for us to be willing to challenge our own assumptions and beliefs concerning those roles, responsibilities, and capabilities.

Notes

1. See "Decision Processes: An Organizational View" in *Information Systems and Decision Processes,* edited by Edward Stohr and Benn Konsynski (IEEE Press, 1992).

2. *Cog•ni•tion:* "the act or process of knowing including both awareness and judgment" (*Webster's*).

3. A *cognitor* is any entity that can perform an act of cognition—e.g., human, group, system. See Fjeldstad and Konsynski (1986).

References

Applegate, L., Cash, J., Jr., & Mills, D. Q. (1988, November-December). Information technology and tomorrow's manager. *Harvard Business Review* Reprint #88601.

Childs, J. (1987, Fall). Information technology, organizations, and the response to strategic challenges. *California Management Review,* pp. 33-50.

Clippinger, J. H., & Konsynski, B. R. (1989, August). Information refineries: Electronically distilling business' raw material to make it more usable. *Computerworld,* pp. 73-77.

Dolk, D. R., & Konsynski, B. R. (1986, November). Knowledge representation for model management systems. *IEEE Transactions on Software Engineering, SE-10,* pp. 619-620.

Drucker, P. F. (1988, January-February). The coming of the new organization. *Harvard Business Review,* pp. 45-53.

Eccles, R. G., & Crane, D. B. (1988). *Doing deals.* Boston, MA: Harvard University Press.

Elam, J. J., & Konsynski, B. R. (1988, Summer). Using artificial intelligence techniques to enhance the capabilities of model management systems. *Decision Sciences, 18*(3), 487-502.

Elofson, G., & Konsynski, B. (1991, Summer). Delegation technologies: Environmental scanning with intelligent agents. *Journal of MIS, 18*(1).

Fedorowicz, J., & Konsynski, B. (1992). Organization support systems: Bridging business and decision processes. *Journal of Management Information Systems, 8*(4) 5-25.

Fjeldstad, O., & Konsynski, B. (1986). Reapportionment of cognitive responsibilities in DSS dialogues. In E. McLean & H. G. Sol (Eds.), *Decision support systems: A decade in perspective.* North-Holland: Elsevier Science Publishers.

Gorry, G. A., & Scott-Morton, M. S. (1971, Fall). A framework for management information systems. *Sloan Management Review, 13*(1), 55-70.

Huber, G. P. (1984, August). The nature and design of post-industrial organizations. *Management Science, 30*(8), 928-951.

Huber, G. P. (1990, January). A theory of the effects of information technologies on organizational design, intelligence, and decision making. *Academy of Management Review, 15*(1), 47-71.

Jaikumar, R., & Bohn, R. (1988a). The development of intelligent systems for industrial use: A conceptual framework. *Research on Technological Innovation, Management and Policy.*

Jaikumar, R., & Bohn, R. (1988b). *The development of intelligent systems for industrial use: An empirical investigation.* Working Paper, Boston, MA: Harvard Business School.

Johnson, R., & Lawrence, P. R. (1988, July-August). Beyond vertical integration: The rise of the value-adding partnership. *Harvard Business Review,* pp. 94-101.

Keen, P. G. W., & Scott-Morton, M. (1978). *Decision support systems: An organizational perspective.* Reading, MA: Addison-Wesley.

Kuo, F-Y., & Konsynski, B. R. (1988, September). Dialogue management: Support for dialogue independence. *MIS Quarterly,* pp. 480-499.

Luconi, F., Malone, T., & Scott-Morton, M. (1985). *Expert support systems.* CISR Working Paper #122. Cambridge, MA: Massachusetts Institute of Technology.

McCorduck, P. (1979). *Machines who think: A personal inquiry into the history and prospects of artificial intelligence.* New York: Freeman.

Newell, A., Shaw, J. C., & Simons, H. A. (1963) Empirical explorations of the logic theory machine. *Proceedings WJCC.* Los Angeles. Reprinted in E. A. Feigenbaum & J. Feldman (Eds.), *Computers and thought* (New York: McGraw-Hill, 1963).

Sprague, R. H., & Carlson, E. D. (1982). *Building effective decision support systems.* Englewood Cliffs, NJ: Prentice Hall.

Stohr, E., & Konsynski, B. (Ed.). (1992). Decision processes: An organizional view. In *Information systems and decision processess* (pp. 27-49). Los Alamitos, CA: IEEE Computer Society Press.

Sviokla, J. J. (1986a, Fall). The business implications of knowledge-based systems: Part I. *DATABASE,* pp. 1-15.

Sviokla, J. J. (1986b, Fall). The business implications of knowledge-based systems: Part II. *DATABASE,* pp. 1-16.

Walton, R. E. (1989). *Up and running.* Boston, MA: Harvard Business School Press.

Zuboff, S. (1988). *In the age of the smart machine: The future of work and power.* New York: Basic Books.

5 THE VIRTUAL ORGANIZATION

Bureaucracy, Technology, and the Implosion of Control

Nitin Nohria
James D. Berkley

How are we to envision the organization of the future? This is the question that has preoccupied many now for decades, although it is usually posed as if for the first time. In fact, prophecies about the "new organization" have been practically an industry unto themselves since at least the 1950s, when Peter Drucker (1959, 1968) first began laying out the vision of a postmodern world run by so-called "knowledge workers." Since that time, the discourse of organizational futurology has been joined by theorists as diverse as Alvin Toffler (1970), Daniel Bell (1973a, 1973b), Shoshana Zuboff (1988), and General Electric CEO Jack Welch (1989). Although typically divergent in their approach and their conclusions, these theorists of the new organization share a common rhetorical framework: The world is changing, traditional bureaucracy is bankrupt, and the future is now—or at least soon.

The problem, however, has always been to articulate a vision of this coming new world that is as resonant as the bureaucratic vision—or in Weberian terms, "ideal type"—that clearly no longer serves as a norm in our society. To a large extent, discussions of the new organization are phrased in negative or differential terms: nonbureaucratic, nonhierarchical, postmodern, post-industrial, and so forth. Current buzzwords such as "knowledge workers"

AUTHORS' NOTE: The authors would like to thank Lynda Applegate, Anne Donnellon, and Charles Heckscher for their comments on an earlier draft of this paper, circulated as a Harvard Business School Working Paper in early 1992.

and "network organization" are evocative, yet also vague and elusive. Perhaps we are still in the situation described by Daniel Bell when he argued that, because of the waning of the archetype of industrial bureaucracy, we were left without a "primary image of work" (Bell, 1973a, pp. 162-163).[1] In Bell's view, the cohesive worldview of the American 1950s—exemplified in the nearly iconic status of factories and large industrial organizations—had all but disappeared, leaving a social void in a world in which these older icons were increasingly seen as anachronisms.

What new organizational archetype might follow in the wake of this last one? Bell himself argued that the emerging sociocultural order would come to be marked simply by a turn back to the individual, and by a new primacy of the individual in the workplace (Bell, 1973a, p. 163). Yet even if this is arguably what has occurred in the intervening years, it is hard to make sense of exactly what such a transition might mean for a theory of organizations. An organizational archetype based on the primacy of individuals quickly brushes up against a set of subtle but unshakable paradoxes: What, after all, could it mean to have a concept of organization based on the preeminence of individuals, and by what means could such organizations be realizable in practice?

Adding to this sense of paradox is the emergence, in recent years, of certain trends that chip away further at our secure notions of what an organization might be. Boundaries between and within organizations have been dissolving, as firms begin to work in novel ways often enabled by new information technology. Consider, for example, the following brief examples drawn from our own field research:

• *Colliers International Property Consultants* (Gladstone & Nohria, 1990). Formed by the merger of two real estate associations on opposite sides of the globe, Colliers brought together 34 technically distinct real estate firms under a common logo and a common computer network. The network permitted a profitable exchange of vital local knowledge on an almost global scale and generated significant commission revenues for member firms. But opinions varied widely in regard to exactly what Colliers was. Was it an organization? Merely a network? An association?

• *Lithonia Lighting* (Berkley & Nohria, 1991). Using information technology packages known collectively as Light*Link™, this major American producer of lighting fixtures began in the early 1980s to tie independent sales agents and other industry players such as contractors and distributors into their own sophisticated information network. By 1991, much of what had taken place through an informal, personal network of interactions now took place through Lithonia's own computer workstations, with the vestiges of the old system targeted for similar transformation. Although there was much debate inside Lithonia about the continued development of Light*Link systems, many in the company firmly believed that the lighting industry's future was "going to be electronic" with a myriad of players networked to each other by information technology.

• *KPMG Peat Marwick* (Gladstone & Eccles, 1991). As of 1991, KPMG—a global accounting firm—had developed a prototype for a computer network that would allow company partners to conduct nearly all their business through computer workstations known as "shadow partners." The "shadow partner" was intended to serve as an electronic assistant capable of handling nearly all of a partner's information needs on a daily basis. Described as a "complete, concise, quality-controlled representation of the company's expertise," the shadow partner was a major, if unresolved, part of the firm's future strategy.

• *Mutual Benefit Life* (Berkley & Eccles, 1991). A large insurance company headquartered in Newark, New Jersey, Mutual Benefit Life pioneered the development of a "case manager system" that could effectively replace an entire collection of clerks with a single person using a PC to underwrite and issue insurance policies. The company's complex and archaic bureaucracy was expected to "wither away" as more and more processes were built in to the workstations of a relatively small number of these case managers. According to executives, the guiding vision was of ultimately creating a "one-person insurance company," where each case manager could handle the company's entire range of services.

In this new corporate world of blurred boundaries, ubiquitous technology, and "empowered" individuals, what counts as an organization? Given these examples, what once seemed stable and self-evident about the very idea of "the organization" now appears obscure and rather arbitrary. In a perplexing way, the central project at both the theoretical and practical levels has come to involve the articulation of a vision of organizational life that is somehow *beyond* organizations.

Based on such evidence, we might posit that what we are witnessing *is* the crystallization of a new ideal type on the order of Weber's theory of bureaucracy (Weber, 1947, 1978). If so, however, the parameters of this new ideal type remain rather undefined, located more in the haze of current discourse than in the observables of current practice. They are more "talked about" than they are completely enacted. Extrapolating from the available evidence, we will discuss this new type as that of a *virtual organization*—an admittedly voguish term that nonetheless serves both to underscore the role of the new technologies and the ontological paradox of the "organizationless organization."[2] Our purpose in the pages that follow is to lay out a vision—in an exploratory, rather than strictly empirical or normative, fashion—of what this new way of thinking and talking about organizations entails.

Weber and Bureaucracy

Rather than jumping into an immediate analysis of the virtual organization, it is helpful to begin by reexamining Weber's theory of bureaucracy. This is the theory that, combined with Taylorism, formed the theoretical backbone of our older rhetorics of organization. To be truthful, any "new" organization would have probably come as a surprise to Weber: However ambivalently, the man cited with the founding modern sociology tended to understand the bureaucratic form of organization as the inescapable telos of modern Western society. Although it is often rightly stressed that the Weberian ideal type indicates a methodological and not a strictly normative ideal, Weber insists at several points in his writings that *only* bureaucratic organization is suited to the otherwise unmanageable complexity of the modern work enterprise.

The basic features of Weber's bureaucratic type can be summarized as follows (Weber, 1947, 1978):

1. A discrete set of "jurisdictional areas" separate and regulated spaces pertaining to clearly differentiated functions within an enterprise.
2. A hierarchy consisting both of the subordination of offices and of individuals, with a resulting separation of levels of planning and execution.
3. A management system based on written documents or "files" and on a staff of people who maintain and transmit these files.
4. An exclusive focus on the organizational roles specific to particular offices, so as to create a neutral, impersonal environment.
5. A stress on technical training, with the use of technical criteria for matters of both recruitment and promotion.
6. An office system comprised of general rules, which are stable, thorough, and learnable.[3]

Weber's principles of bureaucratic organization continue to serve as benchmarks for our understanding of the contemporary work organization. At the same time, it is impossible to deny that the ideal type Weber sought to describe has lost most, if not all, of its rhetorical currency of late. For years—indeed for much longer than we might care to believe—managers and academics alike have sounded the death knell for Weberian bureaucracy while seeking to define new paradigms that might together be labeled "post-bureaucratic." Today, even *within* most firms, one would be hard pressed to find managers defending any of the bureaucratic tenets listed above. In a recent review of the literature, Charles Heckscher (1991) sums up the interesting discursive shift we have recently witnessed:

> Social theorists and popular writers have lamented the trend [of bureaucracy], decrying the soul-deadening nature of bureaucratic work and raising alarms about the world being lost. Until recently, however, the critics of bureaucracy were rarely found in executive positions. The novelty now is that leaders of large organizations see themselves in the vanguard, attempting to create "post-bureaucratic" organizations. . . . And rather than viewing these alternatives as jeopardizing productivity, they see them as a way to make their corporations even better. (p. 115)

Bureaucracy is a bad word in the 1990s, often for quite justified reasons. It is blamed with inefficiency, inflexibility, and general inhumanity; leading business magazines such as *Fortune* have attended to such realizations with a constant flow of articles with titles such as "The Bureaucracy Busters" (Dumaine, 1991). The patron saint of American companies in this war against bureaucracy is General Electric, a massive conglomerate whose CEO preaches against bureaucracy and argues instead for the "boundaryless" company—a company in which, in the words of GE's 1989 annual report (General Electric, 1989), "we knock down the walls that separate us from each other on the inside and from our key constituencies on the outside." Needless to say, the word *conglomerate* is itself verboten inside GE walls.

The new rhetoric of bureaucracy's elimination is stirring and usually well-intentioned. To what degree it finds itself translated into practice, however, is a question that is difficult to answer. We have seen examples of companies engaged in full-fledged "anti-bureaucracy" campaigns where, for the most part, little has changed other than words and rituals used to legitimate how the work is done. Conversely, we have visited companies where the rhetoric of bureaucracy remains unchallenged, yet the actual practice of work appears surprisingly *non*bureaucratic. The confusion only grows when we try to make sense of authors, such as Peter Drucker, who have been proclaiming the advent of the new, post-bureaucratic organization for the last several decades, updating the estimated time of arrival with every new book or article. Clearly, there is a certain point where *talk* about the organization takes its leave of whatever organizational realities exist in the world. This is not to disparage the value of "talk," or of "mere rhetoric." To the contrary, such observations are useful insofar as they help us to understand the language of organization as a *discursive system* whose connections to the empirical world are complex and occasionally even contradictory.

Technology and Society: The Virtual in Context

What happens after bureaucracy's disappearing act? How does this act—real or imagined—set the stage for what is to follow? As a starting point, organizations might be said to become virtual simply by virtue of the giddy new "boundarylessness" preached by figures such as Jack Welch. The realness of organizations wanes—they enter an intermediate realm where they seem, as in Welch's utopian vision, at once real and unreal.

In fact, the term *virtual* has a history and currency that make it uniquely qualified as a way to discuss contemporary issues of organizational structure and design. In the physical sciences, the word *virtual* has been used at least since the mid-19th century to refer to structures and objects whose ontological status lies in the fuzzy realm between fact and apparition we have just encountered. (Hence such expressions as "virtual image," which refers to an image from which light *seems* to emanate but does not in truth do so.[4]) In a more contemporary usage, computers can be said to have *virtual memory* when an external data-storing device such as a disk drive can be employed "as if" it were truly the computer's internal memory system. Likewise, contemporary particle physics speaks of "virtual particles"—particle pairs that evolve literally *ex nihilo* and almost immediately annihilate each other.

Since the late 1980s, new technologies have permitted the concept of virtuality to enter into the popular imagination and everyday life. The success of computer networks such as Internet and Bitnet has allowed people both inside and outside work organizations to experience a form of what has been called *virtual space,* a nonphysical space in which interacting parties never meet face to face and may indeed be downright deceptive about their true identities. On a still more futuristic note, virtual reality systems promise to permit users to enter self-contained three-dimensional simulations of reality. In these three-dimensional virtual spaces, an individual can choose to "be" a different person, or to "explore" a remote or even imaginary locale.

What virtual technologies have in common is their ability to allow a powerful simulation of the physical world by electronic means. The French sociologist Jean Baudrillard (1988) has argued that in recent decades, our entire society has been moving in this direction. According to Baudrillard, our society is in the throes of a passage from a paradigm of *representation* to one of *simulation,* to a technological world in which the distinction between real and unreal ultimately collapses and in which the criteria for "realness" finally become disconnected from any question of ontology. Although the validity of Baudrillard's sweeping hypothesis is open to question, many of the intriguing new features of our everyday world take on new meaning when framed as aspects of such a transition. For example, in the global electronic economy that has been emerging over recent decades, how real is money? In a political system largely dominated by televised sound-bites, how "real" is the democratic polis? Or, returning to the point of our argument here, in a occupational landscape composed of individuals networked through computers, how "real" is the work organization itself? When do organizations cease to exist properly and become virtual?

Of course, one answer to this question is that organizations have *always already* been virtual—that is, that organizations are essentially fictions constructed by human interpretation as opposed to scientifically definable entities. But it is arguable that the emergence of powerful new information technologies such as electronic mail and computer conferencing into our everyday lives has made this fact palpable in a way that it never previously had been. Sandy Stone—one of the pioneer researchers of the virtual realm—has for example noted:

> It is interesting that just about the time that the last of the untouched "real world" anthropological field sites are disappearing, a new and unexpected kind of "field" is opening up—incontrovertibly social spaces in which people still meet face to face, but under new definitions of both "meet" and "face." These new spaces instantiate the collapse of the boundaries between the social and technological, biology and machine, natural and artificial that are part of the postmodern imaginary. They are part of the growing imbrication of humans and machines in new social forms that I call *virtual systems*. (1992, pp. 4-5)

Stone emphasizes the power of technology to reconfigure social space and social interaction. Likewise, to speak of a work organization as a virtual system serves to call attention to the enabling role of technology and to the concomitant transformation of certain organizational fundamentals: personal interaction, the division of labor, and so forth.[5] As the wide-scale introduction of sophisticated IT erodes these features, one encounters "organizational fantasies" that increasingly resemble circulating descriptions of virtual systems: visions of organizations sustained by information technology, organizations where the traditional needs of coordinating people and resources no longer apply, organizations that cease to exist as the rationalized, physical systems Weber had once sought to describe.

In 1992, such ideas made their inevitable way into the mainstream with the publication of the first management book to capitalize on the newfound prominence of the virtual realm. Entitled *The Virtual Corporation* (Davidow and Malone, 1992), its authors' thesis was that new technologies were causing a revolutionary change in what corporations produced and how they worked —and that managers had best to adapt lest they be swept aside in the transition. At the heart of their discussion was the conviction that information technologies were helping to do away with the constraints and limitations that have been inherent to traditional organizations.[6]

Yet aside from the explicitness of its terminology, *The Virtual Corporation* is only a single element of a growing tendency to envision the future organization as a virtual system. As we explained earlier, our intention is to understand the virtual organization as an emerging ideal type—as a distilled trend as opposed to a practical or normative reality. It is, we submit, a *vision* that implicitly guides a great deal of current theory and speculation about organizational structure while standing much of Weber's ideal type on its head. An ideal type of the virtual organization might be said to have the following characteristics:

1. The disappearance of Weber's material "files"—the very ontological stuff of organizations—and their reappearance in flexible and electronic form by means of information technology.

2. The replacement of face-to-face communication with computer-mediated communication as a means of conducting the primary activities of the organization, and a concomitant increase in the role of informal face-to-face communication for purposes of maintaining organizational coherence.

3. The transfer of issues of organizational structure from the realm of the organization of human beings to the organization of information and technology in such a way that, to an observer, the functioning of the organization appears spontaneous and paradoxically *structure-less,* while the functioning of information systems seems at once all-pervasive and faintly magical.

4. The networking of individuals from technically separate firms (such as suppliers, customers, and even competitors) to the extent that clear external boundaries of the organization become difficult to establish in practice.

5. The implosion of bureaucratic specialization into "global," cross-functional, computer-mediated jobs, such that individual members of the organization may be considered holographically equivalent to the organization as a whole.

If an ideal type of virtual organization is thinkable at the present time, its viability is attributable to the seismic shift we have witnessed in technology in recent decades—a shift marked by the development of such things as personal computers, networked databases, and instant forms of telecommunications such as electronic mail. It is not merely that new technology allows new configurations of people and machines, but that our relationship to technology continuously restructures both our thinking and our discourse. As workplaces witness the proliferation of these new "modes of information,"[7] people's expectations and projections about organizational life change just as radically, probably more radically, than the existing organizational environment itself.

Changes in technology, however, do not simply occur in a pristine realm of their own. They are part of the whole social, cultural, and political landscape in which they, and organizations themselves, are situated. There is an affinity, for example, between the virtual organization of PCs and knowledge workers and an extrinsic social discourse that, in Bell's analysis, now values individual self-actualization over deference to large institutions.[8] To put it boldly, issues of social structure and practice are always, at some level, inseparable from issues of technological structure and practice, even when the mechanics of the connection are not especially explicit at the surface. As an analogy to the virtual organization, consider the emergence of the American suburb—at the surface an innovation at the level of social practice, yet clearly intimately related to the technological development of the mass-produced automobile. Today, the social and technological changes taking place are so intertwined that it may be hopeless to attempt to separate them. For instance, Boris Frankel (1987) combines the social and the technological when he lists the following trends as manifestations of an emerging post-industrial ethic: "electronic environments which 'converse with you,' a mass proliferation of demassified political-economic structures, individualized media outlets, [and] the simultaneous decentralization of life and development of a 'planetary consciousness' " (p. 178)

What is at the root of all these developments in contemporary social and technological practice, developments that both surround and participate in the rise of the new organizational rhetoric? One might say that what they have in common is that they are part of contemporary capitalism's tendency to employ technology to make the mechanics of complex organization *occur increasingly behind the scenes,* to naturalize increased complexity through ever more sophisticated orchestrations of knowledge and information.

In its purest sense, this project has to do with the *implosion* of our older structures of coordination and control: a simultaneous miniaturization, concentration, and dispersion of these mechanisms that renders them both less visible and more flexible. Information technology is a vital component of this project, but it exists along side with numerous related developments within everyday life, from customized production to urban planning to mass media. The passage from the rhetoric of bureaucracy to the rhetoric of the virtual organization thus marks not so much a revolutionary technological change as it does the passage to a higher stage in this overarching process.[9] As this occurs, much of the Weberian model is implicitly or explicitly overturned: We witness the vilification of hierarchy, the physical abolition of the "office," the disappearance of office rules, the reintegration of the levels of planning and execution, and other such inversions of Weber's ideal type. New, seemingly revolutionary forms of work are celebrated, such as in scenarios of work-at-home, worker empowerment, and computer networking. At the same time, however, the virtual organization marks new developments in a trajectory begun, but not completed, by bureaucracy.

What Was Bureaucracy Anyhow?

Framing the virtual organization in terms of Weber's theory of bureaucracy permits us to see exactly what is at stake in the presumed transition as well as to see what has remained the same. All too often, a smug picture of the new "information age" casts bureaucracy as a straw man while foreclosing an analysis of the shared deep structure of bureaucratic and post-bureaucratic forms of organization.[10] Often this makes for exciting and motivational rhetoric: the informated late-20th century knowledge worker thus arrives as something of a white knight promising to slay the evil dragon of bureaucracy and to deliver us into the age of post-bureaucratic, nonhierarchical, knowledge-based, utopian labor. However tempting it is to subscribe to such fairy tales, it is important to view information and knowledge not just as recent innovations in the history of work but as constants that have recently come to the fore by virtue of a new conspicuousness.

In a very important sense, all organizations are knowledge organizations, although it would be ahistorical to gloss over the variations in *where* knowledge has resided and *how* workers have been permitted to use it. Traditionally, work organizations have relied on the compartmentalization and expropriation of workers' knowledge in order to differentiate among both levels and functions. Although bureaucratic, such systems are nevertheless knowledge systems. In Weber's (1947) blunt words: "Bureaucratic administration means fundamentally the exercise of control on the basis of knowledge" (p. 339). F. W. Taylor's scientific management—which was to help put Weber's ideal type into practice during the first half of the 20th century—is also explicitly concerned with the organization's role as processor of knowledge. In the words of Frank Webster and Kevin Robins:

> The chief objective of Scientific Management was to annex and control knowledge—both the savoir-faire of the workers and also the more systematic knowledge being produced by increasingly organized research and development—because the possession of knowledge and skill represented the possession of control and power. (1986, p. 309)

Taylor's goal was to isolate the "brain" of the organization from the producing "body" to create a management sector that could serve as a repository and processor of expropriated knowledge (Webster & Robins, 1986, p. 309). Drucker, in fact,, goes so far as to claim Taylor as the founding father of the "knowledge economy," arguing that he was the first to understand that "the key to productivity was knowledge, not sweat" (Drucker, 1968, p. 271).

That Peter Drucker, prophet of the new organization, should find his intellectual roots in F. W. Taylor is perhaps our best indication of the continuities between Taylor's age and our own. Organizations control on the basis of knowledge: They are information-processors, or what could be seen in a metaphorical sense as a kind of human-based computer (Poster, 1990). The Weber/Taylor bureaucracy is a highly structured input-output system, in which a "store of documentary material" (Weber's own phrase) is maintained in order both to interact with the external environment and to control the functioning of the organization itself. In the terms we have been using here, one might say that the bureaucracy functions largely as a *virtual computer,* as an ingenious way of instantiating the mechanistic, highly functionalized workings of a computer in a physical arrangement of people, paper, and rules.

The common view today is that organizations no longer have to serve this purpose, as new forms of control—and IT in particular—have made it possible to manage information in ways much less crude and labor-intensive than the Weberian bureaucracy; we have, so the implicit reasoning goes, managed both to strengthen the control function and to place it still further behind the scenes. If the bureaucratic organization traditionally served as a virtual computer, what is the need for such an organization when "real" IT arrives on the scene, promising manipulations of knowledge previously only envisionable through the mechanisms of bureaucracy? When society as a whole witnesses the emergence of a range of new means of distributed, non-intrusive control (often hinging on IT), what can the perceived role of bureaucracy be other than as nuisance, anachronism, or scapegoat?

What happens, for example, when the organization's store of documentary material becomes electronic? At the highest level of abstraction, one could say that the normal rules of time and space—the rules on which the Weberian bureaucracy is founded—cease to apply. Bureaucracies evolved as responses to a particular set of problems in the coordination of both space and time: They served to manage a flow of knowledge and information at a time when such things were constrained both temporally and spatially. Until the advent of IT, information was tedious to manage, reproduce, and disseminate; as a unique and scarce good, an elaborate spatially extended system needed to exist to control the flow of information from one place to the next. In a sense, the "objective" structure of the bureaucracy, as represented by the organization chart, was simply a reification of the informational infrastructure that by necessity existed within the firm. Different departments held responsibility for the processing and maintenance of different types of knowledge; each maintained different sets of files and lived by complex sets of rules to determine how and when information could flow between other areas. Upper level executives, depending on the upward flow of data from the departments below them, had access to more condensed forms of information that could be used in strategic decision making or in planning. Because information could not be easily organized or transmitted, getting information and communication from one place to another was a prime form of labor in and of itself.

In the virtual organization, however, the file cabinets of bureaucratic ritual disappear, replaced by devices that shatter the traditional physical instantiations of information and knowledge. To an extent, this transition is certainly observable today. When employees in contemporary organizations use electronic mail or build reports from network databases, there is no original, physical reality to which this information refers, unless such reference be to a tangle of code and wiring that, to most workers, remains opaque or even mystical. To adapt the words of Gertrude Stein, there's no longer any there there. Mark Poster has explained the transition thus:

> [When language is made electronic] words cannot any longer be located in space and time, whether it be the "real time" of spoken utterance in a spatial context of presence or the abstract time of documents in a bureaucrat's file cabinet. . . . Speech is framed by space/time coordinates of dramatic action. Writing is framed by space/time coordinates of books and sheets of paper. . . . Electronic language, on the contrary, does not lend itself to being so framed. It is everywhere and nowhere, always and never. It is truly material/immaterial. (1986, p. 85)

These strange properties of electronic information are the foundation of the virtual organization, with effects that multiply in unexpected ways. The consequences are radical and far-ranging: If the formal structure of bureaucratic design hinges on the coordination of time and space, the elimination of time and space as categories is at one and the same time an announcement of the end of the structured organization.

The Disappearance of Structure?

The idea of organizational *structure* is in many ways a legacy of the bureaucratic era, one that has decreased relevance in the "immaterial" world of the virtual organization. Since electronic information appears to evade the laws of what might be called Weber's Newtonian universe—it can be everywhere at once, manipulated instantly and effortlessly—it can be said to be fundamentally opposed to any outward manifestations of structure, whether this structure be conceived of in technological or organizational terms. This is not to say that structure disappears altogether in conceptions of the virtual organization; rather, in the implosive manner already described, it simply withdraws from the realm of everyday experience. Although structure does not necessarily disappear per se, this disappearance at the level of ordinary perception is becoming a part of the dominant discourse of organizations. Even in cases where a firm's own technological infrastructure is not very highly developed, it is enough that this antistructural rhetoric exist in the world at large for it to be replicated within the firm.

For many years, the computer systems used in large organizations tended to replicate the formal structures that already existed in these firms, and lent to bureaucracy a technological infrastructure that figured prominently in many dystopian predictions concerning the impact of technology in the work-place. In a redundant yet probably unavoidable fashion, information systems reinforced the bureaucratic structures that had been earlier introduced to serve the firm's information-processing needs. Computer systems and software adopted the "architecture" of bureaucracy, even though it was precisely this architecture that new technologies would later begin to be able to eliminate. Not surprisingly, the language of information systems became the language of bureaucracy: centralization, hierarchy, command, control.

In truth, early forms of information technology were not powerful enough to do anything other than replicate bureaucratic architectures. Over the last decade, however, the new technologies have lived up to electronic information's inherent ability to overcome the limitations of time and space that made bureaucratic organizations necessary. In computers, relational data-bases and open architectures have allowed organizations to maintain data-bases that, at the user level, appear to have no "real" structure at all: Data is assembled and disassembled on a contingent basis and according to the personal needs of users. Object-oriented programming now promises to allow software code to become modular and reusable. Huge centralized main-frames have given way to so-called "client-server" architectures in which data can be maintained in decentralized networks to be combined and manipulated at the front end. Factory automation systems rely on "distributed" as opposed to hierarchical control. Likewise, electronic mail and electronic conferencing permit employees to develop ever-shifting organizational "structures" that decrease the importance of formal hierarchies and organizational boundaries.

With such changes, organizations have shifted to become more holistic and less highly differentiated. One manifestation of this is the oft-discussed "flattening of the organization," the elimination of the layers of middle management that had existed to coordinate organizational knowledge. At the same time, new kinds of electronic connectivity are encouraging the emergence of more complex and contingent structures, not organizational designs per se, but rather shifting emergent structures that form and dissolve according to the actions of organization members and may even involve members of different organizations. Organizational structure thus becomes a transient by-product of employee action, as opposed to a normative model *for* this action.[11]

As technology withdraws the structures of coordination and control from the plane of everyday life, organizational discourse is coming to extol the absence of structure over its presence. Aspects of this rhetorical shift are already quite evident in the workplace at large, where managers and executives brag about the elimination of hierarchy and the turn to *nonstructured* arrangements of people and information. Leading-edge organizations, even some very large ones, may even willfully give the impression of chaos to the first-time visitor. For example, at one large telecommunications company, employees were proudly self-conscious about the ad hoc style in which work was accomplished and elevated the trait practically to the level of obsession. The introduction of electronic mail had allowed a company whose management style was ad hoc from the first to "formalize" its ad-hocness, with the result that it was almost impossible to make sense of how the company worked. (One director in the MIS function confided that e-mail had become "the driver of the entire company" and noted that she received upwards of 200 messages a day. It was largely through e-mail that this woman was able to launch a major systems change from a relatively low position in the official MIS hierarchy.)

Although some employees bemoaned the lack of procedures and the lack of respect for the discrete responsibilities guaranteed by their job titles and reporting relationships, the de facto disorganization of the company was for most a source of pride, a sort of corporate identity. Another employee, again a director, giddily proclaimed:

> Where we are, its a free-for-all. There's no structure and lots of organizational ambiguity. But the good thing about it is not being limited by organizational structure, and not being constrained by having particular people in particular functions.

This was not hyperbole. Employees *preferred* to send e-mail to one another rather than meeting face to face; because e-mail permitted one to buck the limitations of status and function, not to mention the limitations of having a potentially dissenting face-to-face conversant, anything that could be handled electronically *was* handled electronically, even if people were only yards away. Information flowed so quickly and so densely that each employee often had a totally different picture of the prevailing organizational reality, of what projects were at what stages or even what projects had been formally initiated at all.

While electronic communication is a powerful new form of coordinating people across time and space, it thus also introduces a new kind of static into organizations. Electronic communication disrupts existing hierarchies by making communication less dependent on cues of status, power, and gender (Poster, 1990, p. 117). In addition, electronic communication abhors consensus. Whereas face-to-face groups generally strive toward common agreement, electronic groups may take several times longer to reach decisions (Sproull & Kiesler, 1991), and in some situations may resist forming consensus altogether.[12] Whereas contemporary organizational rhetoric stresses the coordinating potential of the new technology, computer-mediated work can often have something of a reverse effect: Decoupled from the traditional social bonds of the organization, individuals can become lone beacons whose affiliation with the larger picture is more problematic than during the heyday of bureaucracy. It is for such reasons that face-to-face interaction may take on an important and not altogether expected role in guaranteeing consensus and coherence in electronically-mediated organizations (Nohria & Eccles, 1992).

The Apotheosis of the Individual

If the bureaucratic ideal type extolled the logic of differentiation, the ideal type of the virtual organization extols a new kind of holism, a utopian ideal of total connectivity. This holism is, however, ambiguous and paradoxical, since the individual employee actually becomes more important, and in a sense more isolated, than ever before. Whereas bureaucracy sees employees only as instances of an abstract "universal subject," the virtual organization extols the powers of the unique individual, often ascribing idealized or superhuman capabilities to him or her. In a world where reporting relationships and organizational boundaries have lost their former role, every knowledge worker is god.

Of course, the trend to isolate workers from their social surroundings is a long-standing one, with a past that extends back to scientific management and to the basic form of bureaucracy itself. What has changed recently is that the individual worker is no longer bound by a strong sense of *dependency* on other aspects of the organization, and that this new independence is coming to be valued in its own right. New cross-functional jobs, whether or not directly enabled by IT, allow the implosion of different functions into a single employee and permit employees to get an increasingly wide-angled view of the organization. As in the Mutual Benefit Life example recounted at the outset of this chapter, many companies have gutted their bureaucracies and have begun replacing the legions of clerks with "case managers," employees who can use PC networks to carry out a whole range of functions that had typically been separated into distinct jobs.

At its extremes, this cross-functionality becomes something of a fetish, valued not so much for its organizational worth but almost as an end in itself. The very word *cross-functional* can be spoken like a mantra, along with related terms such as *teaming* and *empowerment.* Even when this fetish character is refreshingly absent, the compulsion to push an organization to cross-functional extremes has become extremely powerful. At Mutual Benefit Life, for instance, senior executives spoke of their secret dream of collapsing the entire insurance administration function into a single job, a case manager who could handle the full range of the company's business. Even the name they had chosen for this fantasy project—"the one-person insurance company"—was revealing: In a very overt sense, the rhetoric was of a return to earlier, pre-bureaucratic forms of organization in a thoroughly technological and complex organizational environment. Although case managers did not at the time have the training or the resources to handle *all* the various aspects of the company's business, it is not unreasonable to assume that with more powerful systems and more training such a further collapse of function and hierarchy could be feasible in organizations (Davenport & Nohria, 1994). Insofar as it leads to increases in job-interest and productivity, the goal may certainly be a worthy one.

But in the end, the most interesting thing about the idea of the "one-person company" is not its viability but, rather, the rhetorical form in which the idea is advanced in the first place. After all, the idea of a "one-person company" makes little objective sense. It is hard to imagine a large corporation staging a "withering away of the state" until the entire company consists of a solitary college-educated woman or man at the keyboard of a PC. Rather, we feel the idea is best grasped as an expression of the rhetorical shift away from organizations and toward individuals as the locus of value in the workplace. Introducing the idea of a "one-person company" effects a brilliant collapse of the categories of organization and worker, turning the employee into a kind of holographic model of the organization at large. The case manager, in rhetoric at least, thus *becomes* the company.

Conclusion: Power and Authority in the Virtual Organization

Of course, to speak of a "one-person insurance company" is to occlude the fact that even virtual organizations continue to be *organizations,* that is, complex systems of mutually dependent individuals. The new rhetoric, however, often tends to avoid this basic fact, perhaps out of a belief that such systems are, in Nietzsche's apt phrase, "all too human." In the rhetoric of the virtual organization is envisioned a system that can somehow overcome the complex heterogeneity of the standard organization, either through a mystical integration of discrete individuals (as in the boundaryless and one-person companies) or through the reduction of all interaction to virtual interaction (as in common fantasies of the network organization).

Again, in many contexts, such goals may be worthy ones. There are, however, a number of potential avenues of critique worth exploring. A foremost task is to inquire whether the rhetoric of the virtual organization might possess an ideological subtext that has gone unnoticed. This is a particularly delicate endeavor, since the high priests of the new organization are generally understood as progressives who seek to liberate humanity from the chains of bureaucracy. For a large number of people, however, the new organizational rhetoric increasingly represents nothing more than an attempt to buy out the last bastions of opposition by cleverly declaring that the grounds for resistance no longer exist. The objections from the socialist camp, for example, are trenchant. From Kevin Robins and Frank Webster—two authors who have proclaimed themselves to offer a "Luddite analysis" of the new information technology—we hear the following:

> The very prevalence of these futurist images that now rain upon us from television, bookstalls, and the press induces us to take them seriously. They represent capital's utopia, its promised post-industrial land. . . . One can readily see the ideological role of this planned, post-industrial society, in so far as it represents a dangerous disguise which permits a spurious escape from the anxieties surrounding the decisions and happenings of the present. By offering a potential exit from the ills of the present, electronic futurism floods in to fill an ideological vacuum. (Frankel, 1987, p. 1)

The question of whether the new organization is essentially an ideological disguise runs through a great number of such critiques, critiques that deserve not to be dismissed out of hand. A likeminded complaint could even be levied against Shoshana Zuboff's (1988) widely acclaimed work on the transformative impact of information technology in clerical and industrial settings. On the one hand, Zuboff's *In the Age of the Smart Machine* traces both utopian and dystopian versions of where the "dephysicalization" of work might ultimately lead, and contains meditations on the phenomenology of holistic organizations and computer-mediated work that are undoubtedly important contributions to the literature. On the other hand, Zuboff in the final analysis comes down clearly on the side of the computer and its power to restructure the way we think about space and power in organizations.[13] Of course, to levy the charge that *Smart Machine* thus carries an ideological undertone seems not entirely fair since Zuboff casts herself from the start as a liberal humanist out to catalog the world at a unique historical juncture (Zuboff, 1988, p. xiv). At the same time, however, Zuboff's warnings of certain dark possibilities—of, for example, panoptic power and a new managerial tyranny— should not preclude us from asking what purpose her celebration of the upside of informated labor might ultimately serve. Is it possible, we ask, that holism-celebrating accounts such as hers may ultimately serve as a smoke screen that just makes the survival of certain traditional power relations in organizations harder to see?

If such an idea sounds initially outlandish, it is because most of us find it hard to muster such suspicion toward technological change in the face of its integrative and utopian possibilities. Even those most sensitive to the possible negative effects of technology in the workplace thus often end up arguing that we simply need to reach a certain critical point, a point beyond which technology will be so properly integrated into our daily lives that it will finally have its intended utopian effect. Witness this excerpt from a *Scientific American* article by Mark Weiser of Xerox Parc, an R&D site for the workplace of the future:

> By pushing computers into the background, [new technologies] will make individuals more aware of the people on the other ends of their computer links. This development may reverse the unhealthy centripetal forces that conventional personal computers have introduced into life and the workplace. . . . Even today, people holed up in windowless offices before glowing computers may not see their fellows for the better part of each day. And in virtual reality, the outside world and all its inhabitants effectively cease to exist. Ubiquitous computers, in contrast, [will] reside in the human world and pose no barrier to personal interactions. If anything, the transparent connections that they offer between different locations and times may tend to bring communities closer together. (1991, p. 104)

Here we have the ultimate technological fix: the "computer problem" neatly solved by the development of more, better, smaller computers. On the one hand, there is no doubt that in the coming years, we will begin to see some of the changes of which Weiser (1991) speaks. As technology and control systems continue to develop—and continue to withdraw still further into the background—it is possible that organizational practice may begin to live up more to the utopian visions with which it is increasingly charged. On the other hand, it is possible that we will always require eloquent promises such as Weiser's, much as the donkey requires the carrot dangled just out of reach for it to be led forward.

A final word about this carrot that leads us forward. Our analysis here has stressed that the virtual organization is to be understood primarily as a form of rhetoric, that is, as a *discourse* spoken by managerial professionals—not to mention professors of management—in ways that are not necessarily coterminous with organizational practice itself. Although many of the dynamics attributed to the virtual organization are indeed to be found in actually existing organizations, some might contest that the vision of the virtual organization we have laid out here remains nevertheless a kind of projection, a rhetorical mirage removed from the actual daily activities of organizational life. Yet we wish to reiterate that this last distinction—between organizational rhetoric and reality—strikes us as a misleading one, and our argument has been as much a defense of taking rhetoric seriously as it has been a description of the rhetoric itself. To draw a dividing line between discourse and actuality—labeling one fake and the other worthy of study—is a mistake that has long plagued the social sciences, and organizational science in particular. Against that tradition, it is time to take "mere rhetoric" seriously, as only such an inquiry will grant us true insight into the forces that are already shaping the organizational—or perhaps post-organizational—environment of the next century. Our analysis here has been, we hope, a step in that direction.

Notes

1. In *The Coming of Post-Industrial Society*, Bell writes "The rhythms of mechanization are still pervasive in the United States. . . . And yet, the distinctive archetype has gone. Charlie Chaplin's *Modern Times* at one time symbolized industrial civilization, but today it is a period piece. The rhythms are no longer that pervasive. The beat has been broken" (1973a, pp. 162-163).

2. As we note, recent years have seen a rush to find novel uses of the word *virtual* as a descriptive term. When we began to formulate the virtual "ideal type" in 1991, we suspected that others were likely beginning to use the term for organizational contexts as well. In particular, we are compelled to cite the recent management book *The Virtual Organization* (Davidow & Malone, 1992), discussed below.

3. Adapted from Weber (1978), pp. 956-958. See also Weber (1947), pp. 329-337.

4. This definition of virtual image is taken from *Webster's* dictionary.

5. For an account of how information systems are enabling a reversal in the traditional functional division of labor see Davenport and Nohria (1994).

6. Much of the discussion in *The Virtual Corporation* pertains to the impact of information technology on the production process, a topic not under discussion here. But the authors' discussion of changes in management and corporate structure parallels certain aspects of our formulation of the virtual ideal type, especially with regard to the blurring of boundaries inside and outside the firm. See Davidow and Malone (1992).

7. This term is taken from Mark Poster (1990).

8. For an account of this transition of the American value structure from authority to personal gratification, see Bell's *The Cultural Contradictions of Capitalism* (Bell, 1973b).

9. Although formulated independently, this is the essential idea in James Beniger's historical study, *The Control Revolution* (Beniger, 1986). Beniger sees recent developments in information technology as being the latest stage in a process that began with the control crisis touched

off by the Industrial Revolution. See pp. 426-436. Manuel Castells (1989) has also written on the interrelation of information technology, industrial organization, and social space.

10. Kling and Iacono (1990) offer an interesting analysis of how accounts of a computer "revolution" find ways to gloss over what is problematic in positing such a historical rupture.

11. The turn away from the privileging of structure is now a dominant motif in the contemporary humanities and human sciences, announced initially in Jacques Derrida's "Structure, Sign, and Play in the Discourse of the Human Sciences" (Derrida, 1978). The dissemination of this new post-structuralism—inspired by Derrida and numerous others—has, however, brought it to different disciplines at different times. In particular, the "post-structuralist urge" seems to have reached organizational studies relatively late. See Eccles and Nohria (1990), "The Post-Structuralist Organization" for an argument about the need to privilege action over structure in management.

12. In several experiments, Sproull and Kiesler (1991) found that electronic groups took on average 2 to 6 times longer to reach decisions than analogous face-to-face groups.

13. See in particular the concluding chapter of *In the Age of the Smart Machine*, "Managing the Informated Organization," especially the subchapter titled "Dissent from Wholeness" (Zuboff, 1988, pp. 402-412).

References

Baudrillard, J. (1988). *Selected writings.* Edited by M. Poster. Stanford, CA: Stanford University Press.

Bell, D. (1973a). *The coming of post-industrial society.* New York: Basic Books.

Bell, D. (1973b). *The cultural contradictions of capitalism.* New York: Harper & Row.

Beniger, J. (1986). *The control revolution: Technological and economic origins of the information society.* Cambridge, MA: Harvard University Press.

Berkley, J., & Eccles, R. (1991). Rethinking the corporate workplace: Case managers at Mutual Benefit Life. Case Study N9-492-015. Boston, MA: Harvard Business School Publishing Division.

Berkley, J., & Nohria, N. (1991). *Lithonia Lighting (A).* Case Study N9-492-003. Boston, MA: Harvard Business School Publishing Division.

Castells, M. (1989). *The informational city: Information technology, economic restructuring, and the urban-regional process.* Cambridge, MA: Basil Blackwell.

Davenport, T., & Nohria, N. (1994, Winter). Case managers and the combination of labor. *Sloan Management Review, 35,* 11-23.

Davidow, W., & Malone, M. (1992). *The virtual corporation.* New York: Harper Collins.

Derrida, J. (1978). *Writing and difference.* Chicago, IL: University of Chicago Press.

Drucker, P. (1959). *Landmarks of tomorrow.* New York: Harper.

Drucker, P. (1968). *The age of discontinuity: Guidelines to our changing society.* New York: Harper & Row.

Dumaine, B. (1991, June 17). The bureaucracy busters. *Fortune,* pp. 36-50.

Eccles, R., & Nohria, N. (1990). *The post-structuralist organization.* Harvard Business School Working Paper #92-003.

Frankel, B. (1987). *The post-industrial utopians.* Milwaukee, WI: University of Wisconsin Press.

General Electric. (1989). *Annual Report.*

Gladstone, J., & Eccles, R. (1991). *KPMG Peat Marwick: The shadow partner.* Case Study N9-492-002. Boston, MA: Harvard Business School Publishing Division.

Gladstone, J., & Nohria, N. (1990). *Colliers international property consultants.* Case Study 9-490-049. Boston, MA: Harvard Business School Publishing Division.

Heckscher, C. (1991, Spring). Can business beat bureaucracy? *The American Prospect,* pp. 115-130.

Kling, R., & Iacono, S. (1990). Making a "computer revolution." *Journal of Computing and Society, 1,* 43-58.

Nohria, N., & Eccles, R. (1992). Face to face: Making network organizations work. In N. Nohria & R. Eccles (Eds.), *Networks and organizations: Structure, form, and action.* Boston, MA: Harvard Business School Press.

Poster, M. (1990). *The mode of information: Post-structuralism and social context.* Chicago, IL: University of Chicago Press.

Sproull L., & Kiesler S. (1991, September). Computers, networks, and work. *Scientific American,* p. 119.

Stone, A. S. (1992). Will the real body please stand up? Boundary stories about virtual cultures. In M. Benedikt (Ed.), *Cyberspace: First steps* (pp. 81-118). Cambridge, MA: MIT Press.

Toffler, A. (1970). *Future shock.* New York: Random House.

Weber, M. (1947). *The theory of social and economic organization.* New York: The Free Press.

Weber, M. (1978). *Economy and society.* Berkeley, CA: University of California Press.

Webster, F. & Robins, K. (1986). *Information technology: A Luddite analysis.* Norwood, NJ: Ablex.

Weiser, M. (1991, September). The computer for the 21st century. *Scientific American,* p. 104.

Zuboff, S. (1988). *In the age of the smart machine: The future of work and power.* New York: Basic Books.

6   TRANSFORMATIONAL PROCESSES

Charles Heckscher
Russell A. Eisenstat
Thomas J. Rice

Other chapters in this collection have explored the characteristics, strengths and weaknesses of a possible emergent type of organization. Now the question is: "Can you get there from here?"

Many companies are clearly *trying* to get there—or, at least, to move away from existing patterns, to "de-bureaucratize." It should not be a surprise to say that in our experience this shift is extremely difficult, halting, and subject to many diversions. The central problem is immediately apparent in practice as well as in concept. The starting point for change is a system stressing hierarchy and control; the goal is one stressing participation and involvement. The difficulty lies in jumping the gap: Can one use power to require participation? Or can one use participation to overcome structures of power?

This question is about *transformational processes* rather than decision-making ones—about the creation of a new system rather than patterns of action within a system. The transformation we are talking about challenges the core of the bureaucratic structure: It consists in an alteration in the use of power throughout the organization, moving toward a system coordinated by influence and dialogue.

The closest historical analogy, which may help outline the problem, can be found in the transformation of markets into bureaucracies through the creation of large firms after about 1850. In retrospect, one can see this as a

AUTHORS' NOTE: This essay benefited from discussions with the other authors of this collection and from valuable prodding by Mike Beer.

"bootstrapping" operation in which much movement occurred before it was very clear what it was being moved to. There was no stable or detailed structure for corporations that could have been described in a book such as this one before the 1920s; yet by that time many domains formerly governed by small production units had made the transition to some sort of command organization. Today we are faced with the same issue: Without anything like a complete description of a post-bureaucratic form, many firms are committed to remaking themselves in its image.

This struggle has spawned the recent expansion of process consultation. Bureaucracies have not felt the need for help in the past when they have tinkered with their structure, centralizing and decentralizing authority in an almost predictable cyclical pattern; but something about recent developments has thrown them for a more serious loss. Consider GE, which has been a structural innovator throughout its history: As early as the 1950s its CEO instituted a radical program of decentralization. But even in its most innovative moments in the past it never approached what the current CEO, Jack Welch, is doing: bringing in a large team of outside consultants to guide a process of self-examination throughout the organization in order to build a shared sense of direction.

Such consultants would have been essentially unavailable before the 1960s, and no corporate leader would have put his fate in their hands if they had been around.[1] In the last decade in particular their use has grown very rapidly. But the general significance of these developments remains almost totally unexamined: The literature is primarily by and for practitioners. There is virtually no clear *definition* of process consultation, nor is there systematic and persuasive evidence of its effectiveness in different situations.

The conscious management of process is clearly linked, as an empirical matter, to the generalized attack on bureaucracy that is the subject of this book. It constitutes an alternative to the bureaucratic concept of change, which concentrates on reorganizing and restructuring. Process management (in the sense we will use) is the means of movement from a bureaucratic to a post-bureaucratic world.

A Note on Evidence

Systematic evidence on organization change is *in principle* difficult to collect. "Pure" scientific method requires varying a few factors and observing the results; but in a lengthy change process one can never limit the variation, and one can never be sure what are "results."

First, there are very few good cases to observe. The transformation we are seeking to describe is so far rare, never perfect, and always incomplete—the time frame is too long for the usual span of research. Second, the cases that do exist do not fall into a narrow band; they vary not on a few but on many factors. Given the lack of accepted theory, everyone tries it differently, everyone starts from scratch. The combination of much variation and few cases makes it impossible to trace out cause and effect.

Furthermore, the conceptual problem of change presents the fundamental methodological problem of knowing when to "stop" the chain of cause and effect. One frequently finds that the judgment of the success or failure of some intervention depends entirely on when you ask the question. One year after a new leader comes in, she may be a hero; two years later, a goat.[2] During the current period of rapid economic change it has been particularly evident that an organization that is viewed as effective one year may take a plunge the next; writers who make claims for one or another solution are often embarrassed to read their pronouncements a few years later.

The task now is therefore primarily one of theory. An inductive attempt to gather lots of data and run regressions in the hopes of discovering significant relations is doomed to fail from the simple imbalance of independent and dependent variables. The field cannot be effectively researched until it has been mapped—until good reasons are developed for focusing on particular relations, in order to leverage what little evidence is available into some coherence.

In this context, therefore, our goals are limited: to develop a typology of processes; to sketch the logic for the superiority of the collaborative form; and to describe, in a systematic way, some critical elements.

The concepts are based primarily on the direct experiences of the three contributors to this essay. It has become apparent that secondhand reports are highly unreliable: Because the field is so unorganized, people report with unexamined and unexpressed biases. We use them only with much skepticism. Our base of experience is represented by the cases that follow the body of the essay—long-run change efforts at AT&T, Becton-Dickinson, and the Pine Street Inn; these we present as typical of others that we have been closely involved with, including ones at Dupont, Ford, and Honeywell. We have also conducted research in a number of innovating companies, including Shell-Sarnia (described under an assumed name in the "Lakeville Chemical Company" at the end of this volume) and the Saturn Corporation.[3]

Defining the Problem

Chapter 1 in this book describes the characteristics of post-bureaucratic *structure* in contrast to bureaucracy; we will be using these characteristics as reference points throughout this discussion. Our attention now, however, is on the alchemical process of transformation—of change of state, of *movement*—between the two.

This is one of the most difficult problems in the study of organizations. We are familiar with structural analysis, but there are few tools useful for describing a *pattern of change*. Intervention strategies are a matter of "art": When we try to conceptualize them, it is usually in terms of trying to envisage the future and then create it in the present, only a piece at a time and not too fast.

In the large-scale shift under consideration, the record is not terribly encouraging: By far the largest number of efforts fail. Of thousands of attempts to break the bounds of bureaucracy—from worker participation efforts to cross-functional task forces—only a small percentage can claim more than the most modest success. And even these have generally worked by splitting off into a new "greenfield" organization rather than by transforming from within.

The Practical Paradox of Successful Failures

Most efforts to de-bureaucratize, no matter what the details, run into a wall after a year or so. This phenomenon is so common that it has generated a term among consultants: the *successful failure*. This refers to the pattern in which a dialogue is established, all those directly involved are delighted, both productivity and satisfaction increase—and yet *somehow*, if you come back in a while, the innovation has stalled or disappeared.

This pattern was noted early on in "Quality of Work Life" and "Quality Circle" efforts, early attempts to move toward more team-based systems: Researchers noted that despite the fact that the vast majority of those involved expressed satisfaction, upwards of 75% of the innovations disappeared within 3 years. Even in the most successful cases there was little spread through the rest of the organization. Recently the pattern has repeated in the use of "mutual-gains" or "win-win" bargaining in the union-management arena.[4]

There are two major problems at the root of these failures. The first is the difficulty of creating new levels of trust, especially on a large scale. The legacy of distortions caused by hierarchy almost always interferes with the dialogue that defines a post-bureaucratic order. Anyone who has seen "open door" discussions in traditional companies will recognize the issue: Though the higher-level managers may believe that they are honestly and freely conversing, the lower-level people will soften, shade, distort, or hide their real views. They do not believe they have the capacity to engage their superiors, and they generally also fear retribution for disagreeing. Thus, there may for a time be the *appearance* of new relations, while the old bureaucratic reality simply goes "underground."

Even if such trust does develop within a particular organizational unit—a work group, a task force, a plant—it often proves difficult to translate it into decision-making structures that are widely accepted. Other parts of the organization are apt to view the innovation as irrelevant or threatening. Corporate executives may also stifle innovation (wittingly or unwittingly) through inappropriate management succession decisions or corporate policies.

This form of resistance is also traceable to the persistence of bureaucratic patterns. Peers in different units are not formally responsible for working together; rather they owe their primary allegiance to their functional superiors. Therefore each unit has a basic interest in proving to the superior that it is better than the others. Changes originating anywhere else arouse unease and jealousy—the "not invented here" reaction that is a nearly universal form of resistance.[5]

A second fundamental problem of transition is how to keep the organization functioning during a change process—replacing the control systems of bureaucracy without losing control. The driving impulse in most transformation efforts is the desire to get away from the burden of bureaucratic rules and restrictions; but unless these are replaced with effective alternatives, the system can simply dissolve into inefficiency. The inability to find such alternatives is a prime reason for the tendency to fall back into familiar patterns. To hang onto old controls as long as necessary without blocking the emergence of the new is a very difficult task. Effective dialogue is *necessary* to post-bureaucratic control, but it is not sufficient; processes of organized decision making and follow-up are also needed.

Both of these problems can be seen as matters of *pacing* of change over time. Because an organization cannot transform itself all at once, it needs to find a path that brings in different parts in the right order.

The Theoretical Puzzle of Developmental Change

Underlying these particular and repeated problems is a basic difficulty in this kind of change process: No one really understands what they are moving toward when they start the process. It is a matter of learning something new through practice, of *increasing* the capacity of the system in ways that were incomprehensible within the old order.

This uncertainty is characteristic of all developmental change, but it has never been well explained. Heckscher argued in Chapter 1 that a post-bureaucratic system is a *developmental* leap from bureaucracy, in the sense of having a wider capacity for consistent control. The generation of higher-order systems is one of the most difficult puzzles in all of the sciences, appearing in roughly the same form and essentially unsolved in theories of biological evolution, cognition, and cosmology. The only answer these sciences have been able to find has been *luck*: That is, by pure chance (mutation in biology, a highly improbable confluence of events in cosmology, and so on) something "better" appears and gets a chance to prove its superiority. That is not much of a model for organization change: If we could do no better than random mutation we would have an intolerable level of waste. Biological evolution is measured in millions of years, cosmological in billions: We don't have that much time.

In human learning theory the problem is that the higher-order structure cannot prove its superiority to the satisfaction of the lower until it already exists and has had a chance to exercise its identity for a period of time: The lower cannot "understand" why the higher should be better. Research on cognitive development has demonstrated the way in which less complex systems (for example, the "concrete operations" used by young children) not only fail to grasp more complex solutions, but reinterpret them in terms of what they *can* grasp—and therefore fail even to understand that they don't understand![6]

This "bootstrapping problem," as it might be called, is the core difficulty of the kind of change we are examining. It is constantly visible in the process of organization consulting: People used to bureaucratic systems don't "get" the nature of team-based interactions, and they constantly reinterpret proposed changes in terms with which they are familiar. It is common, for example, for temporary task forces ("skunk works" and other forms), established to cut through bureaucratic red tape, to assimilate to the old order and to become merely another layer in the decision process. It is quite rare for them successfully to establish a new set of norms.[7]

This is the obscure zone in which process consultants operate—cajoling, persuading, training, and steadily pushing toward a vision that (at best) only they can clearly see. They act, in effect, as organization *educators*, with the art and mystery of the educational process. We can't provide a complete theory of how this mystery works in the context of organization change; our goal here is to outline some of its main dynamics.

Linear and Nonlinear Change

One key thing has become clear in all the efforts to effect this transformation: It does not and cannot proceed in a straight line. The classic model of change, which has been explicit or implicit in almost every published writing on the topic, has been that of engineering: Decide what you want to do, then figure out the path to do it. But a *developmental* change of the type we are describing is defined and constrained precisely by the fact that one *cannot* envision it before experiencing it. It is a matter not of clarifying and then implementing a vision but rather of structuring a series of experiences that move toward a vague "sense" of the future.

This understanding has emerged only gradually. Fifteen years ago the key debate among those who sought to promote participation, teamwork, and collaboration was whether to pursue a "bottom-up" or a "top-down" strategy: The former began with pilot efforts at the shop-floor level, which (it was hoped) would spread by imitation and osmosis; the latter relied on the power of the top managers to enforce participation. Both of these are essentially linear conceptions. After a time it became apparent that neither worked: Both led to a kind of encapsulation and isolation of the innovative effort.[8]

The next step seemed logical: to try to bring along the entire organization at once. One of the emblematic stories of the late 1970s, General Motors' Tarrytown plant, actually sent every worker to a week's worth of training in team skills over the course of 2 years—an extraordinary effort involving thousands of workers. Also around that time consultants such as Charles Krone adopted a kind of "blanketing" strategy, covering the organization with facilitators who strictly enforced the new norms at every meeting. Though such approaches produced many converts, they again failed almost completely in generating new patterns of organization.

As this, too, became evident, writers began to explore nonlinear forms of change—ones in which the endpoint was *not* defined clearly in advance. Their prescriptions shared a basic pattern of cyclical spiraling, which can be summarized in three steps:

1. *Fuzzy visioning:* developing a consensus on a deliberately imprecise image of the future—one that sets a general direction of inquiry but that leaves open a large scope of exploration. This phase must penetrate to some degree to all parts of the organization to create a shared anticipation of change.
2. *Experimentation:* trying out various approaches toward the broad vision.
3. *Reflection:* systematic review of the experience and preparation to enter on the next cycle.[9]

Such an approach in a sense compromises between "pure" evolution, in which anything is possible and most things therefore are immediate failures, and the closely managed approach of the engineering model. Biological evolution may occasionally produce two-headed flies, but businesses generally want to avoid that; however, they want to open the possibility of successful changes that they cannot clearly predefine.[10]

The lack of a simple and identifiable outcome makes most managers very nervous. It forces one to put faith *in the process itself*—to adopt a belief that by pursuing the cycle of inquiry and reflection a good solution will emerge. This faith is not widespread—there is far more confidence in the engineering model—and the evolutionary process necessarily tests it severely. The strength of the belief in the process itself therefore becomes a key ingredient in the success of evolutionary change efforts.

The Merits of Collaborative Change

Let us consider top managers of a large corporation facing a challenge that, they believe, will require significant and widespread changes in attitude and structure. What are their choices about how to act?

1. They could restructure by command: move managers around, reduce layers, promote those with skills and values that are seen by the top as needed, push authority down for operational decisions in the organization, change job descriptions and rewards—in general, clean up and reconfigure the organization to meet what the top sees as the new problem.
2. They could focus on an attempt to create a shared commitment to the change through forceful communication from the top, explaining the rationale and strategy—using anything from videotapes to extensive workshops at all levels.
3. They could try to develop the change in a more opportunistic way, without making grand statements to the organization about what is going on. The leaders could seek to build a coalition for change through their individual interactions with organizational "champions," hoping that a gradual accumulation of new approaches would add up to a transformation.
4. They could initiate an open and public process of self-examination without closely predefining the solution, aimed at developing a deeper understanding of the organization's capabilities and the challenges it faces—with the hope that a shared strategy would emerge from the process.

The first of these choices is an example of the use of traditional bureaucratic command. The other three, however, are variants of more open processes, ranging from strongly hierarchical (top-down communications) to strongly collaborative.

Our first thesis is that *only the fourth type—collaborative change—establishes the conditions for a successful transition to a post-bureaucratic model*: It is, in effect, the change process that "matches" the new form of organization. The others may create enthusiasm and a sense of change for a time, but they fail to break through the boundaries that define the essentially bureaucratic paradigm—thereby ending up at best as types of "successful failures."

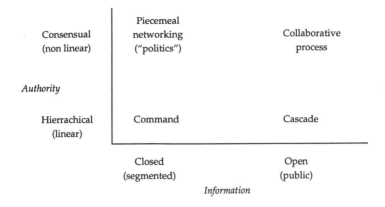

Figure 6.1. Dimensions of Change Processes

Four Types of Process

The four choices sketched above all are defined by two dimensions. The first concerns the sharing of *information*: the degree to which the basic vision of change and its rationale are communicated openly among all members of the organization. The second concerns the sharing of *power*: the degree to which the hierarchical definition of authority is replaced by processes that require consensus across levels.

The classic "command" process is defined by the retention of both dimensions in the hands of formal leaders: That is, they issue commands without seeking agreement, and they do not communicate to the organization the full reasons for their actions. This approach to change can be summarized by the bureaucratic axiom, "Do your job": The change leader communicates only as much as is needed for the job to be done.

The collaborative process goes to the other extreme by opening both dimensions: There is an effort to build change through full, informed consensus among all stakeholders.

But the two dimensions need not go together—in fact, most often they do not. Two major types of change process maximize one dimension at the expense of the other (see Figure 6.1):

1. Shuffling the Structure

Possibly the most common change process is to restructure. This is the familiar way of changing a bureaucracy and so is easily adopted even by those who seek to move away from bureaucracy. It reflects the basic engineering model—define your ends, then seeks the means to them; it is fundamentally linear and nonreflective.

The usual form of this move is "empowerment": you cut a layer of supervision and push their responsibilities down in the organization. The most common move within this type (and most within our experience) is the establishment of autonomous teams. Whether this occurs on the shop floor or within management, this essentially involves transferring to a team responsibilities that were formerly parceled out among individuals who form a natural group within the hierarchy—usually eliminating their supervisor in the process.

Heckscher argued in Chapter 1, in discussing the *structure* of post-bureaucratic organization, that although such a shift feels radical *within* the team, it is easily encapsulated within existing bureaucratic control structures. In this context we can add that as a *process* this approach is limited: It produces change that does not spread easily beyond its initial domain. These efforts tend to be encapsulated and to diffuse very little, eventually withering and dying despite apparent success on their own terms.

The intervention issues in this sort of change are by now well-understood. The building of cooperation within a face-to-face group is not simple, but it can now be duplicated reasonably reliably.[11] The task of building interfaces between a team and the rest of the organization sometimes presents problems of accountability, but these can generally be managed by putting primary responsibility on the team leader, or by parceling out supervisory responsibilities to various team members.[12]

But the relative ease of this change is also an indicator of its lack of penetration of the bureaucratic paradigm. The newly "empowered" structures can easily be *fitted* within a hierarchy, with stable channels of accountability; they merely alter the size and shape of the boxes, as it were, rather than changing their logic. Once they are established, therefore, they tend to become as fixed and inflexible as any other piece of the hierarchy, held in place by the surrounding structure. There is little pressure—despite the early expectations of some—to extend the principle of teamwork beyond the face-to-face group; and restructuring the group for changing circumstances is if anything more difficult than when people are ungrouped.[13]

Something similar can be said of the apparently even more dramatic transfer of power involved in the European systems of codetermination and works councils. The idea of giving direct power for personnel decisions to a body of workers makes American managers shudder; yet the consensus in Europe is that the change has had far less impact than expected and has certainly not shaken the deeply bureaucratic nature of most of the firms involved. They have merely become another layer in the decision process.[14]

The point is that the simple transferal of power does not advance the shift from a bureaucratic order: As a process it remains within the old paradigm. It is easily encapsulated, without creating major waves for the rest of the organization. It is, paradoxically, *less* radical, and creates less tension for the larger organization, than "merely" advisory groups that bring together people from different sectors of the organization.

2. The Cascade

A second highly common change process is what we will call the *cascade,* which involves opening up information but *not* power. The following story could be closely duplicated in dozens of organizations in our experience.

> In one division top management met intensively with consultants and each other for over a year, ending by deciding on the need for a total quality effort focused on pleasing the consumer. They developed a new statement of vision and mission to this effect. Their process for transforming the organization then consisted in holding meetings at which each level explained in great detail what this vision meant and tried to instill the new spirit among their subordinates.
>
> Results: Middle managers a year or two later were extremely versed in the language of "satisfying the customer" and used it at every opportunity. But it had hardly made a difference in underlying attitudes or behavior: In most cases "customer" was merely a synonym for "boss." There was practically no understanding of the real needs of external customers or how middle levels could impact them. Thus they said things such as the following:
>
> "We are terrible in manufacturing. We've focused on meeting the customers' needs all right, but not on the bigger picture of the whole system and the market and the capacity and how we get things out to the market. Manufacturing is not motivated, the people don't care at all about yields."
>
> Or: "I haven't seen a customer yet but I do plan to do so."
>
> The "cascade" had been, as it were, severely watered down as it descended.

Bob Simons, of the Harvard Business School, has found that the large majority of managers who take over a troubled organization begin by developing their own "mission statement" in this way and then scheduling educational sessions down through the organizations.[15] Educators would recognize an old fallacy: the notion that one teaches by pouring a premade idea into students' heads. It doesn't work that way in classrooms, nor does it in organizations.

There are many intermediate types, less thorough than a true cascade, but still moving in this general direction: one might term them corporate communication efforts. The true cascade is an intensive effort to change values from top to bottom of an organization, often involving huge amounts of training. Corporate communication efforts, by contrast, try to spread a word through newsletters and internal publicity, which is generally even less effective.

Like the first type, shuffling the structure, this form of change is essentially *linear* and therefore easy to describe: The end point is quite clearly defined and then implemented through a directive process. A cascade in its true form is not interactive or reflective: It does not leave space for discussions along the way to modify the original definition of the vision. This is why it is attractive to managers who are unsure of their confidence in the new vision.

In general, organizations most likely to adopt the cascade are the bureaucracies with strong internal cultures—the "closed communities" described in Chapter 1. John Akers at IBM seems (though we do not have firsthand knowledge of this) to have used a classic cascade strategy in trying to shake up his bureaucracy. He repeatedly expressed his frustration with his inability to make real change in the traditional patterns of the organization.

The examples cited above (including IBM) indicate what seem to be the typical problems of cascades. First, the values that seem so clear and compelling at the top of the organization lose their "flavor" and sense of meaning as they are pushed down. Second, as a process, it seems to run out of steam once the basic program has reached the bottom of the organization: It has no clear response to the question, "What next?" Like the restructuring path, the cascade has no pattern of development, of interaction; it can only begin again with another mighty "push" from the top. It typically devolves, therefore, into a succession of "programs" heaped on one another.

The resulting responses in the ranks to these efforts are generally combinations of amusement and frustration. As one middle manager put it after a series of culture-change programs, "We just grab the fads. I'm amazed our executives aren't out in California doing scream therapy now." The constant flow of heavy values from above in itself only creates alienation.

The cascade approach is also highly vulnerable to changes in top management. Because the transformation effort is "anchored" at only one point in the organization, it can easily be shifted to another track: The next leader can bring in another "program" as easily as the first.[16]

3. Private Politics and Leadership

A third change strategy is generally less visible, but probably not less common: It works toward consensus, but without an open sharing of information and dialogue. This is the route of *private politics:* of piecemeal consultation and coalition-building in which the leader alone has an overview of the goal. In these processes the leaders work patiently to build agreement—rather than, as in the command or cascade approaches, openly *pushing* their point of view. Nevertheless, their point of view remains the determining force in the process.

A common version of change through private politics has been observed in the actions of new organization leaders. The effective ones do not rely on the formal structure; they find and develop confidants at various levels through the organization whom they can use to test out ideas and plan new strategies.[17] These networks remain poorly analyzed—we know little about their actual effects on change—but they are clearly much more universal than the classic model of bureaucratic communication would lead one to expect.

Much of the literature on *leadership*—at least that which does not recommend a cascade approach—in effect encourages this "private" model of organization change. It recommends that managers listen well to their subordinates and that they focus on developing everyone's full capacities, but it does not suggest true dialogue around what unites the organization.

This model is an improvement on the first two in being nonlinear: The driver of change plays the role of reflecting, adapting, revising, and refining the goals as the process proceeds. The approach can evolve gradually, which is crucial to developmental change.

But this vital flexibility is purchased at a high price. It derives from the fact that the leader does not have to consult with (many) others in order to alter direction. But that also means that the approach creates a built-in resistance to sharing the overall direction, to broadening individuals' views beyond their own "piece" of the transformation. And it is precisely this broadening that is a key feature of the post-bureaucratic approach—providing the capacity for everyone to contribute intelligently to the whole rather than just focusing on their own jobs.

Even more than the cascade, moreover, the private process is vulnerable to changes at the top levels. The cascade at least produces public commitment to a given direction, which may make a new leader think twice about changing direction; but the political route leaves the picture of the future publicly undefined. The top can shift directions without anyone really noticing.

For these reasons the political approach is limited: It may improve morale and the overall functioning of an organization, but it necessarily stops short of a transformation. It may produce an organization in which all members feel their needs are addressed, but not one in which they understand their contribution to the whole. The most ambitious change processes have therefore felt a need for something far more difficult: emphasizing (like the cascade) the dimension of *public* knowledge of the direction of change, but maintaining flexibility (like the political approach) through encouraging reflection and learning at all levels of the organization.

4. The Merits of Collaborative Process

The mark of true collaborative process, in this framework, is that it crosses two boundaries at once: It opens up information and public dialogue *across* boundaries of formal power and status, and it does so in the context of a unifying consensus on basic direction and principles. It is both nonlinear and open. Private discussions across levels and public discussions that are limited by hierarchical relations both fall short.

As one moves away from the lower left-hand corner of Figure 6.1, there is an increase in the amount of time, energy, and investment required to make the process work. Cascading communications processes require elaborate and often expensive series of meetings and publicity events; the networking, or political, approach works relatively slowly to build coalitions and "bring people along." But the most difficult of all is the true collaborative process, which is both open and consensual. This requires a complex iterative series of steps: It does not begin with a decision, as does the cascade, but must work through long and uncertain discussions to reach agreement.

Concretely, what this has meant in various settings is something like this:

• A long and rippling series of discussions focusing around (1) the sense of mission and (2) management principles for the organization as a whole. These involve multiple levels in an open dialogue: That is, the top sets few prior boundaries for the mission. When conflicts or differences develop, they are dealt with by opening up information and exploring the consequences of different courses of action.

It is not uncommon these days for the top management team to engage in this kind of discussion. It is less common, when this has happened, to avoid "cascading" the outcome of the top management process down through the organization rather than opening up a real dialogue. A potential advantage of organizations with unions or other employee associations is that these bodies can provide a prod and a path for pushing the dialogue down, rather than falling back to a cascade.

• More specific discussions around shorter-term priorities and the role of particular parts of the organization. In a logical sense these should follow after a full development of the mission; in practice one cannot put an organization on hold for a year or two, and so the two strands proceed in parallel for some time.

• A consistent use of organizational power—the authority of top leaders—to support and drive the process. Rather than putting their authority behind particular definitions of missions and priorities, or using it to resolve disputes, leaders put power at the service of insisting that everyone follow the process. Thus, for example, they can prevent the use of "power plays" by subordinates, and they can consistently articulate the goal of establishing real dialogue.

The cases described later are efforts to implement such a model, though none fits it perfectly. One notes immediately from these brief analyses how *difficult*, long, and complex the process is. Yet despite this difficulty there are cogent reasons, at least in theory, for favoring the collaborative approach to change.

The two dimensions we have sketched are both important for major transformations. The horizontal one, which we call "openness," produces *unity* that orients everyone in the same direction. The vertical one, which we call "consensus," produces *commitment* that builds credibility and motivation behind the strategy. It is the combination of the two dimensions that should produce the most effective results.

Collaborative processes should produce greater unity by reducing the amount of dysfunctional politics and bringing the existing forms of lateral cooperation more in line with the organization's purposes. Through these processes it becomes possible to talk systematically about the relation between particular actions or interests and the overall strategic direction of the whole, sharing necessary information. Thus, for example, a well-commissioned task force with a sense of its role will (still in theory) be more effective than the informal "behind-the-scenes" agreements that are its functional equivalent in classic bureaucracy. The task force is a part of the larger control systems of the organization in a way that politics are not.

They should improve commitment to implementation by making sure all relevant *interests* are considered. The argument is similar to the one just made: Combinations of interests, like knowledge, are important to effectiveness, and are typically accomplished by informal hit-or-miss means. Good CEO's always have sources by which they get a sense of what the key constituencies think of an idea, but these sources are again built by personal contacts rather than by analysis of the territory. An open process, by contrast, begins with a careful consideration of who can represent those who are affected by or who are involved in implementing the decision.

In addition, collaboration should improve decisions by systematically bringing together those with *knowledge* of the issue. Strategic change involves not only different "specialties" but also different points of view. The top levels may have the most knowledge of environmental and competitive issues, but they are likely to lack the feel for customer response that certain lower-level employees have; they may also miss many aspects of supplier relations and other matters that are in the realm of middle managers, as well as technical knowledge that may be found in Research and Development.

It is for this reason that many studies have found that strategic change does not *in reality* happen according to the bureaucratic model, with the top gathering information and gathering the results. Rather, it emerges from diffuse processes at the middle and lower level, to be crystallized at the top.[18] These processes, however, are poorly understood and controlled; there is no effective guarantee that all the relevant knowledge will in fact be brought into the decision. Much of it is hit or miss depending on personal contacts. A structured collaborative model could be more methodical about bringing the relevant knowledge to bear.

Finally, such processes should increase the level of organizational *learning*. Bureaucracies can learn many things, but they do not learn much about events that cut across lateral or vertical boundaries. For example, the strategic planning process in a typical bureaucracy is conducted according to the chain of command; the outcome, as mentioned earlier, frequently includes decisions that are resisted by the middle levels. In the absence of dialogue about the reasons, the top often gets inadequate understanding; an opportunity for learning is lost.

The question of how systems learn has long vexed scientists both hard and soft. None has answered the question, but one element seems important: Living systems learn in part because, at times, the usual hierarchical pattern of control within the organism is broken. It is difficult to develop a new and more effective paradigm, as long as one remains tightly constrained within the assumptions and logic of the old.[19] Computer systems are slow at learning most tasks when they remain highly "rational" in their programming; by contrast, computer learning is facilitated by such nonhierarchical approaches as the use of "fuzzy logic" and neural networks.[20] Learning in a rational bureaucracy faces the same problem of overly rigid hierarchical control, and collaborative process offers a way out of it.[21]

In the end, the arguments for the superiority of collaboration in managing the *change process* are similar to those given elsewhere in this volume for why collaboration is central to the effectiveness of the post-bureaucratic organization as an *end state*. This is not coincidental. The task of managing large scale organizational change has a similar character to business tasks, such as new product development, that also benefit from collaborative work processes. In fact, one might almost conceptualize the problem of organizational change as one of new product development where the new product is a more effective organizational process. In each case success requires the integration of knowledge and skills that are widely dispersed both horizontally across organizational functions as well as vertically across organizational levels. Thus in each case effectiveness is enhanced by the *unity* of effort, as well as the high levels of *commitment* that result from collaborative processes.

We would expect, by this analysis, that processes limited to either cascading or networking would be weaker than effective collaboration and perhaps unstable in the long run. A cascade creates a unified vision of the future but lacks both the breadth of input and the credibility of the more complex process. It does not effectively combine the knowledge of people at different hierarchical levels, and it does not systematically address conflicting interests. Thus, it should not be surprising to find a good deal of hidden resistance at the end.

A political or "networking" approach may engage more people in real discussion, but in a piecemeal way. Because no unified vision is built, different people will have different understandings of what is going on; therefore they will be less able to work together, and less flexible as the change moves forward, than those who have been engaged in an open discussion of the purposes of change.

Managers may attempt to avoid some of these problems by combining the networking, command, and cascade approaches. For example, a CEO might spend some time informally developing support for his change plan through one-to-one politicking, then use a cascading process of communication to announce a series of changes in the organizational structure. In our experience this approach is quite close to the conventional wisdom embodied in business school curricula and executive development programs. Yet even this more sophisticated approach only mitigates rather than resolves the problems described above. Because the successful movement to a post-bureaucratic organization depends on the commitment, the expertise, and the coordinated activities of multiple organizational levels and functions—not just of the relatively few managers who fall within the CEO's orbit—none of the other change strategies, whether singly or in combination, should be as effective as collaboration.

However—and this is a major qualification—the theoretical benefits of collaboration can be realized only if it *works*. And that is no easy matter: The transformation process is fraught with dangers and blocks. Indeed, it rarely does work, but there has been a gradual accumulation of knowledge to improve the odds.

Implementation: Or, Can It Be Done?

The knowledge of collaborative processes at this point is mostly in the form of "art." There are many descriptions of the change process, but little coherent theory of what works to get past these obstacles.

Several chapters in this collection have stressed the issue of the relation between the *informal* and the *formal* organization. In Chapter 1, we defined the disjunction between these two—the fact that informal cooperation remains "hidden" from the formal organization—as a central weakness of bureaucracy. The most difficult task in the transition is the linking of these two spheres of activity: to *legitimize* collaborative networks and to *decouple* decision making from the formal structure.

From the perspective of those who hold bureaucratic office this is a matter of "letting go" of their authority, and it always creates considerable resistance. This resistance is not a matter of personal irrationality that can be dealt with by replacing individuals; on the contrary, it is quite rational from the point of view of the organization. For the effectiveness of the traditional order depends on the clarity of accountability. Personal resistance to letting go is rarely (in our experience) based solely on selfish individual concerns about power and careers: Rather, it comes from fear that if one lets go, one will be held accountable for acts that one no longer controls. And from the organization perspective, maintaining that accountability is crucial: If decision making is merely "thrown open," chaos will surely follow.

Ironically, despite the intense concerns about accountability in traditional bureaucracies, we are struck by how often we have heard senior managers in these organizations voice their frustration that "no one is really accountable around here." Paradoxically, they find that more tightly compartmentalizing work within departmental or business unit boundaries makes the problem even worse. The reason, as Heckscher discussed in Chapter 1, is task interdependence. If new products do not succeed in the marketplace, who is accountable? Marketing is apt to point the finger at R&D, arguing that they are more interested in technical excellence than in customer needs, although R&D is apt to argue that manufacturing is not skilled and flexible enough to produce its designs at a competitive cost! To the extent that organizational success depends on work processes that cut across parts of the organization, traditional notions of individual accountability no longer apply. Post-bureaucratic organizations use different mechanisms to create organizational focus and disciplined effort, such as shared strategic visions and operating principles backed by rigorous decision making and review processes. Reflecting the reality of task interdependence, accountability for outcomes is apt to be vested in a group rather than an individual.

Although it has been argued throughout this book that this new control system is superior, this does not really help the executives who must give up a set of management tools they well understand for those they do not. They face the challenge of learning to let go *in a way that* enables people in the organization to operate effectively in a new mode.

There are two distinct aspects to the transformation, both difficult and both necessary. The first is creating dialogue among individuals and small groups who are not used to communicating so directly; the second is transforming *institutions* in a way that goes beyond face-to-face interactions. Many efforts have come to grief by emphasizing the first but neglecting the second.

Initiating Face-to-Face Dialogue

The first piece in the implementation of this change process is relatively well-developed in practice, if not in theory. It hinges on one decisive type of event that is repeated many times: This is *the establishment of dialogue among groups that have formerly related through bureaucratic roles.*[22]

We have described the *structural* difference between these two types of interaction in Chapter 1. In brief, in a bureaucratic decision exchange, one party has responsibility for the decision, though another may provide information to assist. In the interactive pattern, responsibility is shared and some form of consensus is needed for a binding decision.

The process of establishing norms of consensus rather than bureaucratic exchange is the heart of the transformation and also the focus of the consultant role. These moments of opening a dialogue occur many times throughout a change process. One quickly becomes aware of how "radical" they are because people are afraid even to enter into them—even though they need make no prior commitments to any outcomes. The news reports of peace initiatives in the Middle East detail the endless arguments over agendas and process even before substantive talks begin; this dynamic is no different than that faced by those who would bring together historically adversarial union and management groups or even hostile divisions of a corporation.

When people agree to enter into dialogue, they know that the power relations will change—and they are not sure how. This is an example of the "bootstrapping" problem identified at the beginning: They cannot see the advantages of a higher-order system until they have entered it, but they fear to enter it until they have understood it.

Thence a reason for the centrality for third parties: They must win from the participants enough trust in their *own* motives—a trust that they are concerned about the welfare of all the actors—that the latter will be willing to "drop their defenses" and enter a game they do not grasp.[23]

The organization development literature presents a reasonably consistent picture of the elements in the creation of dialogue. One can abstract them into three major elements.[24] The first is the *creation of a temporary or experimental space for dialogue*. This includes:

1. Inclusion of representatives of all relevant stakeholders.
2. Initial establishment of a temporary "protected space": usually offsite, confidential, with an atmosphere of uncritical encouragement of experimentation.

3. Development of basic principles of interaction within the group (respect, consensus, etc.).

In this first aspect, consultants play a strong *substantive* role: "insisting," *on their own authority*, on the inclusion of stakeholders and the norms of the dialogue. They generally try to build agreement on these norms, but they do not "merely" facilitate whatever the group wants.

The second element is *the generation of new patterns of interaction among the participants.* Here the consultants drop back from a substantive role, helping the parties to work through some further elements:

1. Exploration of each other's personal values, beliefs, and interests (the development of empathy and understanding).
2. An exploration of the *interdependence* of the parties—often by analyzing the shared environment and how it affects them all.
3. Construction of a common vision of the future.
4. Agreement on basic norms for the relationship.
5. Development of shared goals.
6. Concrete planning of implementation steps.

The third element is the development of *skills* needed to support the new patterns: These include listening, group problem solving, facilitation, and negotiation.

What happens through this process is nothing less than the creation of a new social system. People who have previously functioned essentially "at a distance," with separate goals, linked "objectively" through appeals to power, now enter into a relation in which they can appeal to *shared norms and values*. Hence the stress in these interventions is on discussions of norms, as well as on practicing them in varied exercises and on the skills to support them.

That phenomenon is remarkably seductive to the participants, producing an atmosphere of excitement. People are almost always surprised to find that the "other" group is made up of human beings with the same hopes and fears as themselves—they experience this as a new basis for trust. They are also astonished at their ability through dialogue to reach agreement on goals and plans of action.

It is a process that can bridge quite enormous gaps. The authors have personally seen, for example, frequent transformations of previously bitter relations between labor and management: When one puts these groups together in an offsite context as described, one *reliably* creates a level of trust that one did not initially think possible. We have seen this same magic work often between levels of a company that have never before communicated openly or among bitterly opposed community groups such as environmentalists and corporations.

There are generally crises and obstacles in sustaining this dialogue over time. The pull of the past is extremely powerful: Once out of the protected environment, when people return to their familiar contexts, they may quickly fall back into the belief that discussion is impossible. Third parties must continue to push for continued structured dialogues in order to build the habit and expectation of the pattern.[25]

Typically there are "tests" of the seriousness of the change: One group, usually among the weaker, will raise what it sees as a reasonable request to explore what the reaction will be. Interestingly, these tests are typically very minimal: People begin by asking not for the moon but only for a fruit hanging from a high bough. Examples include settling a key grievance instead of pushing it to arbitration; a desire for more training; holding to an agreed-on date for a meeting; opening the company newspaper to a column by employees or the union; and other requests of this relatively minor level. These are usually easily granted, but the psychological effect is profound: There is a sense that seemingly impenetrable barriers have melted away under the force of reasonable discussion, and trust is increased.

Occasionally issues do develop that are unresolvable in the dialogue—genuine conflicts of interest or of values—which can torpedo the process. The determining question is the degree of perceived interdependence among the parties: If it is high, they can generally find a resolution to such obstacles.[26]

Blockages at this level are, however, relatively manageable. Though the sense of fragility may last a long time, and though there may be frequent "tests" of the new relationship and threats about moving back to familiar patterns, these can generally be overcome by persistence in meeting and dialogue. In our experience the serious problems develop in trying to extend trust beyond the face-to-face relationship: This problem of *institutionalization* is far more intractable than the initial phase.

Notes on the Institutionalization of New Organizational Patterns

Even if the transformative dialogue described above works perfectly, there are enormous hurdles to institutionalizing it in the wider organization. It is, in fact, at this point that the crisis of successful failures most frequently occurs: at the boundary between the enthusiastic conversion of a face-to-face group and the skepticism of others looking on. Pushing out on a large scale is one of the major, as yet unsolved, problems of this transformation.

First there is the obstacle of constituencies. Though individuals may change their views in a face-to-face dialogue, their organizational roles and relationships do not automatically follow. They have constituents who expect them to act in familiar ways, and their ability to lead is threatened if they violate those expectations. Thus, when the initial leaders try to carry their enthusiasm outward, they are quickly "pulled back to reality" by the continuing suspicion and mistrust of those who are connected to them in the bureaucracy.[27]

Then there are a myriad further sources of resistance to change. Any change process faces obstacles, but this type—crossing, as it were, two boundaries at once—must deal with more than the others. In "opening" the leadership vision, top managers are often threatened by the scrutiny of their subordinates; in working toward consensus, all levels are suspicious of the changes in the rules of the game. Thus there is a set of typical crises that include:

1. Resistance by top managers to exposing their feelings and leadership style to examination by those who are lower on the hierarchy. Frequently this is manifested in an argument that the process needs to be more task focused and less "touchy-feelie."

2. Confusion and mixed signals regarding the role of collaborative (cross-level) employee groups established during the change process. These are often established with great fanfare, but then languish for lack of a clear role.

3. Anger from those lower in the organization when they feel the rhetoric of collaboration is violated by those higher up—a sense of betrayal, or breaking of the contract, typically expressed in complaints that the leaders are not "walking the talk."[28]

Finally, if one can overcome these difficulties, there remains the issue of making the organization *work*. Though there may be a relatively clear conception of how control and accountability will be handled in the emergent system, it cannot actually function until all the participants understand the new norms. In this kind of structural change there must be a way of "throwing the switch," of clearly shifting from one set of (bureaucratic) norms to another. In individual learning this is felt as a moment of insight, an "ah-ha." Such insights are key to the success of the face-to-face transformational process, but it cannot be extended farther: One cannot create an "ah-ha" in an entire organization at once.

The Principle of Multiple Dialogues

A major working principle for breaking down the bureaucracy is the *multiplication* of direct dialogue. Because of the intensity of the face-to-face experience, there is a paradoxical but strong tendency to forget that others have not had the same exposure. Thus, the change process puts too much of a burden on the original group, giving them responsibility for developing a design for the change process. But that ends up merely isolating them and encapsulating the effort.

The process can only be kept moving by continually extending direct dialogue to other parts of the organization—bringing together groups who do not normally talk openly with each other. This subverts the bureaucratic process without directly confronting it, and begins to substitute a new principle of dialogue for the old principle of positional authority. In recent years process consultants have developed a number of sophisticated methodologies for broadening the number of actors involved in face-to-face dialogues.[29]

But such extension must occur over time in a number of steps, and it must work steadily to overcome the inertia of the existing structure.

Halfway There: The Parallel Organization

The most common approach of those seeking a collaborative change process is to establish a "parallel organization" of bodies that cut across the hierarchy but that have merely advisory powers. There are several examples in the cases that follow:

1. The Quality of Work Life movement, represented by the AT&T/CWA case, set up teams of workers to make recommendations for change to the management hierarchy, supported by joint union-management steering committees. But there was a clear understanding that neither the union contract nor management policies could be changed except through "normal" channels.

2. The Pine Street Inn established a large number of advisory task forces to make proposals on issues identified through participatory discussions; the management team then acted on the recommendations.

3. The employee task forces (ETFs) at Becton-Dickinson came to have ongoing advisory roles in several divisions.

4. The Local Council at the research laboratory brought together representatives of multiple functions and levels to recommend changes.

In crucial respects these changes were more difficult and subversive of the old order than simple power shifts that might appear on the surface more radical. For example, the establishment of autonomous teams on the shop floor *seems* to be a radical inversion of power: But in fact it is rather limited and easily controlled. The change process is essentially simple: You take out a layer of supervision, and you train a face-to-face group to manage the supervisors' domain of responsibility. Though such a system may require profound behavioral changes both for team members and supervisors, the change can now be reliably accomplished without threatening the functioning of higher levels.

An advisory group that cuts across the hierarchy, by contrast, is harder to contain. It may not have formal authority, but it builds commitment from people with differing power bases who do not fit into an isolable "box." This creates a greater tension with the old order—and therefore has a higher rate of failure.

Both in spite of and because of the fundamental innovation involved in the cases cited, each of them hit a snag that prevented it from moving forward—a period of frustration, tension, and ultimately partial retreat from the ideals of collaborative decision making. The dynamics of these crucial moments are subtle and obscure. Overt confrontation is rare: The usual problem is not, as Marxists might imagine it, that workers try to exercise their new scope of action and thereby provoke a counterrevolution from management.[30] On the contrary, the problem is that they are so convinced of the unchangeability of their subordination that they find it difficult to escape. They *assume* that they will be turned down and *fear* retribution for overstepping their bounds. Therefore they are reluctant even to test higher levels' willingness to "let go"; and when they do, they interpret any resistance or difficulty as evidence of what they "knew" all along—that the top has no intention of really changing. One finds a curiously contradictory pattern of bravado and timidity, of desire for dramatic change and hesitancy in pushing any concrete proposals beyond, or even as far as, the prior limits set from above.

These interaction patterns may seem familiar to anyone who has adolescent children. While each side may intellectually understand the value of establishing a more "adult," equal, and collaborative relationship, there is also a strong internal pull back to the well-understood and comforting roles of superior and subordinate, powerful parental provider and passive dependent child.

The higher managers only occasionally resist openly; given the fragility of the movement, it takes very little of that to stop the process entirely. More frequently, however, the problem is much subtler. The higher levels "bend over backwards" to respond to every request from the advisory bodies, even ones they disagree with; yet the results are ultimately no better. The dynamic that typically develops is this: (1) the lower levels feel that no matter how many recommendations are accepted, "real" change remains frustratingly out of reach; and (2) the higher levels feel increasingly martyred as they give ground (as they see it) out of pure good will, yet do not get the returns of thankfulness that they expect. Sooner or later an issue comes up where the top feels it cannot continue to give, and the process breaks down in rancor.

A small example from among thousands:

> In a research lab, a representative employee council pushed for the establishment of an exercise room. The division head had set an explicit policy against providing exercise rooms. Nevertheless, local management pushed for it and won the right to set one up. The euphoria was brief: The local management felt, and continued to reiterate for years after, that they had made an extraordinary gesture of good faith that merited a return of great commitment; but the council members, instead of remaining grateful, quickly felt that there were many more important issues that were not being addressed. Within six months the energy in the council declined and it faded from sight.

These conflicts, it must be stressed, rarely break out in public: They take the form of *withdrawal* from interaction, amid private grumblings, rather than confrontation. The exceptions are rare. Under some conditions a group finds its voice, as it were, in a meeting *without* the presence of the higher levels: Then they may complain that their bosses are not living up to the espoused principles of involvement, and their accusations may become bitter and heated. Even then, in any direct conversation with the leadership there will be a tremendous withdrawal, and at most only a faint remnant of the original intensity will come through. An example:

> At the Pine Street Inn, a training program brought together middle level managers shortly after an announcement of budget cuts. Very high anger was expressed at this session about decisions made (in their perception) unilaterally by top management. The extent of this anger had not been visible before, and it was never visible again: When higher managers began to ask people about what had gone on, they received extremely watered-down versions of the event.

So at this decisive moment of change—a moment that is repeated many times in a transformative process—the problem of power cannot be ignored. Neither asserting power (making clear that the recommendations are merely advisory) nor generously abstaining from using power (by accepting all recommendations) will overcome the inherent distortion of communication across hierarchical levels. In short, *merely advisory parallel processes do not create enough pressure for change to break through the natural resistances of bureaucracy.* The implication is that some sort of transfer of power is needed.

At the same time, as we have argued, a mere transfer of power *within* the bureaucracy—from one position to another, centralizing or decentralizing—is not the answer either.[31] It is not a matter of cutting more layers of management or giving workers more authority. The issue is more difficult: to *transform* the nature of power so that it is no longer attached to position, but emerges from stakeholder dialogue.

The Contest for Legitimacy

The positive resolution of this critical moment requires that consensus-based bodies outside the bureaucratic hierarchy be treated *seriously*: that is, that they gain a legitimate place in the structure of decision making, rather than a position based on a paternalistic desire to do good.

For management this is a leap from the security of the familiar into a dark and unknown domain. The move away from bureaucracy *essentially* requires those in positions of power to give up control of critical decisions, to turn them over to consensus-based stakeholder groups. It requires a willingness to vest authority not in individual positions but in agreed-on strategic missions, operational principles, and organizational processes. Few are willing to take the plunge without considerable encouragement. Nor would they, as parties responsible for maintaining effective operations, be well *advised* to give up their power without assurance that the new forms will actually work better.

The notion of parallel structures is an attempt to make this leap easier by in effect assuring managers that they can keep one foot on the familiar bureaucratic bank while making the plunge. But the organizational reality is no more workable than that metaphor. Under those conditions, the bureaucratic model has all the advantages over the new model: It fits with people's training and their expected career paths; it has a rich reservoir of experience; it can take many forms without losing its basic stability. The post-bureaucratic model has none of these. Thus, when it is easy to pull back, as in the parallel approach, there is hardly a chance for change.

The pulling back, as we have seen repeatedly, may be complex and subtle. The new may be reinterpreted and absorbed by the bureaucratic paradigm—for example, translating "empowerment" into bureaucratic "delegation"—or it may simply stop at a certain point, contained within a limited "box." It proves, in short, very difficult really to escape the Weberian "iron cage."

Thus we are brought back to the theoretical problem raised at the start of this chapter, of how one can jump from one developmental state to another. The answer appears to be that *the "jump" occurs through combat—but a combat of a certain kind*. It is *not* a matter of a classic Marxist struggle for power between two groups; this, as history has often demonstrated, produces another form of successful failure, remaining within the hierarchical paradigm. Rather, this struggle is between institutions representing *different kinds of authority*: the authority of position versus the authority of consensus.

Here is a story to illustrate:

Shell-Sarnia established early on a "Team Norm Review Board," composed of representatives from the shop-floor teams as well as from the union and management structures. Its role was far from clear: It had no formal authority, yet it was not a mere advisory board. Its legitimacy came from the initial strong statements of intent by management and the union to build something radically new. Somehow it was supposed to create consensus and catalyze the transition to a new structure. That turned out to involve much confusion and struggle.

Early on, for instance, some workers came up with an idea for a reformed shift schedule. *Both* union and management thought this was a bad idea, setting a dangerous precedent, etc.; they sought to squash it. But the TNRB pursued it, gathering opinions and information, refining the proposals, and spurring discussion among the workforce. In the end it made such a persuasive case that the two hierarchies gave in and agreed to try out the new system—which turned out to be a great success by all criteria.

The tension and competition between the old and the new in effect confirmed the power of the latter over the course of a number of such incidents. At critical moments the power of union and management to make *formally binding* decisions seemed weak in the face of the TNRB's ability to make *consensually legitimate* decisions. Gradually more and more decision making on difficult issues passed into this domain of stakeholder consensus coordinated by the TNRB, out of the hands of the more traditional Labor-Management Committee and the two hierarchies.

The leaders of the union and employee representatives recognized how uncertain this victory was—that it could easily have failed, and would have been impossible without the public principles already in place. "The company probably thinks they made a mistake, really, writing down so much at the beginning," suggests one; that written framework, as well as substantial preparation for participative planning, was essential—and, surprisingly, *sufficient*—when the traditional hierarchy turned against the process.[32]

This brief tale brings out several points. First, the process is *necessarily messy* because it involves a competition between two principles. The old hierarchy and the new consensual structures cannot be slotted into neatly distinct domains—that would simply in itself re-create the segmentation of bureaucracy. The creative moments at Shell-Sarnia would never have happened if there was a sharp separation between the advisory role of the TNRB and the authoritative role of management and the union. Instead, the old and the new effectively *duplicate* each other during the transition, covering much of the same ground.

This duplication moves the transformation forward by creating a *contest for legitimacy.* The new structure must win its authority, if it can, by demonstrating that the processes it sets up work better than the traditional ones. This contest forms the bridge between the old and the new—building the role of the stakeholder process, reducing (if successful) the dominance of the hierarchy. It is the answer to the problem of transition—how to give up the old before the new is in place. The answer is that the transition occurs in a fight over time.[33]

The second key point is that the contest cannot be left to brute force or chance. It must be *structured* so that the interactive mechanisms have a fair chance to demonstrate their worth. The phenomenon of successful failures shows how effectively a mature bureaucracy can defend itself from challenges, whether or not it "deserves" to win. The transformation has to shake up those defenses enough that there is a genuine chance for the new principles to make their case in practice.

At Shell-Sarnia the shaking up included the establishment of initial principles advocating radical (though vague) change and the deliberate refusal to "box in" the TNRB. These clues echo sufficiently in other cases to suggest not a full theory but at least a set of mechanisms needed in the transition.

Structuring the Contest: Three Mechanisms

Three elements can be identified from existing cases as creating the conditions for a fair contest:

1. Public Discussions of Principles and Goals (Frequently Reworked). We have seen that there are infinite ways for the process to stop short of success. In order to keep it moving, and to win the confidence of those who are involved, a plausible image of the end state is needed. It will be a reference point to measure progress, and a point of leverage for the champions of the change. Such images have been gradually developing over the past decades; indeed, this book is an attempt to further this tradition. The spread of task forces, matrix organizations, and cross-functional teams has begun to generate a sense that something different might really work—that one can accomplish goals without the hierarchical accountability of a bureaucratic order. One major function of consultants is to help managers build this vision and apply it to their circumstances. Consultants by virtue of their position can maintain a *consistent* picture of the goal through the turbulence of daily business demands and steadily hold that picture up to organizational leaders without getting "caught up in" the pressures of the old order.[34]

The image should not be fixed at the start: In the nature of evolutionary processes, it needs to evolve as the process develops. There is in fact a danger that the top levels will work on too detailed a founding vision; this constrains later possibilities and leaves others feeling cut out. Only the basic direction needs to be stated initially—for example, that the organization is seeking to move beyond bureaucratic decision making, toward a system that involves stakeholders in dialogue. This will seem vague and incomprehensible at first, but will be a template for greater clarity later.

Examples of such images can be found in the most successful new organizational efforts. At Saturn, a group of 99—drawn from all levels of General Motors—developed a set of basic concepts and values that still drive the organization. At Shell-Sarnia, the union and management early on developed a statement of principles that has had a continuing impact.

2. Rotating Stakeholder Representatives in Strategic Discussions. The transition clearly involves not only a "pull," in the form of a public vision, but also a "push," in the form of effective voice from below. The killer moment in most change processes is when management becomes convinced that it has gone far enough. This is where merely advisory processes get derailed: It is inevitable, even with the best of intentions, that management's definition of the proper direction will win out and will close the possibility of real discussion. Then follows the cycle of discouragement and silent withdrawal that destroys trust.

The needed deterrent is a system in which employees can really argue with their superiors. The lower levels need to develop enough self-confidence and clarity that they can break through their own fear of confronting the top, as well as any actual resistance from above. In other words, the pattern of private grumbling and withdrawal must evolve into an open discussion of differences.

This requires, as a central part of the change process, a focus on "empowerment" of an uncommon sort: not pushing responsibility down, but giving people the real sense that they can talk back without retaliation, and that their ideas will be considered seriously rather than dismissed.

Such empowerment is, perhaps surprisingly, more difficult and rare than the simple transfer of power. On the whole, it is easier for a good bureaucratic manager to turn over a larger sphere of autonomy to a subordinate than to tolerate a real argument about his own decisions. The former is part of the logic of the system—bureaucracy is built on the notion of effective delegation—but the latter threatens it fundamentally. The legitimacy of bureaucratic command comes from the *position* of authority and the formal rationality of the process, not from the substantive rightness of the decision. It is essential in holding the system together that subordinates accept that their bosses know more than, have a broader view than, they do; if they had to justify everything the structure would crumble.

But it is precisely this questioning, justification, and breadth of view that distinguishes the post-bureaucratic order. Its key virtue consists in freeing people from the bounds of individual fixed jobs, allowing them to invent and combine flexibly. That in turn depends on an understanding everywhere in the organization of the central purposes and strategies and the ability to argue and debate them freely.

The encouragement of debate can be made still more difficult, paradoxi-cally, by the presence of a union. For unions have dealt with the resistances of bureaucratic management by formalizing and centralizing the structure of voice. All issues, in principle, pass through the official union representatives, who by virtue of their position are protected from retaliation. When faced with the idea of broadening voice beyond the formal structure, these officials often become another obstacle to change. Perhaps the only way to begin the transition to a post-bureaucratic form of voice is deliberately to bring *non*-officials into a direct dialogue with top management. The kind of face-to-face process described earlier builds over time the kind of confidence and ability to argue that is a prerequisite for a shift away from positional legitima-tion. If a cross section of workers and middle managers are, for instance, brought into top-level discussions of strategic management, they are at first intimidated and quiet but gradually come to express a new point of view in the discussions. This is a great lesson in consensus-based decision making for the top managers, and spreads the experience down through at least a small segment of the organization.

Indeed, this is essentially what happened at Becton-Dickinson, as described in the case later: The creation of direct stakeholder dialogue in the Strategic HRM process turned out to be more powerful than anyone expected. Similar mechanisms exist at Saturn and Shell-Sarnia, where through changing con-figurations of task forces many employees are brought into dialogue with higher levels. At Saturn, the union still plays the major institutional role, though it has loosened its control of who may "officially" participate on committees; at Shell-Sarnia the union has long ago pulled back from this control and plays a more coordinating function.

Here the danger to avoid is transforming the representatives into a new kind of official. After a few workers finally develop the confidence and skills to participate in strategic discussions, it is easy to make them a permanent part of the process. Then they become separated from their fellows and simply become another part of the bureaucratic process. Over time there is a difficult balance to maintain between giving people enough time to learn and bringing in enough new people to keep the discussions "fresh."

3. Process Design Teams. The Team Norm Review Board at Shell-Sarnia is an instance of a nonbureaucratic structure that grows up within the old system. The concept is this: The transformation involves the continuous extension and refinement of new processes of decision making. Rather than just reading the process of the hierarchy, there need to be ways of identifying relevant stakeholders and creating an effective dialogue among them. During the change there needs to be *a way of seizing opportunities to create such dialogues* at the moment they are needed. The existing officials of the hierarchy are unlikely to carry this off effectively. Therefore what is needed is a group that crosscuts the formal structure and that *designs better ways of making decisions* that are not being effectively made at present.

The Shell-Sarnia board has ranged widely. It has dealt with many very difficult issues in addition to the shift schedule example cited earlier—from conflict over the relative pay scales of craft and operating workers to the introduction of new technologies in the warehouse. The board does not typically make decisions itself but manages a consensus-building process: setting up task forces, holding plant meetings, seeking credible data, and so on. It has succeeded over time in involving nearly every employee in some aspect of these processes, and it has untied some very challenging knots.

At Saturn something equivalent is done by several Organization Development groups, who have a great deal of "clout"—not formal power, but not mere advisory influence either. They are seen as central to the creation of consensus and the realization of the vision articulated by the original group of 99.

In another organization we are now working with we are trying two versions of this structure. First we have created the position of "transformation manager." This is a well-respected middle manager who has been pulled from his or her line job to take responsibility for coordinating and holding together all the multiform initiatives involved in the change: task forces, work teams, study circles, and so on. The position is in a sense duplicative because the regular line management, including the head of the organization, is *also* responsible for making the transformation; but it was becoming clear that they would not *alone* be able to carry it out because they were "locked into place" by their formal positions. The transformation manager tries to do the same thing, with both the disadvantages and advantages of a nonbureaucratic approach. This manager does not have the formal power to tell people to act differently; but he or she has more freedom to roam across lines and levels than anyone else, even the top manager.

The other "doubled" piece is a transformation *group* called the Process Design Team. This is conceived a good deal like the second Shell-Sarnia body, as a slice that helps to set up new processes for making key decisions. It doubles a more traditional labor-management committee that is also building cooperation among the traditional adversarial organizations.

The three mechanisms described reinforce each other and work together. In the absence of any one of these pieces, the traditional hierarchy will sooner or later reassert its dominance.

As these come together they evolve toward a strategy that might be called *interactive strategic planning*. It is *interactive* in a sense radical to the bureaucratic model—encouraging debate and dialogue among differing sectors of the organization. It is *strategic* in that these debates include the central issues of the business, overcoming the segmentation of focus characteristic of bureaucracy. And it draws everyone into shared *planning,* which serves as a basis for coordinating the newly flexible structures.

Conclusion

The weakness of transformational practice and of theory go hand in hand. Without a clear understanding of the problem, change efforts have been prone to fall into a number of common errors—producing many partial successes, but few real transformations.

The first error is to focus only on the creation of teams and the exciting process of building a new shared understanding within a group. As we have seen, that misses the problem of *institutionalization* and therefore produces at best teams isolated within a hierarchy.

The second is to confuse the establishment of consensus processes with the process of change itself. We have come to understand moderately well how to build consensus on a large scale: The work of the Tavistock group, the Harvard Program on Negotiation, and Interaction Associates (among others) has shown the way.[35] But their successes have come primarily in organizing previously unorganized systems, particularly international or community disputes. The shift *out* of a bureaucratic mold presents a distinct set of problems that have rarely been analyzed at all.

Finally, the lack of available concepts about patterns in time has produced essentially static theories, which formulate the *structures* at the beginning and end points and assume that the change merely involves moving "toward" the latter. Most attempts at a more dynamic interpretation have been limited to identifying the general and repeated phases of movement—unfreezing-change-refreezing, or visioning-experimentation-reflection;[36] they have failed to identify the essential dilemmas and typical turning points particular to the move from bureaucracy.

This chapter represents only a beginning in defining this terrain. It has differed from most treatments of organization change in two ways: by focusing on a relatively specific problem—the transition from bureaucratic to post-bureaucratic systems—rather than on "change" in a universal sense; and by systematically distinguishing models of the *change process* from the *structure toward which change is aimed.* It has distinguished the collaborative model of change from several others, some of which have similarities to it, and has argued why it is essential to this particular transformation. It has specified some of the critical moments typical to this shift, in particular the extension of dialogue and the transformation of power; and it has identified three practical mechanisms of the contest for legitimacy.

This produces some suggestions that are in principle testable: It should be possible to see whether the three mechanisms suggested distinguish successful from unsuccessful efforts. But it will be at best so long before one can make the judgment, and before enough clean cases are available without too many confusing external factors, that one cannot wait for that in practice. The question here is more simply whether this is the best way to make sense of the available evidence.

In this realm, as in all structural development, practice is necessarily outrunning theory: There is a wealth of current efforts with genuinely innovative concepts that have not been sorted out with conceptual rigor. Change could not proceed without such experimentation. It is also important, however, to organize what we know so as to avoid repeating the same mistakes and to focus the central learnings. The error of successful failure has now been made too often; those who seek change therefore need to focus on the pattern of change over time and the mechanisms needed to keep it going against resistance and habit.

Cases

AT&T and the CWA: Quality of Work Life

CHARLES HECKSCHER

This effort from 1980 to 1984 was a relatively early attempt to increase shop-floor participation on a large scale. It built on many efforts during the 1970s that had shown the effectiveness of involving workers in improving their work processes and working conditions. In 1980, AT&T and its unions signed an agreement to encourage such developments throughout the Bell System, which at that time numbered over 600,000 unionized employees.

The image of the effort had two elements: improved union-management relations, and worker involvement. The first was to be achieved through joint committees guiding the process, the second by problem-solving groups on the shop floor. The latter were to consist of about 10 to 15 workers in a single workplace, who would meet for about an hour a week to formulate recommendations for change.

The effort began with discussions at the top of the labor relations and union hierarchies. After the actual contract agreement, these groups met for several months to develop a Statement of Principles framing the effort, including a commitment to jointness, protection of workers from reductions in force coming out of the program, and other basic points.

The project had two broad phases over 4 years. In the first, a series of committees was formed to encourage the downward spread of the concepts. Thus, each operating company developed a joint committee, which catalyzed the formation of committees at the department level, and so on down. At the bottom of this chain were the shop-floor committees, including work teams and their supervisors, which were the object of the effort. In the first 2 years, over 1,200 of these committees were formed, spread quite widely through the system. Each developed its own statement of goals and principles; variation was encouraged within the basic framework of the Statement of Principles. Thus, for instance, there was some experimentation with fully autonomous teams as well as the more limited problem-solving groups recommended in the training.

The second phase involved developing a network of facilitators to support and develop the effort. The National Committee developed a 5-day course for facilitators that was delivered to several hundred people from union and management over a 1-year period.

The final success of the effort is hard to judge, because it was brought to a rather abrupt halt by the dismemberment of the Bell System in 1984. But it was certainly clear at that time that the approach was extremely limited.

On the positive side, the change strategy developed a large number of teams in a short period of time. Frequently the discussions between workers and supervisors produced significant improvements in relationships. In many areas the conversations between unions and management were, or at least felt like, a breakthrough: Groups that had been historically hostile began to consult with each other frequently and openly.

But a study conducted after 4 years confirmed what many of those involved had experienced: The majority of teams quickly reached a "plateau," after which they lost energy and momentum. Though the reasons were not obvious—it was not a matter of open conflicts or clear decisions—the major reported factor was a limitation on the scope of action by the teams. Even without clearly stated hierarchical limits, the teams rarely ventured into territory defined as "managerial."[37] And even with the best intentions, middle managers often had a dampening effect on the discussions.[38]

This was an example of the isolation of collaboration: Dialogue was contained within narrow pieces of the organization. It occurred basically in two places—between workers and their supervisors, and between the union and management in joint committees. In these areas new possibilities were opened up.

But the effort fell short on unity, and therefore did not develop far. Many key parts of the two organizations were not involved in the dialogue at all—the middle managers above the supervisory level, and the vast majority of union members. These "constituencies" never understood the process very well nor joined into its spirit, and they acted as a drag on its development. Nor was the QWL project ever linked in an effective way to a strategy that affected all members of the organization.

The expected consequences of collaboration could therefore be found only in piecemeal fashion: The company as a whole, or even major divisions of it, showed little change in performance. Many teams could tell success stories stemming either from new application of knowledge—ideas from workers about how to do the job better—or from reconciliation of conflict and divergent interests. A certain amount of movement of this type also occurred within the union-management committees, and some innovative agreements were reached. But lacking wider support from the constituencies, the leaders could not move far in translating their discussions into major changes.[39]

The Case of Becton Dickinson

RUSSELL A. EISENSTAT

Becton Dickinson is a multidivisional health care products company. Over the last 15 years, the company has been moving slowly but systematically from a reliance on command to more collaborative management processes. The first step was the institutionalization of a new process for strategy formulation based on discussions between a division president and his staff. This "strategic profiling" process was facilitated by a professional with expertise in both business strategy and process management. Formerly business strategies, to the extent that they were explicit, were primarily the responsibility of the division president and corporate top management. Strategic profiling broadened the collaborative process one level to include the division's functional heads.

The profiling process was judged quite successful internally in developing thoughtful and well-grounded business strategies that had the commitment of the top management team. In fact, the external consultant responsible for developing the process, Ray Gilmartin, was hired by the company, and in 1989 was named CEO. Despite these improvements in strategy development, Gilmartin and others were still dissatisfied with the effectiveness with which these strategies were implemented within BD's divisions. To address this problem, BD developed and implemented a second management process, Strategic Human Resource Management (SHRM).[40] SHRM continued the idea that began with Strategic Profiling, that analyses should be performed collaboratively by the top management team with the aid of external facilitators. However, the process also broadened the scope of collaboration by creating a dialogue between the top management team and a group that was representative of the rest of the organization—an employee task force (ETF). The process consists of the following major steps:

1. The top team defines the major organizational tasks required to accomplish a division's strategic objectives.
2. The ETF is commissioned to interview a representative group of employees about their perceptions of organizational barriers and facilitators to strategic effectiveness.
3. This data is reported back to the top team, along with the results of individual interviews with each member of the top team conducted by two external facilitators.
4. The top team then takes all of this organizational data, and working with the facilitators, develops:
   • A diagnosis of the root causes of the barriers to strategic effectiveness.
   • A model for how the organization should be functioning if it is going to accomplish its business strategy.
   • An action plan for how this model will be enacted.
5. The results of the process are communicated to the employee task force, to corporate management, and then to the larger organization.
6. The process is periodically repeated to assess progress.

BD has been using the SHRM process for almost 4 years. More than half of its divisions have gone through the process, as well as the corporate top management team. Three major conclusions about the movement from command to collaboration can be drawn. First, the lack of collaborative processes has repeatedly been identified during divisional SHRM's as a major barrier to effective strategy implementation. Second, the SHRM process itself has tended to become increasingly collaborative as it has evolved. And third, institutionalizing collaborative processes has proved more difficult vertically than horizontally.

1. Lack of Collaboration Is a Barrier to Strategy Implementation. One of the most consistent themes identified by the various employee task forces has been the difficulties in strategy implementation created by the lack of institutionalized horizontal and vertical collaborative processes. The lack of these processes have been particularly strongly implicated in shortfalls in new product development and product quality.

2. The SHRM Process Itself Has Become Increasingly Collaborative. The extent of collaboration between the employee task force and the top management team has tended to increase as the SHRM process has evolved. The first step was a decision by an employee task force to disregard the consultant's suggestion that they present their feedback using overhead charts. Instead, the task force sat at a table in the center of the room and discussed their findings with the top management team on the outside "of the fishbowl" observing. The profilers observed that this change seemed to give the operating committee a far richer understanding of the issues facing their division than had the previous approach. Consequently it was institutionalized in subsequent SHRM's.

An unexpected consequence of this change in process has been that operating committees have begun to treat the ETF as more of a collaborative partner. In the earlier divisional SHRMs, the results of the top team's deliberations were reported to the employee task force and then to the larger organization using essentially a cascading model. However, the richness of the presentations given by the ETFs using the fishbowl method seemed to encourage a more collaborative engagement with the ETF. Rather than just reporting results to the ETF, the top teams in later SHRMs have generally tested and refined their conclusions based on ETF input. In implementing the results of the SHRM process, the top teams in later processes also have tended to rely more fully on follow-up task forces and committees that include both members of the operating committee and lower organizational levels.

3. Institutionalizing Collaborative Processes Outside of the Formal SHRM Process Has Proved More Difficult Vertically, Than Horizontally. Although divisional top management teams have acknowledged the value of the collaborative discussions across hierarchical levels that occur as part of the SHRM process, there has been substantial resistance to institutionalizing organizational mechanisms for vertical collaboration. For example, in some cases top management teams have stated that they will continue to use the employee task force as an ongoing advisory group to monitor the effectiveness with which the changes proposed as a result of SHRM are implemented. Follow-up discussions with these ETFs have generally revealed an enormous level of frustration with this role—the ETF report that despite the top team's espoused commitment to collaboration, in fact the input of the ETF is largely ignored outside of the formal SHRM process. Members of the top team report that despite their best intentions, the demands of running the business tend to crowd out ETF concerns.

A similar breakdown in collaboration appears to have occurred in the relationships between the divisional top management teams and corporate management. It was initially envisioned that the results of a divisional SHRM would be shared with corporate management and would serve as the basis for ongoing collaborative discussions concerning how the human resources of a given division could best be managed. These reports to top management rarely occurred, and where they have, did not lead to follow-up discussions.

In contrast, as mentioned above, a number of mechanisms for improving horizontal interfunctional collaboration have been instituted. These have generally been more successful in those cases in which they were focused around a clear and immediate business problem and in which the changes did not threaten the power and authority of the divisional top management team.[41]

For example, as a result of the SHRM process, one division created an extremely effective mechanism for interfunctional coordination focused around improving product quality at the plant level. This was an important business problem for the division and was addressed by a team at a low enough organizational level that it did not imply changes in the role and position of the divisional top management team. In contrast, a second division attempted to institute interfunctional product teams. The purpose of these teams was to increase the level of focus on particular product lines and to push responsibility downward from the top management team to middle management so that top management could focus on broader strategic concerns. Despite the top team's stated commitment to this new approach, the members of the teams reported that they were given little more than administrative responsibilities. The problem, revealed in subsequent interviews, was that members of the senior team were concerned that their positions would be diminished to the extent that the teams were empowered. The top team's solution: to cut back the number of teams to those for which there was a clear and compelling business need and to place a member of the top team as the head of each of these remaining teams.

The Case of Pine Street Inn

THOMAS RICE

Context

Pine Street Inn is primarily a shelter for homeless individuals. Each night, the Inn provides for the basic survival needs of 700-900 people—dinner, shower, bed, and breakfast. Primary medical care is available for those in obvious need. In operation since 1968, Pine Street has undergone major changes over the years. Beginning as a soup kitchen in the 1960s, it has become a multiservice organization with a complex vision and an organizational dynamic to match.

Not only does Pine Street provide shelter for the homeless, it seeks to get to the roots of the problem by creating permanent housing and transitional programs needed to move beyond temporary shelter. The homeless population reflects the cumulative erosion of underclass "safety nets" so well documented over the past 15 years[42]—including the emergence of AIDS, poly-addiction, deinstitutionalized mentally ill, youth runaways, handicapped Vietnam vets, and the explosion of working poor. Pine Street Inn faces a daunting challenge.

To address this challenge, the leadership of Pine Street decided to broaden its base of participation in 1986. Demands for services were increasing, the public seemed to be more open to hearing the case of homeless advocates, and it was clear that business as usual was not working. The status quo to that point was top-down command, in terms of our typology. The executive director, who had taken over after the charismatic founder died of a heart attack in 1982, inherited and continued a tradition of unilateral decision making. A "kitchen cabinet" of three board members and the assistant ED served as a shadow management team. Internally, however, decisions were consistently unilateral.

The change process, which was launched in October 1986, was ambitious and dramatic. Ambitious because it sought systemic change in vision, mission, and structure. Dramatic because it sought to consciously change a "command" to a "collaborative" process through the application of collaborative processes from the outset.

What follows is a description of the major process phases employed, the issues raised by the intervention, ongoing challenges to collaboration at the Inn, and some conclusions regarding the evidence we have gleaned over 5 years of close involvement in this case.

Process Phases

The process was set up to move through 12 phases over the life span of the initiative. Each phase has its own dynamics and imperative set of products and unfolds sequentially (more or less) into the next phase, as follows:

1. Start-Up and Scoping. The external consultant interviewed the "client," a representative sample of stakeholders, and built an agreement on the scope and intensity of the intervention. In addition, the consultant provided a "snapshot" of the organizational challenges presented in the interviews.

2. Process Design. A steering committee was made up of a nine-person cross-functional team, including one board member. This team was trained in a common approach to problem solving, facilitation skills, and basics of meetings management. This group designed an overall approach that was geared to open the organization to dialogue and influence all the way from the "guests" —the Inn's term for homeless individuals—to the board of directors.

3. *Visioning the Future.* The steering committee designed and implemented a series of workshops on building a shared vision of the future. All staff, many interested guests, most of the board, and many external stakeholders participated. The intention was to maximize participation and all stakeholder interests. The vision was synthesized into 10 themes, or focal points, for planning.

4. *Issue Identification.* This was the same process as the visioning phase, except that the focus was on the problematic. About 120 issues were registered in a town-meeting style session, facilitated and led by the steering committee, with the help and coaching of the external consultant. These issues were raised in the context of the vision themes already generated and refined at previous sessions.

5. *Education/Training.* The steering committee set up 10 task forces, matched to the vision/issue focal points. Task forces were educated on the issues, joint data collection was legitimized where needed, and a common framework for heuristic problem solving[43] was adopted. The steering committee served as facilitators and coaches, with the chair of the steering committee acting as overall process manager.[44]

6. *Problem Definition and Analysis.* The task forces worked to refine the problem statement into some manageable focal points that can be analyzed in terms of root causes. This analytic work was presented to the original large group for comment, critique, and mid-course correction.

7. *Solution Alternatives/Evaluation.* The task forces returned to incorporate the feedback, begin the task of seeking ideas for resolving or ameliorating some of the root causes, and finally reached a prioritized list against select criteria.

8. *Scenario Development.* Up to this point, the task forces had been encouraged to focus on their select charter. Now was the time to begin a more integrated approach, one in which the discrete work took account of the whole. Various scenarios were advanced, discussed, and refined. The more promising advanced to the next phase, with several task force products synthesized into a critical few.

9. Decision Making. The final set of recommendations were advanced in public to the whole organization, including outside stakeholders. The executive director and his managers announced that they would implement to the extent that resources would permit. However, the final decision on what would be implemented and when rested with the executive director and his management. This was understood and had been reinforced from the start. The steering committee and task forces were strictly influential with no formal power. They did however have the authority to recommend in public their considered and legitimized solution scenarios.

Consequently, the top team accepted 95% of the recommendations (a total of 121 initiatives ranging from minor to major commitments). This planning process took about 1 year before they were ready to implement.

10. Implementation. This phase is still going on, because the 120 recommended actions were categorized into short-, middle- and long-range time frames. They were then built into a 5-year strategic planning process, with the steering committee evolving into an implementation team and later forming the core of a planning board. The latter was designed to function as a monitoring and quality assurance mechanism for the collaborative agreements and principles.

11. Evaluation and Feedback. Each strategic initiative was assigned a lead and accountability rested with this individual for the results specified by the "I team." Periodic reports on progress were built into the process, with the management team scheduling time at quarterly retreats to examine progress against the plan.

12. Redesign/Upgrade for Continuous Improvement. After each iteration of planning and implementation, new learnings need to be incorporated into the next round of organizational processes so that a habit of reflection and adaptation become institutionalized. Leadership needs to ensure that managers and "process owners" are held accountable and rewarded for this. Otherwise, counterproductive patterns soon begin to flourish and hard-won gains are soon eroded.

Pine Street is now in its sixth year of working with collaborative processes and principles. Though successes have been many and rewarding, several thorny problems remain. Each year brings new awareness, new resolve, and discernible progress toward the vision of a collaborative, multiservice organization dedicated to ending the horror of homelessness.

Evidence of Success

As is typical of most change efforts, early euphoria brought a sense of genuine renewal and empowerment to the Inn. This was true for all levels, but especially for the direct care staff and counselors who had felt left out.

Now they were being trained, included, consulted, and heard. Their ideas were legitimized; their immediate issues given real attention. Some irritants that had gone unattended for years were now being fixed in a few days. This was heady stuff. And, of course, it raised expectations that this should go on forever.

The task forces were a success by any standard. They delivered their chartered results: a set of implementable solutions to given problems. They had used an open, collaborative process complete with facilitators who had enough skill to build consensus and ensure that stakeholder interests were respected. Finally, they forged relationships with other people at the inn with whom they'd had little or no working contact before.

This gave rise to warm informal relationships that extended beyond the workplace. It also led to a breakdown of stereotypes that had prevailed between different units and programs through the years of separation.

Another success was the emergence of true interdependence in several problematic areas. An example was the referral system of getting homeless individuals into permanent housing. This process had become thoroughly politicized, with all the attendant fallout: lack of trust between the counselors and the permanent housing providers (known as Paul Sullivan Housing Trust), perceptions of inequities, and turf battles about who could place their favorite people. Over a 6-month period of tough, principled problem solving, a cross-function team worked it out, producing win-win outcomes for all concerned. The agreements still hold, as does the aura of having been part of a successful collaborative effort.

It is not hard to find other success stories stemming from the process. As a result of a collaborative grant-writing effort, the inn was able to capitalize on its experience to win a $3 million McKinney award from the Commonwealth (federal funds originally) of Massachusetts—this to create transitional programs for selected guests. There was consensus that the inn could not have participated in this kind of sophisticated competition before. They attribute their success to the collaborative processes.

Finally, and most important, the executive director agreed to build a management team and make "real decisions" openly. Budget decisions are shared, the books are open for all managers to see, and major decisions of capital spending and master planning are in the team domain. A shift has clearly taken place within the management team. It is fair to say that Pine Street is no longer run as a command organization. It is, however, equally fair to say that the inn has not arrived as a model of collaboration. In fact, several episodes and recurrent issues provide ample evidence that gains are in constant danger of being undermined or canceled.

Evidence of Limitations

Some issues were raised at the very outset and remain endemic. Others are linked to seasonal stresses, and still others are directly correlated with situational snafus that are clearly in violation of collaborative principles.

In the first category, the problem of inclusion is a major issue. Who should be the decision makers (how many, under what conditions, with how much authority and influence), how is the final decision made, and what is the rationale? Another in this category is the issue of workload—how to find time to be collaborative and to adhere to a principled approach in the face of incredible stress. In other words, how to "walk the talk."

Finally, and related, is the problem of process proliferation coordination, communication, and skill. The organizational tendency is to post "the process" as the solution to every problem, small or large, while ignoring the requisite need for coordination, communication between stakeholders, and competence to handle the group dynamics and associated politics. One unanticipated side effect is that many disappointments are blamed on "the process" and "collaboration" has become a target for those in search of a scapegoat.

The other set of issues is more predictable. Winter comes around. Under the stress of dealing with a surging, relentless sea of pain, traditional fissures in the Pine Street culture show up. Direct care staff, close to the guests and protective of their vulnerability, favor a non-interventionist approach. The management and many of the "professional" staff—administrators, medical and psychiatric personnel—favor an interventionist approach, which includes setting recovery goals for guests and holding out expectations of improvement for those who are ready to participate. As the inn grows more complex, this duality is exacerbated, especially in the battle for declining resources.

The first category of issues can be traced directly to the violation of norms of collaboration. Once, with the budget slashed by close to 15%, the management team decided it was their responsibility to make the choices of where to cut. No participation was invited. The response was close to a primal scream throughout the organization. The management team acknowledged its error, apologized, and opened up the budget process. It has taken 2 years and several principled personnel departures to soothe the backlash. Trust has not yet been fully restored. Other minor violations occur all the time, as with any set of norms. This is, of course, evidence that collaboration is becoming institutionalized, however imperfect it may be in day-to-day practice.

Conclusions

Any overall conclusions about the success of collaboration at Pine Street must be mixed. Empirically, we know that 83 of the 120 initiatives from the beginning task forces have been implemented with excellent impact. The inn is successfully holding its own in the face of a hostile public and a declining federal state budget allocation. The executive director felt confident enough to take a sabbatical this year (1991-1992) although the inn is launching a $25 million plus capital campaign. The Paul Sullivan Housing Trust—the permanent housing arm—is more integrated than ever and they are well on their way to getting "beyond shelter" to a genuine attack on the root causes of the problem.

Yet, staff turnover remains high and morale is tenuous. As newcomers arrive to replace the tired or burned out, they are not always successfully socialized to the principles and methods of collaboration. (Thus a tendency to erode a set of cumulative gains.) In addition, the snafus continue under pressure of time and daunting mission. Recently (December 1991), several members of the management team registered their perception that the acting executive director—who was the original and ongoing champion of collaboration— was being closed and arbitrary. They've scheduled a session to air the issue at their next management team meeting. Hopefully, one more agreement will be reached. As with any ideal type, the form is evolving. Like others, it seems to involve no magic answer to the question of how to build unity into any commitment while delivering organization results.

Notes

1. For an excellent history of this field, see Weisbord (1987). He tends to treat Frederick Taylor as an ancestor of process consultation, but that certainly stretches the term beyond the way we are using it here. A survey of books in the Harvard holdings find no references to *process consultation* before 1969.

2. Or vice-versa: Some cooperative efforts were defeated in the short run and flourished in the long run. James Q. Wilson gives several ones in his book on *Bureaucracy* (1989; e.g., the Marshall Plan, p. 56). Gouldner (1955) points out that the iron law of oligarchy must necessarily be matched by an iron law of democracy; and indeed the whole history of democracy is a broadscale example of this phenomenon.

3. Much of the experience of Interaction Associates, which is "cutting edge" in this field, remains available only in proprietary documents; but some papers are available from the company— see Straus (1990); Rice (1990). Other cases that Russ Eisenstat has worked on are summarized in Beer, Eisenstat, and Spector (1990a). Charles Heckscher has conducted research at Shell-Sarnia (see Heckscher, 1988; ch. 7) and Saturn.

4. On the phenomenon of successful failures, see for instance Walton (1975); Goodman (1980); Goodfellow (1981); U.S. Department of Labor (1985); Heckscher and Hall (1992).

5. See, for example, the extremely rich description of interdepartmental relations in Pettigrew (1973).

6. Jean Piaget demonstrated the inability to grasp higher-stage problems in the cognitive realm; Lawrence Kohlberg (1973) found the same in the domain of moral reasoning.

7. See, for example, Donnellon (1991).

8. Walton (1975) represents the moment at which this lesson emerged into general consciousness. There was also at that time a small effort to try a strategy of "middle-out"—but that ended no better!

9. Though we are not aware of these steps having been presented in exactly this way, it would not surprise us if they had: The basic concept of such a cycle is by now widespread. Works that explore this kind of "spiral" or cyclical pattern include Argyris (1967) (as usual, Argyris was well ahead of the game); Beer, Eisenstat, and Spector (1990a); Grobstein (1973); Pattee (1973b) (in the context of the natural sciences); Friedlander and Brown (1974); Rutherford (1975); Pava (1986); Pettigrew (1987); Spector (1987); Schlesinger Jick, Johnson, and MacIsaac (1991).

10. One older and famous model of phases in the change process is Kurt Lewin's "unfreezing-change-refreezing." This formulation does not clearly move away from a linear conception: The "refreezing" can be, and in our experience usually is, defined from the beginning by those who drive the change process, rather than being allowed to evolve with experience. The clearly evolutionary approach is relatively recent.

11. We will take up the functioning of face-to-face consensus groups in more detail below. See also Hackman (1990); Lippitt and Lippitt (1978); Schein (1969, 1990); Dyer (1987); Merry and Allerhand (1977); Fox (1987); Argyris (1970). Note that we are here referring to teams that are built from existing groupings within the bureaucratic hierarchy—such as the subordinates of a single supervisor. Cross-functional teams, as Donnellon (1991) shows, present much more fundamental difficulties.

12. Some such teams, as they mature, take an almost facetious pleasure in assigning the insignia of rank to one of their members so the "outside" will know who to deal with, while minimizing their importance internally.

13. On the difficulty of adapting team systems, see Lawler (1990); on the problem of diffusion, see Walton (1975).

14. See, for example, Tannenbaum and Rozgonyi (1986); Thimm (1980); Furlong (1977).

15. Simons (1991). See also Davis (1984) for a strong advocacy of the cascade approach.

16. For further analyses of problems with the cascade approach, see Beer, Eisenstat, and Spector (1990b); Schaffer (1988).

There are secondhand (to us) reports of possibly successful cascades, such as Xerox's massive "Leadership through Quality" effort or Johnson and Johnson's reevaluation of its mission. But Xerox's cascading program stalled out after a year or two and later took quite a different, more complex path; J&J's was highly interactive, with a great deal of "process" involved in encouraging lower levels to genuinely argue about the values, rather than adopting what came down. Thus these moved into the realm of the more complex, participatory, and nonlinear process that we are calling "collaborative." On the cascade phase of the Xerox case, see Schlesinger et al. (1991).

17. On the use of private networks by managers, see e.g., Mintzberg (1973); Kotter (1982); Stewart (1982); Pettigrew (1973).

18. On the nonhierarchical nature of real (as opposed to theoretical) strategic planning, see Bower (1970); Pettigrew (1987); Burgelman (1983); Mintzberg and McHugh (1985); Hayes (1986).

19. See Kuhn, *The Structure of Scientific Revolutions,* for a number of examples of the seeming confusion and lack of "intellectual control" that characterize the movement from one scientific paradigm to the next.

20. See Pattee (1973b). Pattee's description of programming is beginning to be dated, as experiments grow with nonhierarchical programming styles that are more effective at learning. But this development only proves the point.

21. Another way of putting this point is that collaboration helps create "double loops" that facilitate learning. See Argyris and Schon (1978).

22. A group of action researchers at MIT's Organizational Learning Center has been engaged in an ongoing action research process that has demonstrated the power of dialogue as an instrument for organizational change and learning. See Isaacs (1993) and Schein (1993).

23. Psychologists have developed a number of techniques to establish this trust with their clients; some of these cannot be applied to organization development, to the detriment of the latter. Most important is the matter of pay: As Freud noted, making people pay for your advice is an important element in getting them to take your advice on faith. But in organization consulting, with rare exceptions, only one party of those to be brought together (usually top management) is paying. Thus the rest of the parties lack the positive motive to rely on the intervenor and actually have an increased reason for suspicion.

24. See, for example Gray (1989), Spencer (1989), and Rice (1990) for treatments that converge on similar elements.

25. One description of resistance emerging after initial euphoria—what might be called the "morning-after effect"—can be found in "After Apollo's Night of Unity, Optimism Is Tempered" (1992).

26. The issue of perceived interdependence is dealt with at greater length in Chapter 2 of this book, "Defining the Post-Bureaucratic Type."

27. For an analysis of the constituency problem in changing union-management relations, see Heckscher and Hall (1992).

28. The case descriptions at the end of this chapter provide examples of the complex dynamics of these three crises.

29. Recent examples of complex dialogue on a large scale include General Electric's "Work-Out" process and AT&T's Network Systems' "Ask Yourself," both of which create highly interactive contexts for different parts of the organization to analyze the need for change, and the "future search" conferences used by a number of practitioners of sociotechnical systems redesign. See Ashkenas and Jick (1992); Weisbord (1987).

30. Though this did happen in one quasi-Marxist analysis by Kaus (1973).

31. See also Anne Donnellon's (1991) study of cross-functional product development teams, which similarly concludes that their success depends on a much more extensive change in the hierarchy than is immediately apparent.

32. See the case "Lakeville Chemical Plant" later in this book for more details.

33. Thomas Kuhn (1970), in *The Structure of Scientific Revolutions,* suggested that scientific paradigms replace one another through a similar contest for legitimacy. For a time the old and new paradigms coexist, each with their advocates, until one or the other gradually proves its superiority in explaining scientific phenomena.

34. This consultant role is analogous to that of a psychoanalyst as described by Freud: The core of the therapeutic process is that the therapist *refuses to be drawn into* the roles and interaction patterns that the patient projects but instead *steadily* presents a cultural pattern or vision that provides an anchor for development.

35. On large-scale collaborative processes see, for example, Williams (1982); Weisbord (1987); Gray (1989); Forester (1989); Van De Ven (1980).

36. Or, we might add, "storming-norming-performing." There is a small literature of stages in organization change (as opposed to repeated phases within it), but it has been fragmentary and not focused on the particular transformation we are examining, from bureaucratic to post-

bureaucratic systems. Therefore its concepts have not been very useful for practitioners or theorists in this field.

37. The explicit prohibition on discussions of contract-related items seemed to be a less significant restriction.

38. U. S. Department of Labor (1985).

39. On the constituency problem, see Heckscher and Hall (1992).

40. The process was developed by two external consultants, Michael Beer and Russell Eisenstat, at Becton Dickinson's request.

41. This is consistent with the findings of Beer, Eisenstat, and Spector (1990a).

42. See Harrington (1984), Hirsch (1989), and West (1993).

43. Doyle and Straus, *How to Make Meetings Work* (1976).

44. The role of process manager is critical to the success of any collaborative process. We have found the neglect of this role to be a serious mistake.

References

After Apollo's night of unity, optimism is tempered. (1992, December 19). *New York Times*, p. 25.

Argyris, C. (1967, February). Today's problems with tomorrow's organizations. *Journal of Management Studies*, pp. 31-55.

Argyris, C. (1970). *Intervention theory and method: Behavioral science view*. Reading, MA: Addison-Wesley.

Argyris, C., & Schon, D. A. (1978). *Organizational learning: Theory of action perspective*. Reading, MA: Addison-Wesley.

Ashkenas, R. N., & Jick, T. D. (1992). From dialogue to action in GE Work-Out developmental learning in a change process. *Research in Organization Change and Development, 6*, 267-287.

Beer, M., Eisenstat, R. A., & Spector, B. (1990a). *The critical path to corporate renewal*. Boston, MA: Harvard Business School Press.

Beer, M., Eisenstat, R., & Spector, B. (1990b, November-December). Why change programs don't produce change. *Harvard Business Review*, pp. 158-166.

Bower, J. L. (1970). *Managing the resource allocation process: A study of corporate planning and investment*. Boston, MA: Harvard Graduate School of Business Administration.

Burgelman, R. A. (1983). A process model of internal corporate venturing in the diversified major firm. *Administrative Science Quarterly, 28*, 223-224.

Davis, S. M. (1984). *Managing corporate culture*. Cambridge, MA: Ballinger.

Donnellon, A. (1991). *The meaning of teamwork*. Mimeo, Harvard Business School, Boston.

Doyle, M. & Straus, D. (1976). *How to make meetings work*. San Francisco: Berkeley.

Dyer, W. G. (1987). *Team building: issues and alternatives*. Reading, MA: Addison-Wesley.

Forester, J. (1989). *Planning in the face of power*. Berkeley, CA: University of California Press.

Fox, W. M. (1987). *Effective group problem solving: How to broaden participation, improve decision making, and increase commitment to action*. San Francisco, CA: Jossey-Bass.

Friedlander, F., & Brown, L. D. (1974). Organization development. *Annual Review of Psychology, 25*, 313-341.

Furlong, J. C. (1977). *Labor in the boardroom: Peaceful revolution*. Princeton, NJ: Dow Jones Books.

Goodfellow, M. (1981). Quality control circle programs: What works and what doesn't. Chicago, IL: Mimeo, University Research Center.

Goodman, P. S. (1980, August). Realities of improving the quality of work life: Quality of Work Life projects in the 1980s. *Labor Law Journal, 31,*(8), 487-494.

Gouldner, A. W. (1955). Metaphysical pathos and the theory of bureaucracy. *American Political Science Review, 49,* 496-507.

Gray, B. (1989). *Collaborating: Finding common ground for multiparty problems.* San Francisco, CA: Jossey-Bass.

Grobstein, C. (1973). Hierarchical order and neogenesis. In H. H. Pattee (Ed.), *Hierarchy theory: The challenge of complex systems* (ch. 2). New York: George Braziller.

Hackman, J. R. (Ed.). (1990). *Groups that work (and those that don't): Creating conditions for effective teamwork.* San Francisco, CA: Jossey-Bass.

Harrington, M. (1984). *The new American poverty.* New York: Penguin.

Hayes, R. H. (1986, April 20). Why strategic planning goes awry. *New York Times.*

Heckscher, C. C. (1988). *The new unionism: Employee involvement in the changing corporation.* New York: Basic Books.

Heckscher, C., & Hall, L. (1992, January 3-5). Two levels of mutual-gains intervention. *Industrial Relations Research Association, Proceedings of the 44th Annual Meeting* (pp. 160-178). Madison, WI: IRRA.

Hirsch, K. (1989). *Songs from the alley.* New York: Ticknor & Fields.

Isaacs, W. N. (1993, Autumn). Taking flight: Dialogue, collective thinking and organizational learning. *Organizational Dynamics,* pp. 24-39.

Kaus, R. M. (1973). *Job enrichment & capitalist hierarchy.* Cambridge, MA: Harvard University.

Kolberg, L. (1973). Continuities and discontinuities in childhood and adult moral development revisited. In P. Baltes & K. W. Schaie (Eds.), *Life-span developmental psychology: Research and theory.* New York: Academic Press.

Kotter, J. P. (1982, November-December). What effective general managers really do. *Harvard Business Review,* pp. 156-167.

Kuhn, T. (1970). *The structure of scientific revolution.* Chicago, IL: University of Chicago Press.

Lawler, E. E., III. (1990, Autumn). The new plant revolution revisited. *Organizational Dynamics,* pp. 5-14.

Lippitt, G., & Lippitt, R. (1978). *The consulting process in action.* La Jolla, CA: University Associates.

Merry, U., & Allerhand, M. E. (1977). *Developing teams & organizations: Handbook for consultants.* Reading, MA: Addison-Wesley.

Mills, D. Q. (1991). *Rebirth of the corporation.* New York: Wiley.

Mintzberg, H. (1973). *The nature of managerial work.* New York: Harper & Row.

Mintzberg, H., & McHugh, A. (1985). Strategy formation in an adhocracy. *Administrative Science Quarterly, 30,* 160-197.

Pattee, H. H. (Ed.). (1973a). *Hierarchy theory: The challenge of complex systems.* New York: George Braziller.

Pattee, H. H. (1973b). Postscript: Unsolved problems and potential applications of hierarchy theory. In H. H. Pattee (Ed.), *Hierarchy theory: The challenge of complex systems* (pp. 129-156). New York: George Braziller.

Pava, C. (1986). New strategies of systems change: Reclaiming nonsynoptic methods. *Human Relations, 39,*(7), 615-633.

Pettigrew, A. M. (1973). *The politics of organizational decision-making.* London: Tavistock.

Pettigrew, A. M. (Ed.). (1987). *The management of strategic change.* New York: Basil Blackwell.

Rice, T. J. (1990). Managing organizational change: The challenge and the promise. Cambridge, MA: Interaction Associates.

Rutherford, S. V. (n.d., c. 1975). The Leland experience: Educational change through institutional renewal. Mimeo.

Schaffer, R. H. (1988). *The breakthrough strategy.* Cambridge, MA: Ballinger.

Schein, E. H. (1969). *Process consultation.* Reading, MA: Addison-Wesley.

Schein, E. H. (1990, Spring). A general philosophy of helping: Process consultation. *Sloan Management Review, 57,* 57-64.

Schein, E. H. (1993, Autumn). On dialogue, culture, and organizational learning. *Organizational Dynamics,* pp. 40-51.

Schlesinger, L., Jick, T., Johnson, A. B., & MacIsaac, L. A. (1991, Rev. June 19). *Xerox Corporation: Leadership through quality (A) & (B).* Harvard Business School Case 9-490-008.

Simons, R. (1991, October). *How new top managers use formal systems as levers of strategic renewal.* Paper presented to 11th Annual International Strategic Management Society Conference, Toronto.

Spector, B. (1987, May 5). *HRM transformations.* Mimeo, draft. MIT, Sloan School.

Spencer, L. J. (1989). *Winning through participation: Meeting the challenge of corporate change with the technology of participation.* Dubuque, IA: Kendall/Hunt.

Stewart, R. (1982). Managerial behavior: How research has changed the traditional picture.

Straus, D. (1990, May). Process management: Planning to plan to do. Mimeo. Interaction Associates.

Tannenbaum, A. S., & Rozgonyi, T. (Codirectors). (1986). *Authority and reward in organizations: An international research\.* Ann Arbor, MI: Survey Research Center.

Thimm, A. M. (1980). *The false promise of co-determination: The changing nature of European workers' participation.* Lexington, MA: D. C. Heath.

U.S. Department of Labor. (1985). *Quality of work life: AT&T and CWA examine the process after three years.* Washington, DC: Department of Labor, Bureau of Labor-Management Relations.

Van De Ven, A. (1980). Problem solving, planning, and innovation (Part 1: Test of the Program Planning Model; Part 2: Speculations for theory and practice). *Human Relations, 33,* 711-740, 757-779.

Walton, R. E. (1975, Winter). The diffusion of new work structures: Explaining why success didn't take. *Organizational Dynamics,* pp. 3-22.

Weisbord, M. R. (1987). *Productive workplaces: Organizing and managing for meaning, dignity, and community.* San Francisco, CA: Jossey-Bass.

Williams, T. A. (1982). Search conference design.

Wilson, J. Q. (1989). *Bureaucracy: What government agencies do and why they do it.* New York: Basic Books.

7 THE PARADOX OF QUALITY MANAGEMENT

Commitment, Ownership, and Control

Janice A. Klein

Total Quality Management (TQM), with its legendary emphasis on utilizing the knowledge of all employees, could be seen as one of the most prevalent and positive examples of the post-bureaucratic organization currently in practice. It has certainly been touted as an essential element of worldwide competitiveness. After Japan showed how quality could win market share away from entrenched industry giants such as in the U.S. automobile industry, American managers concluded that their futures depended on TQM. But recently, a series of reports (e.g., "The Cracks in Quality," 1992 and "Total Quality Is Termed Only Partial Success" [Fuchsberg, 1992]), have noted the inability of Western companies to successfully introduce TQM. A number of potential reasons have been cited, including inexperience, lack of top management support, a desire to find a quick fix, and unwillingness to focus on the long term.

A common thread, however, in successful implementations is the ability of an organization to involve all levels of the workforce in the quest for TQM. This requires engendering employee commitment toward the improvement process. The methods for generating such commitment, however, vary across companies and across nations, particularly Japan and the United States. In the United States, it has been generally accepted that if employees are to feel commitment toward their job, they must possess some sense of ownership

AUTHOR'S NOTE: The author would like to thank Harvey Kolodny and Therese Flaherty for their helpful comments.

over decisions that affect their workplace. This has implications for how teams and individual team members' jobs are designed.

Another underlying principle of TQM is the reduction of process variability through improved control over the process. This requires employee acceptance and conformance to established standards or procedures, which may not be of a particular employee's choice. As a result, a paradox can be created between the need for operating discipline and employee empowerment over operating decisions. If ignored, this paradox can lead to confusion within the workforce over potentially competing objectives, namely, empowerment versus conformance. This chapter focuses more on this paradox than TQM per se. But once managers begin to address this paradox, they will have a better chance of implementing TQM in North America.

The chapter begins by looking at the various sources of employee commitment and the link between commitment and ownership. It then compares team structures in Japan and the United States to better understand how commitment is generated at the workplace. Next, the need for control is discussed. Last, the chapter concludes with a look at how control fits with Japanese-versus American-style commitment. This, in turn, has significant implications for the success of TQM in American organizations.

Generating Commitment

Walton (1985) popularized the use of the term *commitment* to describe a comprehensive set of organizational principles and practices designed to create a partnership between labor and management to improve organizational performance. But what really is commitment and how is it generated? The *American Heritage Dictionary* defines commitment as "the state of being bound emotionally or intellectually to some course of action." To a large extent, employees' commitment to their jobs, and, in particular, to continuous improvement is based on their perceived psychological contract toward work, that is, what they expect to receive in exchange for the effort they expend on the job. The sources of this commitment stem from organizational loyalty, manager-subordinate relationships, peer relationships, and/or the work itself.

Organizational Loyalty

Some employees are committed to outstanding job performance and continuous improvement because they believe that their company will reward them for their efforts in terms of employment and opportunity for skill development and promotions. They trust that their company will provide them with an equal or better job if they find a way to eliminate their current work activities. Here, the reciprocity is at a *systems level*, that is, employees believe that the organizational policies are looking out for their best interests. Even if they dislike their job assignment or their immediate supervisor, they will do a good job because they are convinced that the "top management" (via their actions in expanding the business, which translate into future job opportunities) or the company's human resource practices (e.g., no lay-off policies) will fairly reward them for their contribution.[1]

Company loyalty has been a cornerstone of traditional Japanese culture. This is, in part, due to the messages sent by Japanese corporate leaders. For example, Honda patriarch Soichiro Honda recognized that an organization's main purpose was to serve its people, rather than its people serving the organization (Taylor, 1991). Furthermore, as Nakane (1973) noted,

> The attitude of the employer is expressed by the spirit of the common saying, "the enterprise is the people." This affirms the belief that employer and employee are bound as one by fate in conditions which produce a tie between man and man often as firm and close as that between husband and wife. Such a relationship is manifestly not a purely contractual one between employer and employee; the employee is already a member of his own family, and all members of his family are naturally included in the larger company "family." (p. 15)

Although many tend to regard such policies as uniquely Japanese, there are several U.S. companies, including Motorola and Poloraid, that have had long-standing policies, including guaranteed employment security, that have traditionally generated intense company loyalty. In addition, many policies, typically labeled paternalistic, create a sense of loyalty to one's company.

Manager-Subordinate Relationships

Personal relationships between an employee and his or her supervisor often lead to high levels of commitment. As Kotter (1982) noted, a key general manager activity is building relationships between superiors and subordinates. In so doing, many managers incur the loyalty of their employees by looking out for their best interests, even if it means buffering employees from upper management or company policies. Here the psychological contract is based on a *personal relationship* between a manager/supervisor and his or her employee or work group. When this occurs, employees will do, within reason, whatever their manager requests of then. This reciprocity or mutual dependence (Emerson, 1962; Gouldner, 1954) has been referred to as "deal-making" (Klein, 1984) or "effort bargains" (Kaboolian, 1990).

Peer Relationships

Relationships between group members can also lead to high levels of commitment to the work of the team. Peer group pressure can play a major role, particularly in self-managing work groups in which peers must look out for each other's interests in the absence of a supervisor. Here, employees may strive to find ways to make their jobs more efficient if they see that it will improve the working conditions of their peers. As with manager-subordinate relationships, there can be a fair amount of "trades" made between workers. Some employees may find certain jobs more appealing, whereas their peers may prefer other assignments; as a group they are able to cover all activities more efficiently by swapping assignments.

There is also a sense of belonging to a group that generates a level of commitment to one's peers, often placing the group's interests above one's own. Such group interest appears to be more influential in Japanese than American culture:

> The power and influence of the group not only affects and enters into the individual's actions; it alters even his ideas and ways of thinking. Individual autonomy is minimized. When this happens, the point where group or public life ends and where private life begins no longer can be distinguished. There are those who perceive this as a danger, an encroachment on their dignity as individuals; on the other hand, others feel safer in total group-consciousness. There seems little doubt that the latter group is in the majority. . . . With group-consciousness so highly developed there is almost no social life outside the particular group on which an individual's major economic life depends. The individual's every problem must be solved within this frame. Thus group participation is simple and unitary. (Nakane, 1973, pp. 10-11)

The Work Itself

Many employees also feel a sense of commitment to work itself, that is, they are personally committed to doing a good job because the job provides them with a sense of accomplishment. As such, the psychological contract is with the work and is based on the employees' perception as to their *individual* ability to achieve their desired outcome. Since human beings vary in their motivations, these outcomes are very personal in nature and can cover a broad spectrum of desires. Some employees are motivated by money and will strive to improve their output if they perceive a direct link between their job performance and their compensation or future promotion; this is particularly prevalent in individual piecework incentive factories. Other employees have personal pride in their craft or profession; it is out of a sense of personal dignity that they try to improve their performance.

However, some employees feel a sense of commitment when they have an opportunity to personally influence or contribute to job-related outcomes. To this end, Hackman and Oldham (1980) identified three key conditions necessary for jobs to generate high levels of internal work motivation—meaningfulness of work, responsibility for outcomes, and knowledge of results.

Ownership

Over the years, commitment and ownership have become almost synonymous in the organizational behavioral literature. It has also been argued that a sense of ownership leads to commitment. The underlying premise is that if you have a stake in the outcome (that is, ownership), you will be more inclined to put your heart and soul into achieving that outcome (i.e., commitment). Here, commitment is linked primarily to the work itself; company policies and management styles must be congruent with the work system, but they are not the primary source of "ownership." Since most employees are not owner-operators, in the purest sense of the term, i.e., personal ownership of the enterprise (excluding ESOPs), several proxies for ownership have developed:

1. Autonomy. Hackman and Oldham (1980) identified autonomy as the core job characteristic that fosters increased feelings of "experienced responsibility for outcomes of work." To this end, they argued that scheduling one's own work and determining one's own work methods are determinants of the degree of one's autonomy, or ownership of one's tasks.

2. Voice in Decision Making. Hackman (1986) used the term *self-managing* to describe work units whose "members have responsibility not only for executing the task but also for monitoring and managing their own performance." Others have used the labels "self-directed work teams" (Orsburn, Moran, Musselwhite, & Zenger, 1990), "high-commitment teams" (Walton, 1985), and "high performance teams" (Hanna, 1988)—the list goes on and on and on! The basic premise is that employees who make decisions about their daily activities will feel more ownership toward those activities.

3. Creatorship. At this level of "ownership," employees become "organizational citizens," who not only manage their daily activities but also co-create their work environment (Frank, Rehm, & Pasmore, 1991). This is similar to Hackman's (1986) self-designing groups.

4. Gainsharing/Profit Sharing. Short of providing a stake in the company, many organizations have begun to compensate workers for production gains. Whereas gainsharing strives to create a sense of workforce ownership over their operation's performance, profit sharing provides a larger sense of ownership over the company as a whole.

Commitment Without Ownership

Many observers—journalists, practitioners, as well as some academics—have assumed that *teams* and *employee empowerment* mean the same thing in both Japan and North America. The words are the same, but the use of the words is quite different. For example, Japanese lean production plants[2] are noted for their team-based production systems where employees are cross-trained to perform all jobs in the team. In addition, team members are responsible for quality, minor maintenance, and continuous improvement. Similarly, production workers in U.S. plants, designed around team structure (e.g. "high commitment" or socio-technical work systems), are trained to do a wide range of team tasks and assume responsibility for the daily management of their team. But one American manager who had the unique opportunity to have worked in both a lean production Japanese transplant operation and a U.S. corporation's high commitment plant commented that team members at the Japanese transplant factory were "more committed" than employees at the high commitment plant. He went on to say, *"There is less ownership but not less commitment.* It's like the difference between leasing and owning your home. You are committed to taking care of the house in both cases" (emphasis added). If employees in the Japanese transplant operation did not feel a sense of ownership, what then was the source of their commitment?

Commitment in traditional Japanese companies appears to be based on loyalty—first to the nation, second to the company, third to the family, but all are closely intertwined. As Gregory (1985) noted,

Efficiency became a transcendental cause . . . the purpose of efficiency was not mainly to increase profits of the enterprise for the enrichment of shareholders, but rather to build a "rich nation and strong army" . . . it was in the national interest, it took preference over short term profitability in the hierarchy of management objectives. . . .

Indeed, every Japanese school child came to understand the compelling logic that, since Japan has no natural resources, the nation has to survive from the wealth it creates in production. (pp. 10-11)

Thus, when Japanese employees work hard for their nation, they, in turn, work hard for the good of their company and ultimately for themselves. The homogeneity of the workforce helps to make this a widely held view. This is further substantiated by Vogel (1987) in his description of Japanese ideology:

> Employees are expected to work hard and to make some sacrifices when it is in the company's interest. In turn, management will look after the interests of employees, help them grow and develop, and give them a substantial share of the benefits of the company's success. (p. 157)

Womack, Jones, and Roos (1990) also came to a similar conclusion concerning employee commitment in Japanese lean production operations:

> Lean production, by contrast, is inherently a system of reciprocal obligation. Workers share a fate with their employer, suppliers share a fate with the assembler. When the system works properly, it generates a willingness to participate actively and to initiate the continuous improvements that are at the very heart of leanness. (pp. 248-249)

Although one can find American companies where employees believe that their company or management is looking out for their best interests, the vast majority of American workers are quite skeptical of top management's motivations. As a result, a greater emphasis is placed on generating commitment through the design of work itself. This "American-style" commitment is also an outgrowth of our individualist society. We value autonomy and tend to believe first in the individual and second in a personal relationship that we have some control over; only as a last resort do we place any faith in a larger organization to look after our own interests. Trust is a key factor here. Company loyalty and personal relationships require placing trust in others and having less personal control over one's own destiny. Furthermore, the company policies that breed loyalty depend on financial stability, company growth, and a willingness by the corporation to place greater emphasis on the long-term prosperity of the firm, while commitment based on personal relationships (manager-subordinate or peer) requires a supportive corporate culture. Both of these are often in short supply in many American firms. It should be noted that many contemporary Japanese corporations are encountering similar difficulties in engendering trust as their economy weakens. (Schlesinger & Kanabayashi, 1992). Hence, it appears that organizational loyalty may be difficult to sustain with today's economic pressures.

"High Commitment" Versus
Lean Production Team Structures[3]

A closer look at "high commitment" versus lean production team-based organizations reveals significant differences, particularly in the level of decision making delegated to the teams and in the types of tasks assigned to team members. For example, the idea of eliminating first-line supervisors and holding a team of production workers responsible for daily management decisions is foreign to Japanese idealogy, as Vogel (1987) noted:

> Workers do not share in management. Management is often frank in sharing basic information about a company, but in the end the decisions are in the hands of management. This is considered necessary for timely and effective responses, and it is generally accepted that management is looking out for the interest of workers. (p. 157)

First-level managers are highly valued in Japanese operations because they are the conduit for communications and the ultimate caretaker of the company's culture. They also play a pivotal role in training and quality circle activities, including assisting and guiding employees in the submission of suggestions for process improvements (Yasuda, 1991). Jaques (1991), in defending the need for a managerial hierarchy, noted,

> The Deming miracle in Japan was achieved by building quality, just-in-time working, and continuous improvement into the process, that is, instituting accountability in the managerial system, where these ideas flourish to this day. (pp. 538-539)

Another major difference lies in the type of tasks assigned to team members, as shown in Figure 7.1, which compares traditional Tayloristic and craft models with lean and high-commitment team structures. Production jobs in high-commitment operations designed around sociotechnical principles typically include such vertical tasks as work scheduling and job assignment, selection of new team members, and administrative record keeping. As a result, team members get an opportunity to broaden their understanding of the business in general and "manage their team" as if it were a small business, and organizations are able to minimize overhead costs by reassigning tasks typically performed by support personnel to production teams.

Production jobs in lean production factories, however, rarely include many of these tasks. The manager in the Japanese transplant operations who described high levels of commitment without ownership described what he observed to be the differences in job design:

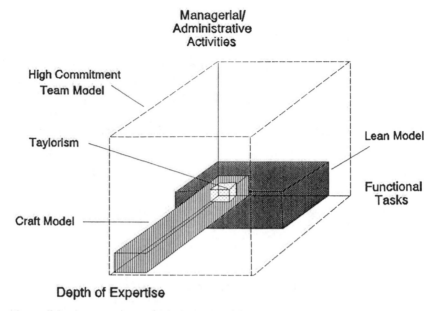

Figure 7.1. A comparison of job design models
SOURCE: Adapted from Klein (1993)

There is an equal amount of communication in both plants relative to sales and quality. Team member jobs at [the Japanese transplant] have a narrower focus in that they do not worry about suppliers or production control, but they do more vertical tasks related to the improvement cycle, such as, housekeeping (4S's), maintenance (adjust & modify), Kaizen, and tracking scrap. Team members at [the Japanese transplant] have more process ability to modify the job. Although team members at [the sociotechnical plant] had a broader understanding of the plant, all the vertical tasks diluted their responsibility. As a result, they were not as focused. Employees at [the Japanese transplant] have a higher sense of urgency relative to quality, efficiency, and getting production out.

Although lean production workers are not directly involved in broad business-related activities, they do attend training sessions on such subjects as sales and customer demands. This knowledge, coupled with on-the-job rotational training across multiple teams (especially immediate customer-supplier teams within the factory), develops the skills needed for generating meaningful process improvements (Koike, 1987). In addition, Japanese production workers are often given a high level of employee discretion relative to work methods. Koike (1987) noted that it is often said that "there are no manuals in Japanese industry." But this, he noted, is a bit misleading:

When new machinery is introduced, there is always a manual that describes how to operate a particular machine or conduct a job. As time passes, however, workers are apt to devise better ways to do the job and surpass the manual. This is why it is usually said there are not manuals in Japanese firms. Again, this shows that in practice workers on the shop floor have the power to change the way jobs are conducted, which is one of the foundations of QC circles. (p. 307)

Employee discretion over work methods, however, must fall within the boundaries of standardized work methods (Adler, 1992; Klein, 1991). To the casual observer, standardized work appears to be a reincarnation of Taylor's scientific management: employees must strictly adhere to detailed job procedures. There are, however, two significant differences:

1. *Dynamic Taylorism*: Taylorism advocates "one best method" and that method remains fixed until there is a change in equipment, product/process specifications, etc. In contrast, standardized work is based on stabilizing the procedure so it can then be improved upon. Hence, the "best method" is a moving target. Standardization serves two purposes: (1) it is the basis for learning (Adler, 1992), and (2) it prevents backsliding, that is, it "locks in" improvements (JUSE Problem Solving Research Group, 1991).

2. *Taylorism Without an Ego*: Traditionally, industrial engineers were assumed to be the sole experts in setting work methods. In contrast, at Toyota, team members are taught the mechanics of setting standards. It is the team members, themselves (at times, in conjunction with engineers), who establish the methods. This recognizes that a major source of knowledge concerning the process resides in the people doing the job.

Both of these dimensions suggest that employees in lean production operations possess a great degree of control over their work methods. But in contrast to Hackman and Oldham's (1980) definition of autonomy (i.e., *individual* control over work methods), standardized work requires that employees strictly conform to the work methods that are developed through *group* consensus. This is necessary to assure process control.

Control

An underlying premise of TQM is the reduction of non-value-added activities that stem from any variability within the process. Hence, the JUSE (Japanese Union of Scientists and Engineers) Problem Solving Research Group (1991) noted, "It goes without saying that with quality control comes price control, production control, delivery control, safety control, *human resource control*, and other types of control" (pp. 5-6, emphasis added). That statement encompasses a broad range of activities to make the point that variability occurs throughout an organization, not only on the shop floor. There are two generic areas—organizational control and operational control—that must be considered in achieving successful TQM.

Organizational Control

Organizations must maintain some form of behavior control to assure organizational, as opposed to solely individual, goals are attained. Traditionally, this was achieved through rules and policies. Walton (1985) used the phrase "management by control" to characterize traditional workforce management, where management "controlled" every aspect of an employee's workday. Organizational control need not be oppressive, however. Empowered organizations, that is, those designed to generate high levels of employee commitment, use norms, values, or principles as controlling mechanisms (Fisher, 1986). Walton would call this "managing by commitment," which amounts to providing control without being controlling.

Operational Control

Control in an operations management sense refers to process control, where process variability is held to a minimum. Juran and Gryna (1970) used the term to refer to "the process we employ in order to meet standards. This process consists of observing our actual performance, comparing this performance with some standard, and then taking action if the observed performance is significantly different from the standard" (p. 3).

In both cases, to have control, one must have discipline. But there is discipline in the sense of control or punishment, and there is also discipline in a way of thinking. A look at *Webster's* dictionary reveals six definitions for discipline:

1. (Obs.) Instruction
2. A branch of knowledge involving research
3. Training that corrects, molds, strengthens, or perfects
4. Punishment; chastisement
5. Control gained by enforcing obedience or order, as in school or army; hence, orderly conduct
6. Rule or system of rules affecting conduct or action

Unfortunately, we tend to focus on the second half of the list as opposed to the first three definitions, which denote those aspects of discipline necessary for continuous improvement and organizational learning. For example, Peter Senge (1990) uses the term to describe "a body of theory and technique that must be studied and mastered to be put into practice. A discipline is a developmental path for acquiring certain skills or competencies" (p. 10). Although both uses of the term may be needed to assure organizational and operational control, managers have a choice as to which to emphasize.

Controlling behavior, however, often creates a tension between the goals of an individual and those of the organization as a whole. Juran (1964) recognized the potential for this conflict and likened it to that of political control where citizens consent to be governed by a central body. Problems, according to Juran, arise primarily where the ruling body, in this case management, does not take into consideration the needs of the employees:

> "Aren't controls an infringement of the freedom of the individual?" Indeed they are. The individual starts it by bartering quite a chunk of his freedom for a job. He barters another chunk to belong to a team. If the manager responds by living up to his end of the bargain, there are no hard feelings—everyone has gained. If the manager fails, the loss of freedom becomes conspicuous, and the trouble begins. (p. 351)

Just as there are several sources of commitment, there are also different ways to achieve organizational and/or operational control. In many ways, they parallel the four sources of commitment discussed earlier. An organization can achieve control through centralized rules or principles. Managers can also impose control via their managerial style. Team dynamics can impose control over individual team members. And, lastly, individual job procedures control how employees perform individual tasks.

The choice of method in achieving control and cultural conditioning can have a major impact on employee commitment. For example, in traditional Japanese culture, individual interests are secondary to the best interests of the group. Nakane (1973) described the importance of the group in Japanese society:

> The limits of individual freedom of action are fixed in such a way as to ensure that the activity of the individual will not breach group limits. Freedom is allowed only in directions allowed for in group decisions. Action should be always for the group, not calculated in terms of the individual. (p. 86)

The downside is "group think," where individual ideas are lost. Also, if the culture has created a need for conformity, dissent from group norms is discouraged. This is often the case in traditional Japanese society, as noted by Nakane (1973):

> In particular, a junior takes every care to avoid any open confrontation with his superior. Such attempts lead to the point that a flatly negative form is rarely employed in conversation: one would prefer to be silent than utter words such as "no" or "I disagree." The avoidance of such open and bald negative expression is rooted in the fear that it might disrupt the harmony and order of the group, that it might hurt the feelings of a superior and that, in extreme circumstances, it could involve the risk of being cast out from the group as an undesirable member. Even if there are others who share a negative opinion, it is unlikely that they will join together and openly express it, for the fear that this might jeopardize their position as desirable group members. Indeed, it often happens that, once a man has been labelled as one whose opinions run contrary to those of the group, he will find himself opposed on any issue and ruled out by majority opinion. No one will defend him in any circumstance. (pp. 36-37)

The difference between Japanese and American work systems was succinctly summarized by a recent visitor to Japan who observed, "Japanese work systems put a stress on individuals, while American individualism puts a stress on companies." The issue is not to replace one system with the other, but to reduce the stress on both individuals and companies.

Commitment and Control

The question is not "control versus commitment," but rather how to develop commitment while maintaining operating control. The paradox of commitment and control is what Roethlisberger (1977) called a false dichotomy: "the overcomplication in thought of an oversimplification in fact" (p. 139). To begin with, the concepts of commitment and control have been over simplified by a romantic view of Japanese manufacturing practices (Zipkin, 1991). Many have erroneously assumed that the employee participation described by TQM experts is equivalent to employee involvement or empowerment in high-commitment work systems (Klein, 1989, 1991). From a control perspective, there is also a need to differentiate between variability resulting from random versus assignable causes; random causes are unavoidable and cannot be eliminated (JUSE, 1991). TQM aims to eliminate variability due to assignable causes, while utilizing individual employee knowledge and commitment to manage random variability. As Lund, Bishop, Newman, and Saltzman (1993) recently noted, "Control means investing a person with responsibility, know-how, and means to intervene in a process when conditions indicate the need to do so" (p. 274).

The paradox is also an overcomplication because it only arises when commitment becomes synonymous with individual ownership. Provided the commitment is based on loyalty, control is a duty that employees are expected to perform. Similarly, when commitment is based on a relationship with a superior, control is an exchange employees are usually willing to accept. Further, when commitment is based on a relationship with peers, controls are accepted as a method to maintain harmony within the group. But when commitment is tied to individual ownership and autonomy, a conflict can arise.

What then can U.S. managers who want to preserve American individualism while instituting controls necessary for TQM do? As mentioned earlier, loyalty to the company is not a uniquely Japanese concept; many American companies have generated high levels of employee loyalty through longstanding human resource policies which protect the interests of employees. These companies tie the long-term job security of employees to the need for process controls and TQM.

If a company is not in the position to provide employment guarantees, its managers must find other means to convince employees that they are in the same boat together. This may include an equality of sacrifice in both salaried and hourly workforce reductions, a narrowing of the gap between executive and shop floor compensation, an increase in the use of ESOPs, and a greater sharing of profits. Where production levels fluctuate, managers must find innovative ways to minimize the negative consequences toward the workforce. Several U.S. team-based operations are staffing their factories so that up to 25% of team members' time, on average, is spent in training or performing vertical tasks. As a result, employees vary their daily tasks based on production loads. Another company is establishing a core of part-time employees who agree to be available on-call in exchange for training and benefits.

Where circumstances minimize the opportunity for organizations to engender company loyalty[4], managers and supervisors can still build significant commitment to continuous improvement through manager-subordinate loyalty; often employees follow managers to new assignments, both within or outside a firm. Such loyalty must be built over time; managers must consistently demonstrate that they recognize the value of their employees' knowledge and contribution.

Job design can also be used to generate employee commitment, primarily to the work itself. The involvement of workers in broader business activities, such as is done in many high-commitment work systems, provides an avenue for educating team members as to the importance of TQM. Increasingly, team members, especially in continuous process operations, are being given increased responsibility for costs, process stability, and troubleshooting through the use of computer controls. In such operations, operators are provided with sufficient data to make judgment calls that were once the exclusive domain of managers and engineers.

But TQM does put limits on individual autonomy. As such, more weight must be placed on collective autonomy of teams with a recognition that there are limits to independent decision making (Klein, 1991). Employees are adults and understand the responsibilities of working within an organization and the need for coordination and, at times, compromise. Commitment to TQM and continuous improvement is ultimately pride in doing a good job. Hence, it is commitment to work itself, but not in the traditional sense of individual autonomy or ownership. Commitment must be based on relationships, both to one's manager or to one's peer group as well as to oneself. This, in turn, relies on a supportive organizational culture, human resource policies (e.g., performance evaluation and reward systems) that reinforce commitment, and management/leadership styles that promote a TQM team environment.

Notes

1. Similarly, some employees tie their loyalty to their trade union. Here, union members will follow their leadership's work-related recommendations because they believe the union will look out for their best interests.

2. *Lean production,* which has become synonymous with the Toyota Production System, was the term used by Womack, Jones, and Roos (1990) to describe the philosophies and practices of Japanese automobile manufacturing companies.

3. This section draws heavily on Klein (1993).

4. Some companies, such as fast-food chains, recognize the realities and benefits of employee turnover in certain jobs.

References

Adler, P. S. (1992). The learning bureaucracy: New United Motor Manufacturing, Inc. In B. M. Staw & L. L. Cummings (Eds.), *Research in organizational behavior.* Greenwich, CT: JAI.

Emerson, R. M. (1962). Power-dependence relations. *American Sociological Review, 27,* 31-40.

Fisher, K. K. (1986, Fall). Management roles in the implementation of participative management systems. *Human Resource Management,* pp. 459-479.

Frank, G., Rehm, R., & Pasmore, W. (1991, June). *Developing citizenship for the active organization.* Ecology of Work Conference Proceedings.

Fuchsberg, G. (1992, October 1). Total quality is termed partial success. *The Wall Street Journal,* p. B1.

Gouldner, A. W. (1954). *Patterns of industrial bureaucracy,* Glencoe, IL: Free Press.

Gregory, G. (1985). *The logic of Japanese enterprise.* Institute of Comparative Culture Business Series, Bulletin No. 92. Tokyo: Sophia University.

Hackman, J. R. (1986). The psychology of self-management in organizations. In M. S. Pallak & R. O. Perloff (Eds.), *Psychology and work: Productivity, change, and employment.* (pp. 89-136). Washington, DC: American Psychological Association.

Hackman, J. R., & Oldham, G. (1980). *Work redesign.* Reading, MA: Addison-Wesley.

Hanna, D. P. (1988). *Designing organizations for high performance,* Reading, MA: Addison-Wesley.

Jaques, E. (1991, October). Managerial leadership: The key to good organization. *The World & I,* pp. 535-542.

Juran, J. M. (1964). *Managerial breakthrough: A new concept of the manager's job.* New York: McGraw-Hill.

Juran, J. M., & Gryna, F. M., Jr. (1970). *Quality planning and analysis: From product development through use.* New York: McGraw-Hill.

JUSE Problem Solving Research Group (Ed.). (1991). *TQC solutions, the 14-step process, volume I: The problem-solving process.* Cambridge, MA: Productivity Press.

Kaboolian, L. (1990). *Shifting gears: Auto workers assess the transformation of their industry.* University of Michigan, Ph.D. dissertation.

Klein, J. A. (1984, September-October). Why supervisors resist employee involvement. *Harvard Business Review.*

Klein, J. A. (1989, March-April). The human costs of manufacturing reform. *Harvard Business Review,* pp. 87-95.

Klein, J. A. (1991). A reexamination of autonomy in light of new manufacturing practices. *Human Relations, 44*(1), 21-38.

Klein, J. A. (1993). Teams. In J. Klein & J. Miller (Eds.), *The American edge* (pp. 70-88). New York: McGraw-Hill.

Koike, K. (1987). Human resource development and labor-management relations. In K. Yamamura & Y. Yasuba (Eds.), *The political economy of Japan—Volume 1: The domestic transformation* (pp. 289-330). Stanford, CA: Stanford University Press.

Kotter, J. P. (1982). *The general managers.* New York: The Free Press.

Lund, R. T., Bishop, A. B., Newman, A. E., & Salzman, H. (1993). Designed to work: Production systems and people. Englewood Cliffs, NJ: Prentice Hall.

Nakane, C. (1973). *Japanese Society.* Tokyo: Tuttle.

Orsburn, J. D., Moran, L., Musselwhite, E., & Zenger, J. H. (1990). *Self-directed work teams: The new American challenge.* Homewood, IL: Business One Irwin.

Roethlisberger, F. J. (1977). *The elusive phenomena.* Cambridge, MA: Harvard University Press.

Schlesinger, J. M., & Kanabayashi, M. (1992, October 8). Many Japanese find their "lifetime" jobs can be short-lived. *The Wall Street Journal,* p. A1.

Senge, Peter M. (1990). *The fifth discipline: The art and practice of the learning organization.* New York: Doubleday/Currency.

Taylor, A. (1991, December 30). A U.S.-style shakeup at Honda. *Fortune,* pp. 115-120.

The cracks in quality. (1992, April 18). *The Economist,* pp. 67-68.

Vogel, E. F. (1987). Japan: Adaptive communitarianism. In G. C. Lodge & E. F. Vogel (Eds.), *Ideology and national competitiveness: An analysis of nine countries* (pp. 141-171). Boston, MA: Harvard Business School Press.

Walton, R. E. (1985, March-April). From control to commitment in the workplace. *Harvard Business Review,* pp. 76-84.

Womack, J. P., Jones, D. T., & Roos, D. (1990). *The machine that changed the world.* New York: Rawson Associates.

Yasuda, Y. (1991). *40 years, 20 million ideas: The Toyota suggestion system.* Cambridge, MA: Productivity Press.

Zipkin, P. H. (1991, January-February). Does manufacturing need a JIT revolution? *Harvard Business Review,* pp. 40-50.

8 BUREAUCRACY

Can We Do Better? We Can Do Worse

Frederick M. Gordon

Any organization, if it is to succeed, must coordinate the activity of numerous individuals to achieve organizational goals. Organizations differ in how they do this. Bureaucracy, as has been said at several points in this book, coordinates activity by a system of formalized roles, next-level-up supervision, and so on. A competing, less bureaucratic, and less formally structured model—typical of major Japanese corporations and popularized in this country by Ouchi, Peters, and Waterman, and others—coordinates activity by a consensus around values and aims, which originate in managerial leadership. This, Charles Heckscher calls the *closed community* model. In this book, authors for the most part want to go beyond this closed community model to a yet less formally structured model, which Heckscher calls the *interactive* model. Like the closed community, the interactive model is based on consensus about organizational values and aims. But this consensus emerges from unconstrained dialogue among all organization members and is not promulgated from the top. Indeed, leadership is itself informal, based not on organizational position but on influence, which moves in a fluid manner from one individual to another depending on the problem at hand and the experience and judgment that different people can bring to bear.

AUTHOR'S NOTE: I would like to thank Charles Heckscher, with whom I have discussed these problems over 15 years; Anne Donnellon, with whom I have just begun to discuss them; Peter Gumpert, my research collaborator in work that underlies many of these arguments; and Robert Gordon, president of The Store 24, Inc., for his comments on the ideas developed here in the light of his experience with his own business organization.

195

Heckscher sees this new, interactive model as superseding the more paternalistic closed community. Although the closed community model predominates in Japanese industry and in virtually all large U.S. corporations ("Defining the Post-Bureaucratic Type," Chapter 2 in this volume), its problems are said to be too great for it to prevail. Heckscher therefore calls it a "false variant" of post-bureaucracy, which will yield to the more capable interactive type.

In what follows, I will take a closer look at the interactive type and its closed community competitor. I will specifically question whether the interactive model, with its unformalized leadership, won't tend to lose control of the divisive forces that both bureaucracy and the closed community are able to contain. I will ask how the interactive model of post-bureaucracy might be strengthened. And finally, I will ask whether an alternative nonbureaucratic model—neither interactive nor closed community—might have some advantages that the others lack.

The Issue of Formalized Leadership

The key difference between the interactive model and the closed community is in the role of managerial leadership. In the closed community, top management restricts the domain of participation by reserving to itself the role of formulating and promulgating organizational values and aims. Although all levels of the organizations are involved in discussing these issues, the organization can hardly be called democratic. Key advocates of the closed community model are explicit about this: They maintain that democratic participation about basic organizational direction doesn't work and shouldn't be tried. Stanley Davis, a prominent theoretician and consultant, is typical though more explicit than most in his views (Davis, 1984, p. 7):

> During all my work on corporate strategy and culture over the last five years, I have learned that guiding beliefs are invariably set at the top and transmitted down through the ranks. Also, any effort to change them must be led by the chief executive officer (CEO). These are not judgments, but observations.
>
> Since American culture is built on democratic values and beliefs, one might rightly expect its organizations to develop them from the bottom up. Yet I have never encountered a large corporation in which the guiding beliefs were created or fundamentally changed by the rank and file.
>
> The significance of this observation for setting and implementing strategic direction in a company cannot be overstated. Culture, and therefore strategy, is a top down affair.

Richard Hackman takes a similar view (Hackman, 1986, pp. 101-102):

> Except in self-governing performance units . . . ,the overall directions for performance are established by representatives of the larger organization in which a performing unit operates. Those who own an enterprise for example, or who act on their behalf, have the right to determine organizational objectives—to say, in effect, "This is the mountain we will climb. Not that one, this one. And while many aspects of our collective endeavor are open for discussion, choice of mountain is not among them."
>
> Will such an assertion de-power and alienate organization members? On the contrary, having a clear statement of direction tends to be empowering.

Similar views are also expressed by Beer, Spector, Lawrence, Mills, and Walton (1984, p. 82), Peters and Waterman (1982, p. 6), Naisbitt and Aburdene (1985, p. 20), and, in a more muted form, by Ouchi (1981, p. 102). Top management, with varying degrees of sensitivity to the values, aims, customs, and sensibility of organization members, defines values and aims that are then promulgated downward, forming what is hoped to be an effective consensus. Participation is encouraged within certain bounds, beyond which lies leadership authority that is accepted as legitimate. Leadership resolves internal differences and maintains consensus; the emergence of faction represents the failure of leadership's consensus-building function and is not allowed.

Hackman (1986), gives three reasons why direction-providing managerial leadership is constructive and empowering (p. 102). "First," he writes, "it *orients* organization members toward common objectives." "Second, clear direction *energizes* people, even when the goals that are articulated may not rank highest on members' personal lists of aspirations." "Finally," he writes, "a clear statement of direction *provides a criterion* for unit members to use in testing and comparing alternative possibilities for their behavior at work." The flip side of Hackman's positive message would seem to be the warning that *lack* of such leadership would result in *disorientation*: shared objectives would *not* emerge from democratic debate. It would *de-energize* people: The lack of leadership would encourage discordant voices; energy would be dissipated in fruitless contention. And the organization would have no clear criteria for behavior at work: Different groups with different aims would adopt different standards and norms.

As suggestive as Hackman's writing is, he offers here no explanation for why these negative tendencies should occur. Why shouldn't participatory democratic organizations, such as the interactive type, produce strong consensus that would orient people, energize them, and provide the basis for coordination? In what follows, I will use social psychological research findings to suggest why the interactive model may have difficulties.

Problems With the Interactive
Post-Bureaucratic Type: Some Suggestions
from Social Psychology

Any organization that exceeds the size of a face-to-face interactive group tends to generate subgroups. These subgroups may be formed on the basis of proximity, function, previous friendship, race, gender, or various other things. Research on "minimal groups" (Turner, 1978) shows that even when group members have *nothing* in common save that they are somehow identified *as* a group, they will generate in-group bias and out-group prejudice. This in itself is probably not yet enough to disrupt the functioning of an organization. As Roger Brown points out, "the in-group preference of the minimal group is . . . moderate" and "would produce only very mild perceptions of inequity and no real anger or aggression—just a lot of grumbling discontent" (Brown, 1986, p. 582). But to this discontent are added four social psychological dynamics that may escalate intergroup antagonism and make it more damaging.

These are: First, leaders emerge who maintain and strengthen the identity of the group and its sense of its own strength and ability (McClelland, 1975, p. 262). Second, group leadership employs this enhanced sense of group self-importance to intensify competition with other groups, both *psychologically* (having the group compare well with other groups) and *materially* (getting for the group resources commensurate with the group's conception of its own merits) (see Goethals & Darley, 1987). Third, this competition enhances the status of leaders, because it makes more valuable their internal identity-enhancing and external resources-securing efforts. Because of this, those who enjoy leadership roles have an interest in the perpetuation of political competition for organizational resources. And, fourth, the group-based competition for organizational resources leads to allocations that are based on political clout and not merits. These are seen as being unfair, and it is this violation of people's sense of equity that creates the most damaging hostility (Brown, 1986, pp. 582-583).

This escalating pattern of competition and hostility between groups introduces organizational inefficiency in several ways. It creates the irrationality that Weber saw in pre-bureaucratic forms, namely, subgroups with parochial interests who resist centralized authority and jealously guard their own rights and prerogatives (Weber, 1947, p. 242). In a *democratic* organization, however, a much broader domain is opened up for political competition than in the case of Weber's "traditional authority"; for the rights of each group are not something "given," to be guarded and maintained. Rather, rights, entitlements, and status can be *increased* through competitive pleading. Thus, there are strong motives for contests over allocation of resources, contests that demand large amounts of organizational time and effort. In short, the organization tends to engage in zero-sum (or worse) struggles within itself at the expense of producing a product.

These competitive relations between organizational subgroups might have *some* positive effects similar to interorganizational competition, but overall their effects are extremely damaging to organizational morale. Subgroup bids for organizational resources present to decision makers (in this case, the democratic body of the organization) strongly motivated arguments about which course is the best; these might, at least theoretically, improve decision making. On the negative side, however, the competitors, unlike competitors from different organizations fighting it out in the marketplace, have to interact cooperatively with one another day-to-day. When competition escalates, for example, when one group would do the equivalent of "putting the other bunch out of business," intraorganizational relations become so poisoned as to make the organization nearly dysfunctional.

Laboratory research has shown that when competition escalates into a pattern of injury and retaliation, the fact that overall performance is hurt is not a deterrent to competitive behavior. Even when parties are themselves hurt by the level of destructive competition, they will continue to retaliate (Deutsch, 1973). Reviews of the cooperation-competition literature show that competition tends to be inferior in productivity to cooperation not just because it is an inferior motivator but probably more because it leads to obstructionist behavior and sabotage (Miller & Hamblin, 1963).

To prevent these spirals of dysfunctional behavior, there is a tendency for groups, especially in face-to-face interactions, to allocate resources equally (Deutsch, 1985, pp. 140-147). But this creates inefficiencies of a different kind: Organizational resources are not allocated to those who can employ them most efficiently. Further, the tendency is to placate ill-feeling by allocating resources *generously* to contending internal groups. This is done at the expense of other priorities, such as return to shareholders or payments for services to parties external to the company. This is the pattern of the U.S. Congress, which mitigates conflict over allocations among its members through pork-barreling and bloating the size of the budget at the expense of the taxpayer and efficient service delivery. Ever increasing generosity toward all insiders—at some outsider's expense—can mitigate zero-sum competition.

All of these tendencies toward inefficiency are addressed and countered by bureaucracy, and indeed, re-bureaucratization will often be chosen as the way to straighten out such an organization. Competition for resources is reduced by putting allocation decisions in the hands of superiors who do not share the social identity of the group and are bound by the professional norms of rational calculation. By having decisions about allocation of resources, promotion, pay, and termination made for each organizational level at the next level above, the group-promotive leadership is deflated and rendered relatively functionless. And the leader's ability to build a self-promoting, solidaristic group identity is thwarted by putting the power to decide members' welfare in the hands of an outsider from whom it would be imprudent to rebel.

Bureaucratization breaks the resistance of self-promotive groups and puts the organization at the disposal of those at the top who have an interest in overall organizational efficiency. It would therefore be my inclination to say that the interactive form of post-bureaucracy, except under atypical conditions, rather than superseding bureaucracy would fail to equal it. Interactive post-bureaucracy would relinquish the efficiencies and even the sense of administrative fairness that bureaucracy has achieved and mire itself in intergroup competition and politically driven resource allocation.

Is the Closed Community
Really So Weak, or So Closed?

If interactive post-bureaucracy, as it has been defined, is likely to be a change for the worse, are we then left with bureaucracy? Is the closed community really as weak as Heckscher claims? The closed community is characterized by four features:

1. Consensus about organizational goals, leading to the overcoming of divergent subgroup goals, particularly the avoidance of polarization of workers and managers.[1]
2. Some concept of the organization as a community, which entails the use of peer sanction to encourage and insure adherence to and execution of shared goals.[2]
3. The use of local knowledge and intelligence at every level of the organization, especially the lower levels (from soliciting workers' views and suggestions to workers' problem-solving groups that can call on technical experts and choose their own projects).[3]
4. Leadership that generates and symbolizes the values and aims of the organization.[4] The result of such leadership is the generation of an organizational identity that supersedes subgroup identity and weakens factional leaders. *Organizational* identity would appear capable of overcoming the irrationalities of intraorganizational competition. Group leadership *does* emerge, but its aim is not to define subgroup identity and further subgroup interests; rather it consists of those inspired by organizationwide purpose who try to further it (Burns, 1978, p. 20). People are not competing for organizational resources because shared identity (Ames, 1981), altruism (Turner et al., 1987), and superordinate goals (Sherif, Harvey, White, Hood, & Sherif, 1961) engender strong interest in organizationwide success.

The function of control—which bureaucracy performs through next-level-up surveillance—is performed by the closed community organization more efficiently. Once the organization has a shared social identity, everyone has a stake in monitoring the behavior of others. Our research finds increased surveillance in such groups (Gumpert & Gordon, 1993). The people who have a stake in seeing that decisions are carried out are not one's superiors, as in bureaucracy, but one's peers. Peer pressure is stronger because the buffers that are built between organizational levels (solidarity among workers in responding to the commands of superiors) no longer exist.

Closed community organizations can also respond to problems more quickly and flexibly than bureaucratic organizations. So long as the aims and values of the organization are the governing principle for all subunits, these subunits can be trusted to make more decisions on the spot, without referring issues to higher-ups. On the one hand, each member can be trusted to act in the commonly shared interests of the organization. On the other hand, members are less motivated by seeking approval from superiors but are oriented more by the success of the organization.

Despite these strengths of the closed community model, Heckscher points to a series of weaknesses from which they suffer. These he thinks serious enough to make the future of these organizations ultimately disappointing. But are these weaknesses really so bad, or so inescapable? Consider them in turn.

1. Narrowness of Values Impedes Change

Heckscher writes that "the values that hold the system together, being relatively narrow and specific to the company, can become barriers to needed change" ("Defining the Post-Bureaucratic Type," Chapter 2 in this volume). He gives examples about dress codes and neatness and uniformity of appearance, as well as basic definitions of organizational purpose. But rules about dress, demeanor, formal terms of address to show respect and rank, as well as other idiosyncratic indicators of organizational belonging are not the exclusive province of closed community organizations. These features are *more* prominent in bureaucratic organizations. Relative to bureaucracy, closed community organizations are relatively *in*formal. Dress codes are relaxed, overt signs of rank are abolished, access to higher-ups is increased (see, e.g., Peters & Waterman, 1982, pp. 121-125).

One should distinguish those aspects of cultural unity that pertain to superficial matters—which the closed community probably suffers from less than bureaucratic ones—from those aspects of cultural unity that have to do with basic corporate aims and values. Here the closed community does differ from bureaucracy in that it tries to establish organizationwide consensus on basic aims and values. It is difficult, however, to see how this is a crippling limitation.

For one thing, the very gains that this kind of organization has made over bureaucracy are due to the fact that it can create a culture that shares values and aims. It is this which motivates people, enables different parts of the organization to coordinate with one another, and allows people close to the action to make decisions without consulting superiors. For a second thing, there is no reason why the aims and values of an organization have to be "narrow" or "inflexible." Organizations like this, with consensual values, may be slow to adopt and change basic strategies because consensus requires a prolonged period of organizationwide discussion. But, once the organizational mission has sunk deep roots, there is greater flexibility, because common understandings allow quicker decision making than in bureaucracy.

Nor is change even in basic organizational values and aims overwhelmingly difficult. Especially with strong, legitimated leadership, the proposal of new directions may engender broad discussion and arrive at a consensus around a new strategy. It is not clear that the old type of bureaucratic American corporations, with the relative freedom of top management to change strategic direction, has been quicker to exploit new opportunities than Japanese companies with their consensual decision making. It is at least arguable that companies such as IBM, which Heckscher uses as an example of the closed community, failed not because top management was unable to act decisively but, as Drucker (1993) has written, because it acted very decisively in the wrong direction.

But finally, however cumbersome the closed community is, it is probably *more* flexible than the interactive post-bureaucratic type. In interactive post-bureaucracy, the lack of organizationwide leadership and the emergence of competitive subgroups mean that discussion about basic values and aims is more poorly focused and is burdened by sub-agendas of intergroup rivalry or is hampered by conflict avoidance.

It is interesting in this regard to consider a consulting case that Ouchi (1981) presents in *Theory Z*. Ouchi is, as I said, an exponent of closed community—he calls this kind of corporation Type Z. The management to whom he was consulting was considering whether a strong management team needed a CEO at all, or whether it could go forward on the basis of peer consensus. Ouchi, first advocating the consensual line, was later convinced that the consensual team would make the organization *less* open and flexible, whereas strong leadership would make it *more* so. Although this case relates to the management team versus a CEO, I think that it applies easily to the peer-governed whole organization versus the CEO. He writes:

A thoroughly integrated Type Z company needs a strong leader. Indeed, a Type Z company can dangerously close itself to change and to the outside world in a culture of its own. With a strong leader balanced against an equally strong management team, new directions can more readily be discussed, argued, and considered. (p. 171)

2. Resistance to Outsiders

In closed communities, Heckscher writes, one has "the tendency to close off to the outside—to see oneself as better than the environment," and this "reduces flexibility across company boundaries" ("Defining the Post-Bureaucratic Type," Chapter 2 in this volume). *Any* organization with a sense of its own identity tends to have an in-group bias and out-group prejudice. This organizational pride may be a necessary component of high morale and motivation. But in-group bias is not necessarily an obstacle to collaboration with outsiders. Negotiative strategists emphasize that the differences in *interests* do not require that one be unwilling to *understand* another's positions or arrive at bases for collaboration that reflect the other's interests (Fisher & Ury, 1981). Indeed, strong organizational self-interest can motivate such understanding and collaboration.

It should be noted, however, once again, that whatever problems the closed community might face would be faced by the interactive form of post-bureaucratic organization as well. Both are based on organizational consensus and both have the tendency, which must be consciously overcome, to be inward-oriented.

3. Problems of Guaranteeing Security

It is claimed that "the promises of security on which such closed cultures depend introduce major rigidities into the system that only very large companies can tolerate, and nowadays not even them" ("Defining the Post-Bureaucratic Type," Chapter 2 in this volume). An altruistic dedication to making a contribution to the organization with which one identifies requires that the organization be dedicated to the welfare of its employees. It is probably true that the closed community is at a disadvantage in this regard as compared with bureaucracy; when one merges one's identity and goals with those of the company, it hurts much more to be put out.

But the closed community is probably more flexible in this regard than the interactive form of post-bureaucracy. In the closed community, leadership can often convincingly convey to employees the crisis in which the organization finds itself and the requirement for layoffs if the organization is to survive. But the interactive post-bureaucratic organization may find layoffs almost impossible. Insofar as groups become self-promotive and compete with one another, it becomes more and more difficult to find anyone who can speak with legitimacy for the interests of the *whole* organization. The organizational need to "get rid of people" becomes a competitive zero-sum struggle in which each group, solidaristic in itself, tries to protect its own at the expense of outsiders. The internal antagonism that this would generate would make it almost impossible for the organization to function.

As a defense against this kind of tension, organizational subgroups tend to adopt an informal agreement never to threaten seriously one another's vital interests. That is why determination of compensation—which arrays organization members along a scale of better and worse—has never in my knowledge been performed effectively by a participative democratic process. Termination of employment might very well fall under even more severe taboos; interactive post-bureaucratic organizations may find it virtually impossible to lay members off.

4. Problems in Leadership's Ability to Engender a Consensus

In Chapter 6 of this book, "Transformational Processes," Heckscher describes the way that closed community organizations create a unified culture by a "cascade" strategy. Top management of such organizations develops a "mission" and disseminates it to the rest of the organization through a series of meetings. The process, he claims, is not very effective: "Educators would recognize the old fallacy: the notion that one teaches by pouring pre-made ideas into students' heads. It doesn't work in the classroom, nor does it in organizations." But is this the way that leadership works in the closed community model? McClelland, a social psychologist frequently cited by closed community advocates, in his studies of organizational leadership, finds organizational leadership to be much more involving, transformational, and legitimate. At the same time, he does not minimize its top-down aspects (McClelland, 1975, p. 260):

> [The leader's] message is not so much: "Do as I say because I am strong and know best. You are children with no wills of your own and must follow me because I know better," but rather, "Here are the goals which are true and right and which we share. Here is how we can reach them. You are strong and capable. You can accomplish goals." His role is to make clear which are the goals the group should achieve, and then to create confidence in its members that they can achieve them. John Gardner (1965) described these two aspects of the socialized leadership role very well when he said that the leader "can conceive and articulate goals that lift people out of their petty preoccupations, carry them above the conflicts that tear a society apart, and unite them in the pursuit of objectives worthy of their best efforts."

The motivating power of the cascade approach is not that top management pours information into people's heads by repetition. The psychology involved is very different; several elements are required. First, organization members must have a high regard for the top organizational leadership. Leadership must be seen as the people who have succeeded in the past, and who can do so again. But high regard is not in itself motivating. So long as management is viewed in an "us-them" way, a highly capable management may even demotivate organization members by intensifying the perceived potency of the "them" in the us-them rivalry and making employees more resistant to managerial direction.

The second element that is needed to make the cascade approach work is that the "us-them" must be superseded by the "we." And that—not learning by repetition—is the real aim of the cascade approach. By soliciting support from the rest of the organization, top management is using the respect that the organization has toward them in their organizational role to motivate performance, because the leadership, through sharing that purpose, creates or affirms the "we." The opportunity to be a member of the "we," to be included in the group with a highly respected management, raises the prestige, self-esteem, optimism, and sense of personal capability of every member of the organization. Research shows that for people in groups with group identity ("we" groups), the sense of empowerment and self-esteem depends on group membership rather than individual achievement (see Ames, 1981). These groups have the highest sense of empowerment and capacity and are among the most productive (see Gumpert & Gordon, 1993).

If the line of reasoning developed up to this point is correct, it seems that although interactive post-bureaucratic organizations are destined to fall short of bureaucratic ones, closed community organizations with respected leadership are likely to surpass them.

Is There Another Way?

The argument presented here against post-bureaucracy turns on the claim that in organizations that are bigger than a face-to-face group, subgroups will form with in-group bias and out-group prejudice. It is that tendency which bureaucracy overcomes by governing groups *from outside*. It is the emergence of bias and prejudice that generates group-promotive leadership and intergroup competition that hurts organizational efficiency. This pattern would not occur if groups somehow would never form, or, if they did, were without bias and prejudice. This might be possible if people resisted the assumption of group identity and maintained a clear and objective perspective. Is it possible that this might happen? Several devices might help.

Professionalism

If people identified first and foremost with their professional grouping and had primary respect for its leadership, tendencies for parochial allegiance to corporate peer groups might be balanced. This might occur if professional training were intense, if professional identity were stressed, and if there were ongoing contacts between the employee and the professional group.

It is unlikely that professional groups would become important motivators unless they had sanctioning or promotive power over their members. To do so, the professional organization would have to be the repository of not only severe negative evaluations, for example, censure or expulsion, but of positive evaluations of people's work. This is possible to do in certain occupations; for example, skilled tradespeople under union hiring practices are given an exam and experienced-based skill level that determines rate of pay and authority. It is hard to imagine how exam or other evaluation procedures would be implemented, however, for more complex and less standardized job types.

Personnel Reshuffling

When membership in work groups is temporary and new assignments depend on evaluation of organization members outside one's own group, in-group bias and out-group prejudice are diminished. One is concerned about how peers on the outside, who will later govern one's opportunities, think about one's objectivity, sense of fairness and, regard for *their* interests. This encourages perspective-taking (Kohlberg, 1969). The effect is similar to the role of bureaucratic supervisors' balancing narrow group interests by holding the power of promotion *outside* the group. With intergroup mobility, the supervisor is replaced by all those peers who are potential collaborators in future projects and teams.

Training to Overcome In-Group Bias

Group parochialism might be overcome by bringing the problem out into the open, having groups become aware of the psychology involved, and getting training in negotiation and conflict resolution. Organizational consultants typically do that. Techniques include image exchange in which each group explains publicly how it views itself and how it views other groups; committees that crosscut the organization so diverse viewpoints are melded in a new cohesive unit; the public flagging of stereotyping, denigration, derision, and cynicism as out of bounds; and so on. All of these, and many more, have become part of the consultant's bag of tools, and all counter the psychology of internal division.

Respect for the Organization

In paternalistic or closed-community organizations, factionalism is overcome by the feeling of shared identity, of the "we." The power of this feeling of collectivity is governed by the fact that included in this collective "we" is a highly respected management. This management symbolizes the collective purpose of the community and is its most powerful source of binding judgments about norm compliance. The interactive model lacks such leadership, and is in danger of having a weak organizational identity or one that dissipates entirely. When this happens, the tendencies toward intergroup rivalry come to predominate.

Groups with informal leadership structures have a harder time maintaining organizational respect. In order to do so, they must probably be *more* careful than closed communities in building genuine consensus, in establishing trust, and in avoiding personal antagonism and conflict.

Another Model: Socialized Rivalry

A different approach to the problem of small-group self-interest is to embrace the psychology of in-group bias and out-group prejudice instead of trying to overcome it. It may be possible to structure organizations so that parochialism and bias are channeled into constructive directions and also tempered by organizationwide interests. In *A Proposed Model of a Democratic Productive Organization* (Gordon, 1988), I sketch out such a system. The design includes the following features:

1. Work groups would compete for organizational resources based on proposals that are dependent on local knowledge and that aim at improvements of efficiency and quality.
2. Each work group would have at its disposal a certain amount of management expertise and technical assistance that it could use in developing its own projects.
3. The initiative for these innovations would be local, but the evaluation would be through an objective, impartial board of experts.
4. Compensation would be structured so that increases in productivity are shared between the innovative group and the rest of the organization. This compensation system would be a hybrid between reward proportionate to group achievement and equal reward.
5. Validation of resource allocation to groups would take place through organizationwide debate and democratic approval of the recommendation of the panel of experts.
6. Local group leadership would be moderated in its parochialism and narrow self-interest by a career track that would promote leaders beyond the group.

The effort of this model, which might be called *socialized rivalry,* is to encourage small-group esprit even at the cost of in-group bias, and to channel the competitiveness into organizational efficiency and to moderate it by an organization-wide perspective. The model creates small groups with their advantages: high motivation and orientation toward success, high internal control and discipline, task enjoyment, mutual support and cooperation. But, at the same time, it avoids the negative tendencies of small groups: destructive intergroup competition, lack of openness to information or expertise from the outside, conformism, and the suppression of creativity and individual initiative.

The model solves problems of intergroup competition because under the hybrid group-based compensation system, groups would have a self-interest in the allocation of resources in an economically efficient manner. Specifically, although each group would have an interest in the allocation of resources to itself, this bias is sharply limited *only to itself*. In the case of *all groups besides itself*, each group would have an interest in efficient resource allocation, for efficient allocation of economic resources—funding the most productive groups—maximizes one's income under this gain-sharing arrangement. So, a culture would develop through democratic organizationwide meetings in which the majority would vote for rational allocation, and coalitions would be very difficult to put together that would skew allocations in a self-interested direction. The hybrid system of compensation does not appear, on the basis of our research, to create antagonistic competition but rather to engender relations that are highly cooperative (Gumpert & Gordon, 1993).

The model of socialized rivalry solves the problems of conformity, suppression of initiative, and closedness to expertise through a mild competitiveness between groups. This competitiveness would generate social comparison about which group does best. This would put pressure on group leaders to become dynamic, instead of defensive, to use the technical and managerial help that is offered, and to encourage the initiative of group members. The mild competitiveness of this distribution system seems to create an attitude of creativity, informality, and expressiveness, coupled with high productivity, and protects the self-esteem, assertiveness, and expressiveness of low performers better than any other system (Gumpert & Gordon, 1993).

Conclusion

The aim of this chapter has not been to argue the ultimate workability of any organizational model. It has rather been to point to certain problems in organizational design—problems stemming from in-group bias and out-group prejudice. This is a problem that bureaucracy was set up to solve and does so with considerable effectiveness. Those who want to go beyond bureaucracy would have to show that their models could also meet this challenge. The closed community, I believe, can do this. It has demonstrated this by its practical success and I believe that I have given a theoretical account of how it can resolve the problems arising from internal organizational division. But the interactive model has neither demonstrated theoretically how it might solve this problem nor done so by its practical success. Both are necessary for it to be credible. I have also summarized an alternative model of how theoretically the problem of internal division might be resolved. The practical workability of this model is, of course, untried.

Notes

1. See Charles Heckscher's "Defining the Post-Bureaucratic Type," Chapter 2 in this volume. Most key writers in the field concur in this characterization of the closed community; see, for example, Peters and Waterman (1982), p. 77; Davis (1984), pp. 8, 87; Naisbitt and Aburdene (1985), pp. 12, 22; Ouchi (1981), p. 55; Beer et al. (1984) pp. 52, 82.

2. See Charles Heckscher's "Defining the Post-Bureaucratic Type," Chapter 2 in this volume. For other major writers in the field, see Peters and Waterman (1982), pp. 240, 267, 320; Davis (1984), pp. 120-123; Naisbitt and Aburdene (1985), p. 36; Ouchi (1981), pp. 54-55; Beer et al. (1984), p. 56.

3. See Charles Heckscher's "Defining the Post-Bureaucratic Type," Chapter 2 in this volume. For other major writers in the field, see Peters and Waterman (1982), pp. 271, 321; Davis (1984), p. 49; Naisbitt and Aburdene (1985), p. 38; Ouchi (1981), p. 185; Beer et al. (1984), p. 83.

4. See Charles Heckscher's "Defining the Post-Bureaucratic Type," Chapter 2 in this volume. For other major writers in the field, see Peters and Waterman (1982), pp. 82-86; Davis (1984), p. 8; Naisbitt and Aburdene (1985), p. 20; Ouchi (1981), pp. 104, 171, 192; Beer et al. (1984), p. 193.

References

Ames, C. (1981). Competitive versus cooperative reward structures: The influence of individual and group performance factors on achievement attributions and affect. In *American Educational Research Journal, 18*(3), 273-287.

Beer, M., Spector, B., Lawrence, P. R., Mills, D.Q., & Walton, R. E. (1984). *Managing human assets.* New York: The Free Press.

Brown, R. W. (1986). *Social psychology: The second edition.* New York: The Free Press.

Burns, J. M. (1978). *Leadership.* New York: Harper & Row.

Davis, S. M. (1984). *Managing corporate culture.* Cambridge, MA: Ballinger.

Deutsch, M. (1973). *The resolution of conflict: Constructive and destructive processes.* New Haven, CT: Yale University Press.

Deutsch, M. (1985). *Distributive justice: A social psychological aproach.* New Haven, CT: Yale University Press.

Drucker, P. F. (1993, October 21). The five deadly business sins. *The Wall Street Journal,* p. A18.

Fisher, R., & Ury, W. L. (1981). *Getting to yes: Negotiating agreement without giving in.* Boston, MA: Houghton Mifflin.

Gardner, J. W. (1965). The antileadership vaccine. *Annual Report of the Carnegie Corporation of New York.* New York: Carnegie Corporation.

Goethals, G., & Darley, J. (1987). Social comparison theory: Self-evaluation and group life. In B. Mullen & G. Goethals (Eds.), *Theories of group behavior* (pp. 21-47). New York: Springer Verlag.

Gordon, F. M. (1988). *A proposed model of a democratic productive organization.* Unpublished manuscript.

Gumpert, P., & Gordon, F. (1993) *Cooperation vs. competition—A poor dichotomy for research.* Manuscript submitted for publication.

Hackman, R. (1986). The psychology of self-management in organizations. In M. S. Tallack & R. O. Terloff (Eds.), *Psychology and work: Productivity, change and employment* (pp. 89-136). Washington, DC: APA.

Kohlberg, L. (1969). Stage and sequence: The cognitive-developmental approach to socialization. In D. A. Goslin (Ed.), *Handbook of socialization on theory and research* (pp. 347-480). New York: Rand McNally.

McClelland, D. C. (1975). *Power: The inner experience.* New York: Wiley.

Miller, L. K., & Hamblin, R. L. (1963). Interdependence, differential rewarding, and productivity. *American Sociological Review, 28*(5), 768-778.

Naisbitt, J., & Aburdene, P. (1985). *Re-inventing the corporation.* New York: Warner Books.

Ouchi, W. (1981). *Theory Z: How American business can meet the Japanese challenge.* Reading, MA: Addison-Wesley.

Peters, T. J., & Waterman, R. H., Jr. (1982). *In search of excellence.* New York: Harper & Row.

Sherif, M., Harvey, O. J., White, B. J., Hood, W. R., & Sherif, C. W. (1961). *Intergroup conflict and cooperation: The robbers' cave experiment.* Norman, OK: University Book Exchange.

Turner, J. C. (1978). Social categorization and social discrimination in the minimal group situation. In H. Tajfel (Ed.), *Differentiation between social groups.* London: Academic Press.

Turner, J. C., with Hogg, M. A., Oakes, P. J., Reicher, S. D., & Wetherell, M. S. (1987). *Rediscovering the social group: A self-categorization theory.* New York: Basil Blackwell.

Weber, M. (1947). *The theory of social and economic organization.* Edited by Talcott Parsons. New York: The Free Press.

9 CONSTRAINTS ON THE INTERACTIVE ORGANIZATION AS AN IDEAL TYPE

David Krackhardt

"Some men see things as they are and say, Why; I dream things that never were and say, Why not."

Robert Kennedy, 1968.

Expressed in the theme of this book is a hope, a desire for a better organization than the one we have experienced for generations, the infamous bureaucracy. I am sympathetic with this hope. All of us who have studied organizations have encountered the debilitating effects of bureaucratic forms, whether managed well or not. And progress is made, as the Kennedy quote above suggests, by dreamers who are willing to let go of the way of the past and peer into the neverland of what could be.

Dreams motivate. They liberate us from the institutional constraints of history and social inertia so that we can explore new, unimaginable landscapes. But dreams also conveniently leave out the obstacles and problems that reality so rudely interjects. Thus, dreams do not guarantee success. And although the last two words "Why not" from the above quote are presumably rhetorical, one could take them literally and suggest that dreams should be scrutinized for loopholes. The answer to the question "Why not?" may just be, "Because it won't work."

It is not my purpose here to prejudge the viability of the post-bureaucratic form. But, if it is to succeed, we must explore the obstacles to its evolution, the possible constraints to its existence. If we can anticipate the sources of resistance to its survival, we will have a better chance of nurturing it along until it can predominate among its alternatives.

This chapter is built around two questions: (1) Can the ideal post-bureaucratic form, as posited in this book, exist? and, (2) If it could exist, would we want it to?

Constraints on the Existence of Interactive Forms

The characteristics of interactive forms are described in the Heckscher-Applegate "Introduction" and narrowed down in the Heckscher chapter "Defining the Post-Bureaucratic Type." Although I see differences in the various chapters about what this ideal type might entail, there are characteristics that emerge as dominant in this proposed form.

Foremost among these defining characteristics is the reliance on informal relations, or associations, that cut across, or perhaps replace, formal channels established by the organization. This theme is prominent in the definition of the organic organization (Burns & Stalker, 1961): "The organic form . . . is characterized by . . . a network structure of control, authority, and communication."

In the interactive form, this characteristic is taken one step further: "It is a matter of knowing who to go to for a particular problem or issue" ("Defining the Post- Bureaucratic Type," Chapter 2 in this volume). This theme is localized to the team level, where the definitions and boundaries of teams are adapted to meet the current needs of the organization. Moreover, the interactive relations are extended beyond the organization to include highly mobile personnel, joint ventures, and other forms of collaborations beyond the traditional organizational boundaries.

I would start by noting that there are three "laws" of social systems that are likely to place great constraints on the likelihood that the "ideal" interactive form could exist. These laws are the Law of N-Squared, the Law of Propinquity, and the Iron Law of Oligarchy.

The Law of N-Squared

The Law of N-Squared simply states that the number of possible links in a social system goes up approximately as the square of the number of elements in the system. With 10 people, there are 90 possible links (=10×9, assuming asymmetric links are possible); with 20 people there are 380 possible links; 100 people produce 9,900 possible links; 1,000 people produce 999,000 links; and so on.

It is quite easy to extrapolate from these numbers to note that any organization of a moderate size (say, 1,000 employees) has no chance of being a fully connected network (cf., Harrison, in press). At Harvard University, for example, to expect that a every professor's secretary be connected to the Harvard baseball team's assistant batting coach is unreasonable. There are cognitive and time limitations on the employee's part that prevent this from occurring. Not only is this asking too much of the employee, it is asking too much of the organization to ensure that all n-squared connections are extant.

In contrast, one could argue that the ideal is simply a lack of barriers to links and not a full set of activated links. That is, if a particular secretary has a task that requires information from the batting coach, then the question is how easily the secretary could access the coach to get the information. In this case, the interactive form would be characterized by many (but not all) temporary connections, presumably randomly distributed throughout the organization.

If we allow for this milder definition of barriers rather than a complete set of activated connections, we may still refer to the effective barriers produced by lack of knowledge of who the person should be going to for any particular piece of advice. The interactive form has no advantage over the traditional bureaucracy if everyone still only interacts with their supervisor out of ignorance of others as a resource.

But, what if everyone has access to an information technology—a kind of superdirectory—that tells them which person is the best to go to for help or advice. Now, the Law of N-Squared presents a different kind of constraint. As noted in the introduction to this book, such an ideal type may not result in egalitarian interactions, because some people are more expert than others. In this eventuality, what we observe is that the unlucky soul who knows the most, is the best resource, will be inundated with interactions. The constraint, then, is not that people are unable to go to whomever they want; it is that the recipients of these requests will not have the personal resources to handle all the traffic. After all, even the best organizational form cannot squeeze out more than 24 hours in a day.

Thus, the Law of N-Squared, I argue, is an immutable constraint on the interaction capabilities of the organization. But, even if it were not, the organization would still have to face the next two laws of social systems that constrain equal access.

The Law of Propinquity

The Law of Propinquity differs from the preceding law in that it was deduced from consistent empirical findings. This law states that the probability of two people communicating is inversely proportional to the distance between them. In fact, the results often imply a stronger statement. In a study of R&D labs, where intergroup communication is essential to the groups' vitality and productivity, Tom Allen (1977, pp. 236-240) found striking evidence across a set of seven labs: "One might . . . expect [communication frequency] to decay at a more than linear rate [with distance]. It is the actual rate of decay that is surprising. Probability of weekly communication reaches a low asymptotic level within the first twenty-five or thirty meters."

One might expect that such face-to-face communications are affected by distance because of people's unwillingness to transgress the physical distance necessary to communicate beyond that. What has been surprising is the more recent research results that point to the robustness of this law even with the widespread use of modern communication technology, such as the phone or electronic mail, where physical distance should not create such a firm barrier. As Kraut, Galegher, and Egido (1990) have noted:

> Many studies have shown that communication frequency declines sharply, even exponentially, with the distance between the potential communicators, and that this decline is relatively independent of the technology through which the communication is occurring. . . . These findings can be partly explained by the idea that individuals who need to communicate are geographically clustered, and that the association of proximity with communication frequency is an artifact of this clustering. But data indicate that the association between communication frequency and proximity holds even when the need for communication between collaborators is held constant. (pp. 10-11)

I observed an example of this in a major investment bank in New York. As part of a larger reorganization, a group of 24 specialists from different parts of the firm were put together as a team to facilitate communication and reduce response time for problem solving. This group was considered a high-powered team that would lead the way out of the doldrums that the division found itself in.

Because of space constraints, different parts of this team were located in three different nearby buildings and on three floors in each building. The understanding was that the team members, each versatile with computer mail, would all communicate with each other on a regular basis, either by phone, e-mail, or in person (walking between buildings was common).

I asked each member how often they communicated with other members of the team. There was a strong preference to talking to people on the same floor. More than 60% of the communication occurred within the same floor, and most of the rest within the same building.

Moreover, I asked people to list the names of other members of the team whom they do not currently talk to very often, but who would be of help to them in getting their job done if they did talk to them. I call this the "cry for help" question. The first interesting result was that people listed more names in response to this question than they did to the question about who they actually talked to, even though a primary purpose of forming the group was to encourage more communication. Second, the pattern of these "cry for help" nominations was even more strongly related to physical proximity. Only one of these responses was to someone within the same floor of a building; and 86% of the nominations bridged across buildings. That is, although some communication leaked from one building to the next, the barriers to effective communication access were highly related to physical proximity—despite the formal admonitions to communicate more and the advanced communication technology at their disposal.

What implications does this law have for the ideal interactive form? At a minimum, this law underscores a difficulty organizations will have in establishing unrestricted communication access, since the laws of physics prohibit everyone crowding into a sufficiently small space. It is quite likely that, no matter what the social, cultural, and formal norms are about being a "completely connected network," communication patterns will localize geographically.

The Law of N-Squared is a mathematical law with biological limitations. The Law of Propinquity exposes physical limitations. But perhaps the most intractable laws are those that deal with the inherent way humans relate and respond to each other: the social laws. The past 100 years of social science has produced precious few such laws, because of the ubiquitous inconsistency and creativity in human behavior. But the Iron Law of Oligarchy has been so named because it seems to recur despite the best efforts of good-willed participants to suppress it. I now turn to this third constraint on the viability of the interactive form.

The Iron Law of Oligarchy

The term *oligarchy* is literally translated from the Greek to mean "rule by the few." It is this inequality in power that the interactive form attempts to squelch. Yet some social theorists, including Michels and Pareto, have observed that groups, even devoutly democratic ones, seem to evolve into an oligarchical structure, with power relinquished by the majority to a small handful of "leaders."

Pareto (1942, vol. 1, p. 62) argued that democratic socialism led to a new "elite" class of leaders, called the "political class." He lauded the leaders who were able to stand up to the masses and their criticisms of their rule; such was a display of courage and demonstrated that the leader deserved his or her status. But Pareto's view was that this elite class, in a democratic socialist state, would be fluid, and this fluidity would keep the rulers from straying far from the interests of the nonruling class.

Michels (1915/1949) went further. In a carefully documented historical account of democratic socialist experiments, he noted that differential interests develop within any social system:

By a universally applicable social law, every organ of the collectivity, brought into existence through the need for the division of labor, creates for itself, as soon as it becomes consolidated, interests peculiar to itself. The existence of these special interests involves a necessary conflict with the interests of the collectivity.

> Nay, more, social strata fulfilling peculiar functions tend to become isolated, to produce organs fitted for the defence of their own peculiar interests. In the long run they tend to undergo transformation into distinct classes. (p. 389)

His sympathies were with the democratic socialists. But he begrudgingly concluded after reviewing the evidence of many well-intended attempts at true egalitarian reform: "Thus, the majority of human beings, in a condition of eternal tutelage, are predestined by tragic necessity to submit to the dominion of a small minority, and must be content to constitute the pedestal of an oligarchy" (p. 390).

Michels's pessimistic theory comes only after a volume of detailed observations of conditions that lead him to his inevitable conclusion. He noted that cooperative effort through organization (i.e., division of labor) is more efficient than individuals in accomplishing complex goals. He outlined the technical infeasibility of all the members of the cooperative being aware of and making decisions regarding all matters of concern to everyone. He also noted the psychological advantages to having a political leader: People like a leader who can inspire them, organize them to accomplish more than they could otherwise. And finally, he noted that these same leaders, once virtuous and selfless, become addicted to their power and engage in behaviors that perpetuate it rather than benefit the followers who thrust them into power in the first place.

The modern question for us as organization theorists, then, is whether these preconditions and forces, psychological and sociological, still operate today. Certainly, we would not deny that organized cooperative effort is more efficient. Nor would we argue, I think, that it makes sense for everyone in a collective of any reasonable size to have all information contained in the whole system and to collectively discuss and participate in every decision.

What about Michels's claim that people like to abdicate their power to leaders? This may be a point of contention. But I know of no evidence to suggest that it is not true. Although clearly people do not like the feeling of being "controlled" (Langer, 1983), they do like being inspired by the Martin Luther Kings and John Kennedys of the world. That is, although they will not abdicate their power to just anyone, once they find someone whom they can trust (and depend on), they gladly abdicate.

I am reminded of the work of McClelland (1987; McClelland & Burnham, 1976). He made a career out of developing people's "need for achievement," a sense of fulfillment derived from facing a challenge and accomplishing a task by yourself. Yet, to his surprise (and dismay, I think), he found that achievement motives did not contribute to the success of the large organization manager. Rather, he found that the key to success was a high need for power. More striking, he found that managers who exhibited a high need for power (and who used it judiciously) had the most satisfied subordinates. He concluded that having a powerful superior enabled the employees to be more effective themselves, giving them a stronger sense of accomplishment.

McCarthy (1987), in a study of worker participation in a high-tech manufacturing firm, found that programs designed to increase participation in the workplace were regularly resisted by the very people who were to supposedly benefit from these programs. Although she found several reasons for this resistance, one that dominated was that employees did not want the increased responsibility of participating in more decisions than they already had to make. They had work to do, and these additional responsibilities were not part of the psychological contract in their job.

Finally, there was the experiment by the grand master of participation, Douglas McGregor, author of Theory Y management. It may be recalled that he spent several years as president of Antioch College implementing his Theory Y participative management philosophy. Antioch is a progressive liberal arts school, a prime candidate for such an experiment. If it could succeed anywhere, it should succeed there with a highly self-motivated, achievement-oriented, intellectual student body and faculty. But, as McGregor was to later admit, his attempt at creating a Theory Y culture and organization failed, and he returned to his post at MIT as a professor.

What about Michels's last condition, that is, the inevitable psychological "metamorphosis" that leaders undergo when they become ensconced in their position of power? Again, I know of no systematic evidence to refute this suggestion. However, stories abound about failures. For example, Rath Meat Packing was a company bought out by the employees. Employees sat on the board of directors, and the former union president became president of the company. Within 3 years, the president became a bitterly distrusted leader who returned to the hated practices of the previous management, including the practice of laying employees off in order to make the firm more efficient and preserve his job (Hammer & Stern, 1984).

Michels was writing about social movements and governments. But the forces behind his Iron Law of Oligarchy are equally applicable to organizations of all types, including business organizations. Whether his law is immutable or only represents a formidable challenge to the formation of a true interactive form is a question we cannot answer. But it is at least a formidable challenge.

Although these three "laws" are compelling in themselves, I will offer a fourth barrier to the emergence of the ideal interactive form. This argument does not constitute a law, as provided in the prior three examples, but it does constitute a credible objection. The objection stems from what we know about networks in organizations.

The Property of the Emergent Organization

An inherent principle of the interactive form is that networks of relations span across the entire organization, unimpeded by preordained formal structures and fluid enough to adapt to immediate technological demands. These relations can be multiple and complex. But one characteristic they share is that they *emerge* in the organization, they are not preplanned.

I propose that we must first agree on the fundamental process by which these networks emerge before we can agree on what effect they might have. To clarify this point, I will outline a model network formation based on a three-dimensional model of relation types. I will characterize these relational dimensions as dependence, intensity, and affect.

By *dependence* I mean the degree that one person is dependent on another in the performance of his or her task or work assignment. A relation that characterizes a high degree of dependence indicates that the relation is critical to the person in order for the person to effectively do their job. Low dependence indicates a relation that may be incidental to the accomplishment of their work.

Such dependence may change from one time to the next. And dependency does not guarantee interaction. That is, one could be dependent on another for information but the former does not have access to the latter.

Intensity is the extent to which the two parties interact with each other, both in frequency and duration. Strong intensity would be characteristic of coworkers who work side-by-side each day, collaborating in their work. If such collaboration facilitated their respective work performance, then such links would also be highly dependent. If their interactions were merely social, and their work performance is not enhanced by these interactions, then their relation would be characterized by strong intensity but low dependence.

As Granovetter (1973) has so well articulated, low intensity ties, or weak ties, are not necessarily dysfunctional for the firm. First, they are relatively low cost to the individuals to maintain. Second, weak ties, relative to strong ties, tend to form between distal parts of the organization. And finally, two people with a strong tie tend to have access to the same information and the same sources of information, making their tie redundant. By contrast, weak ties often provide sources of relatively new, different, even contradictory information. This richness allows weak ties frequently to be the source of creative, innovative, and adaptive exchanges.

Affect, the third dimension, captures how a person feels about another in the relationship. Such evaluations can vary from strong (trust, love, hate, reverence) to relatively mild levels, even indifference. Note that the focus here is on the strength of the affect as well as whether it is positive or negative.

Again, the relationship between two people can be characterized by strong or weak feelings with any combination of dependency and intensity.

However, I propose that overall patterns tend to emerge over time as a function of the relationship between these three factors. The process by which these emergent networks form is my next point of departure.

Dependency → Intensity

Task dependence creates a demand, a need for interaction. An employee faced with a need for information, or resources, or permission, will attempt to fill that need by seeking someone who can provide it. If the dependence persists, interaction with that person who fills the need will increase over time.

Intensity → Affect

One of the most enduring findings in social psychology is that prolonged interactions induces affective evaluations, even emotional responses. Two people who interact only sparingly can maintain neutral evaluations of each other. If they are induced to interact frequently, they will tend to form stronger emotional bonds through the experience. Over time, each party learns what to expect from the other, resulting in feelings of trust, respect, even strong friendship.

Sometimes these experiences form negative emotional bonds. One party may "learn" that another is untrustworthy, unreliable, perhaps sinister in intentions, or just unlikable. But, whether the feelings are positive or negative, they tend to grow in strength as the parties interact more frequently.

If the frequent interaction results in stronger positive evaluations of the other person, this will reinforce the connection, inducing more intense (frequent and durable) interactions. It will also tend to reinforce the dependency, especially the perception of dependency, since the employee feels comfortable that the need created by the dependency can be readily filled. Thus, a relationship characterized by positive affect will tend to endure, and that link in the network will be *stabilized*.

Conversely, a negative evaluation will tend to encourage the employee to reduce the frequency and duration of interaction. If the dependency is sufficiently strong, reduced interaction may not be an option. In such a case, the employee will be motivated to reduce the dependency in the relationship (for example, by finding another means of getting the information or resources, or by reducing the perceived need for the information or resources). Thus, negative affect will tend to shorten the life of—or *destabilize*—a link.

In aggregate, then, structures of relations will emerge as a result of this process. Those parts of the structure that are reinforced with positive affect will form a stable core to the overall network. Unstable links will tend to disappear over time and be replaced by others.

What are the implications of this model for the interactive form? It suggests that networks are not particularly fluid over time. In particular, the parts of the network that depend on *trust*, a key to several authors in this book, are particularly stable. Trusting relations take time to form, and then once formed are difficult to break.

There is evidence that the network that people see and recall is the stable part of the network, and not the transitory, low-intensity part. That is, the network that people experience as helping them, or the network they actively draw on to do their work in the organization, is the network of stable, recurring relations.

Given this is true, then the idea of a fluid, truly organic network structure may be difficult to obtain. People as a matter of habit and preference are likely to seek out their old standbys, the people they have grown to trust, the people they always go to and depend on, to deal with new problems, even though they may not be the ones best able to address those problems.

I now turn to the final point I raised at the beginning of this chapter: If we *could* wave a magic wand and create a purely interactive organization, would we want to?

Constraints on the Idea of the Ideal

Simon wrote a small piece in 1962 called "The Architecture of Complexity," in which he proposed that many social, biological, chemical, and physical systems share a tendency to be "hierarchical." By hierarchical he meant that these systems were "nearly decomposable" into subsystems, which in turn were decomposable into smaller subsystems, and so on.

His claim was not based on simple observation, however. He noted that such hierarchical systems were inherently more robust against adverse outside forces. As an example, he described two watchmakers. The first had a process that was very fast but required that all 100 parts in the watch be assembled in one sitting. He could assemble a watch in an hour, if he were not interrupted. The second had a process that was slower (it took 2 hours to assemble the watch), but was based on building 10 subassemblies to the watch that could remain completed as each subassembly was finished. That is, if he were interrupted after half an hour, he might have completed 2 subassemblies that would not be lost as a result of the interruption.

Simon then shows how the second "hierarchical" watchmaker would be able to make in order of magnitude more watches in a year than the first, given even a modest interruption rate. Thus, according to Simon's theory, hierarchies are evolutionarily superior to alternative forms of systems. His paper started a minifield in systems theory called *hierarchy theory.* Simon is not the only proponent of hierarchies as more efficient and fit for environmental competition than nonhierarchical forms. Although I think we all believe that there are dysfunctions to hierarchical forms, there are some efficiencies also. Burns and Stalker (1961) recognized this in their original formulation of the organic versus mechanistic dichotomy.

One approach has been to suggest that organic forms may be more effective in some environments whereas mechanistic and hierarchical forms are better in others. But I suggest a second approach. It is possible that organizations are inherently inefficient in either extreme. Overly bureaucratized organizations are too rigid to deal with the fast-changing world. But overly dense networked firms have inefficiencies of their own. I have found, for example, in a study of a set of bank branches, that the density of communications relations is negatively (although not strongly) related to profitability in the branch. My follow-up interviews in those branches with dense communications also reveal low morale and a good deal of experienced chaos.

Perhaps, then, there is a curvilinear relation between the degree of interaction of an organization and the organization's effectiveness. This would lead us to a new path of research. Perhaps the attributes defining the interactive form have different curvilinear shapes, with each having a different maximum point on the curve. Discovering those maximum points is not as theoretically appealing as holding up an ideal type to which we all aspire. But in the long run it may be the more profitable path.

References

Allen, T. J. (1977). *Managing the flow of technology: Technology transfer and the dissemination of technology information within the research and development organization.* Cambridge, MA: MIT Press.

Burns, T., & Stalker, G. M. (1961). *The management of innovation.* London: Tavistock.

Granovetter, M. (1973). The strength of weak ties. *American Journal of Sociology, 78,* 1360-1380.

Hammer, T., & Stern, R. (1984). *Labor representation on company boards of directors: Effective worker participation.* Working paper. New York: Cornell University.

Harrison, B. (in press). *Lean and mean: The changing landscape of corporate power in the age of flexibility.* New York: Basic Books.

Kennedy, R. (1968, June 9). *New York Times,* p. 56.

Kraut, R., Galegher J., & Egido, C. (1990). *Informal communication and scientific work.* Working paper. Pittsburg, PA: Carnegie Mellon University.

Langer, E. J. (1983). *The psychology of control.* Beverly Hills, CA: Sage.

McCarthy, S. A. (1987). *Theoretical and empirical perspectives on nonparticipation at work: Levels of nonparticipation in a Company Quality Circle Program.* Ph.D. dissertation. Cornell University, New York.

McClelland, D. (1987). *Human motivation.* Cambridge, UK: Cambridge University Press.

McClelland, D. C., & Burnham, D. H. (1976). Power is the great motivator. *Harvard Business Review,* pp. 100-110.

Michels, R. (1915/1949). *Political parties: A sociological study of the oligarchical tendencies of modern democracy.* Glencoe, IL: The Free Press.

Pareto, V. (1942). *The mind and society.* New York: Harcourt, Brace.

Simon, H. A. (1962, December). The architecture of complexity. *Proceedings of the American Philosophical Society, 106,* p. 5.

10 ALLEN-BRADLEY'S ICCG CASE STUDY

A Commentary

Nitin Nohria
James D. Berkley

O'Rourke always said that the second repositioning of Allen-Bradley would make the first one look like child's play. But I don't think any of us knew how difficult it would be.

Rodolfo Salas, Senior Vice President, ICCG

Allen-Bradley's Industrial Computer and Control Group (ICCG) presents an intriguing example of the changes typically associated with the "coming of the new organization." ICCG, based in Highland Heights, Ohio, is a manufacturer of control systems for industrial automation. The story of what happened there between 1986 and 1990 should ring familiar: Under the pressure of new technologies and customer expectations, a traditional industrial firm undertakes a radical transformation of its organizational practices. In ICCG, this transition takes many manifestations: team-based management, an emphasis on interfunctional and interorganizational collaboration, increased use and integration of information technology, a thought-provoking concentric

AUTHORS' NOTE: Research Associate James Berkley prepared this case under the supervision of Assistant Professor Nitin Nohria as the basis for class discussion rather than to illustrate either effective or ineffective handling of an administrative situation. Harvard Business School case No. N9-491-066 (12/20/90). Copyright © 1990 by the President and Fellows of Harvard College. To order copies, call (617) 495-6117 or write the Publishing Division, Harvard Business School, Boston, MA 02163. No part of this publication may be reproduced, stored in a retrieval system, used in a spreadsheet, or transmitted in any form or by any means—electronic, mechanical, photocopying, recording, or otherwise—without the permission of Harvard Business School.

organization chart, and a general turn to "softer" control systems. The experiences of ICCG are instructive for two reasons. First, they present a usefully condensed picture of the complex interrelation between technological innovation and organizational change. Second, they raise fundamental questions about the status of the "new" organization as a concept. Do the changes at ICCG yield a truly new organization? Are these changes sustainable? Might they in some ways be more rhetorical than actual?

Technology and Organization

The organizational changes that occurred at ICCG were prompted by a general technological transition at Allen-Bradley during the 1980s. Commonly referred to as "the second repositioning" of Allen-Bradley, this transition is perhaps better seen as two transitions in one. The first component was Allen-Bradley's decision, articulated by then-CEO Tracy O'Rourke, to pioneer the use of computer-integrated manufacturing, or CIM, in its own organizations and factories. The second was Allen-Bradley's decision, again articulated by O'Rourke, to become a premier provider of CIM systems to companies interested in using computer-integrated manufacturing themselves. Both of these transitions would require a rethinking of how information circulated in ICCG and how the group would be structured.

CIM poses a challenge to the tenets of bureaucratic organization. The CIM philosophy dictates that organizations develop a single closed loop of information connecting its manufacturing function with sales, engineering, marketing, administration, and others. Traditional bureaucracies, however, are relatively rigid systems designed to ensure order and control; they do not easily support the real-time decision making and information flows that are part of the CIM vision. CIM requires that information be instantly available wherever it is needed, regardless of bureaucratic considerations of function or formal position. It also requires that employees have a holistic, cross-functional view of the organization. Initially, ICCG presented the exact opposite situation: Information was locally isolated in specialized departments that had little communication with each other. This problem was particularly acute in the manufacturing and engineering functions. Overcoming these barriers hinged on a relatively unsupervised cross-functional alliance headed by Jeff Kent and Greg Mesko, who worked together to develop a system that would let information pass freely between the two functions.

Yet ICCG was not only using CIM. It was also selling CIM, an activity that set in motion its own set of challenges to ICCG's traditional bureaucratic organization. The new corporate strategy of selling CIM solutions to customers dictated a new attention to collaborative product efforts both inside and outside the organization. Recall that in brief, the CIM strategy consisted in Allen-Bradley reinventing itself as a provider not of "boxes" but instead of computer-integrated "solutions" for its customers. Instead of simply delivering a mass-produced product to a customer, the firm now intended to work to provide customized systems that could integrate the entirety of a customer's manufacturing processes with its broader information systems. The Pyramid Integrator project was ICCG's first foray into the sort of collaboration that this new strategy entailed. To develop the Pyramid Integrator, almost 100 people from Allen-Bradley worked along with people at DEC to come up with a major new product that could serve as the cornerstone in a customer's CIM system. The point made by ICCG's then-vice president that Pyramid Integrator was a "people integrator" aptly describes the subtleties of the situation: The Pyramid Integrator would integrate the people in the companies who used it, yet it also served to integrate the people in the companies who designed it. Like the Kent-Mesko initiative, people on the Pyramid Integrator team attributed a large part of its success to the fact that the special project had received little formal direction from above.

Formalizing Innovation

By the late 1980s, ICCG was seeking to turn the out-of-the-ordinary character of the Kent-Mesko and Pyramid Integrator teams into everyday occurrences. Thus began a series of transitions whose purpose was to formalize the spirit of collaboration and integration that underlay these first venturings into CIM as a business philosophy. What had been the exception with the initial, experimental projects, they now sought to make the rule.

One of the most important changes ICCG undertook in this regard was the transition to a broad system of team-based management. After an extremely successful pilot project to develop the T60 workstation (a computer workstation for factory-floor applications), a two-tiered team system was introduced through the group. Cross-functional project teams would see product development through from "womb-to-tomb," while a smaller number of business teams would oversee clusters of project teams without interfering with their daily activities.

An equally major change came with Rody Salas' introduction of a concentric model of ICCG's organization. The new model placed new emphasis on groupwide integration and the dissolution of intra- and interorganizational boundaries. Existing boundaries between the groups' three internal product divisions were eliminated, along with divisional responsibilities for profit and loss. The concentric rings corresponding to the former divisions expressed the relationship between ICCG's "core" business in programmable controllers and its value-added services to customers. Locating suppliers and customers in an orbit around these inner businesses (along with peripheral functions such as human resources and finance) conveniently captured the dissolving of the boundaries that had traditionally separated ICCG from the world. Perhaps the most striking element in this round of changes was the shift of theoretical attitude that seemed to underlie them: Whereas the old organizational chart represented ICCG as a formal and logical system, the new one represented ICCG as a single organism, a "virtual organism" in real-time interaction with its environment.

Drawing Conclusions

It is instructive that for many, the introduction of the concentric model of ICCG's organization seems definitive "proof" of the firm's adoption of a new organizational paradigm. Yet in the end, it is difficult to draw conclusions about the final meaning and import of the transitions that occurred at ICCG in the years up to 1990. On the surface, all that was solid had melted into air. Divisions had been eliminated, the bureaucratic hierarchy tossed out, a new era of integration and "boundarylessness" formally initiated. Distinctions between managers and nonmanagers had become harder and harder to uphold. Comprehensive employee handbooks could no longer be distributed because the working environment had become so dynamic. Increasingly, control at ICCG was now being effected through broad, cultural campaigns, such as the four "behavior principles" that quickly became ubiquitous throughout the company.

Yet we may ask whether these changes were exactly what they seemed, and whether they could prove effective in the long run. And here the answers are far from definitive. The transition to firmwide teaming had met with mixed results: Some employees seemed terrified, others seemed merely to be collecting team memberships as ends in themselves. The changes involving managerial authority were similarly ambiguous: Real distinctions between managers and nonmanagers continued to exist, although it had become difficult to articulate exactly what they were. Finally, the teaming structure itself was ambiguous: Project teams were empowered to take projects from "womb to tomb" but the important role of milestone reviews, business teams, and executive councils threatened to turn the teaming system into bureaucracy by a different name.

Cynics might proclaim that ICCG's "transformation" amounted to nothing more than old wine in new bottles. Once the initial excitement settled down, what would prevent a three-tiered system of councils, business teams, and project teams from becoming just as bureaucratic (in the bad sense) as the system it was designed to replace? What would make the new organization chart much different from the old one, especially once its compelling theoretical nuance became old hat? How would it really change the way business was done? Where was the post-bureaucratic progressiveness of awarding "I did it just right!" T-shirts to newly empowered employees when, for all intents and purposes, these employees were still very much subordinates?

Firms such as ICCG do not need to address all these questions when they undertake processes of organizational transformation—but these questions do need to be addressed eventually. As we see it, ICCG was headed for some lessons in the paradoxes of the new organization. One set of lessons would have to do with how far down into the formal organization the new rhetoric of integration would go. Even in a company of teamwork and integration, they would need, for example, to make difficult decisions about compensation and performance measurement practices, about control mechanisms, and about the actual distinctions between managers and nonmanagers.

Another set of lessons would have to do with the paradoxes that come whenever innovation is formalized and institutionalized. ICCG's early experiments with innovative management techniques such as teams were highly successful. Both the Pyramid Integrator and T60 projects helped pave the way for later adoption of teams as ICCG's normal mode of operation. But ICCG would need to consider the costs, as well as the benefits, of making cross-functional teams the basis of organizational practice. Did it make sense to use the team structure for all projects, rather than just certain key ones that cried out for it? Would teaming become less effective once it had lost its contrast to "normal" management? Would ossification set in as managers found new ways to consolidate control in business teams and executive councils? Would executives become frustrated with the amount of control that seemed to be relinquished for good? With the benefit of hindsight, we can say with certainty that these questions—and particularly the last one— were crucial ones for ICCG. By mid 1992, we found, Rody Salas had left ICCG and the team structure had been scrapped in favor of a system in which teams were only used in certain key projects where they were seen as crucial to the business.

There are no right or wrong responses to any case study, particularly a case study with as many components as we have here. In general, however, we think that there is one particular and hopefully uncontroversial conclusion that needs to be drawn. This has to do with the role of pragmatism in the new management. To put it bluntly, organizations *are* as organizations *do*. In judging the ideas that have been implemented at Allen-Bradley's ICCG, what is of primary importance is that we examine not their theoretical form but their manifestation in actual practice. An idea such as team-based management, or, for that matter, a circular organization chart, can have multiple translations into organizational reality. The organizational impact can be light or considerable. Their effects can be confusing or enlightening, paralyzing or liberating. In any such situation, the proper question to be asked is: What are the effects of this innovation on the ways people think and act *in this particular situation?* At Allen-Bradley in 1990, the answer to this question was still unclear. Teaming, integration, and customer-focus were more than a rhetorical gloss on practices that were essentially business as usual. And clearly, the new CIM technology—adopted both as process and as selling strategy— was requiring a revision of organizational practices. But there was not yet a firm sense of the relative balance of management fundamentals and management innovations, and the innovations had yet to be tested for more than a few months as a firmwide way of doing business. As is true for most organizations who have taken the leap into the appealing ideas of the "new management," the real challenges were just beginning.

Allen-Bradley's ICCG: Repositioning for the 1990s

Although situated a few miles from downtown Cleveland, the tinted glass doors at the Highland Heights, Ohio, offices of Allen-Bradley's Industrial Computer and Communication Group (ICCG) bid the visitor welcome in eight languages and several different alphabets. After passing through them, one was met by a row of clocks mounted above the reception desk: One showed the time in Amsterdam, another the time in Tokyo, the third the local time in Cleveland. In all, the entrance lobby projected the image of a stream-lined enclave of internationalism: the clocks, multilingual framed posters, even a display of the flags of nations using Allen-Bradley products.

Traditionally, a supplier of industrial control devices to the manufacturing industry, Allen-Bradley, a Milwaukee-based company acquired by Rockwell International in 1985 for $1.65 billion, had moved swiftly to embrace a dizzying array of new techniques in both manufacturing and in management. In the past decade, this had meant pioneering the use of computer-integrated-manufacturing (CIM), and later the introduction of a product—the Pyramid Integrator—that gave customers the ability to bring factory floor data into their information systems. Now under the slogan "Reaching Higher in the 90s," ICCG was instituting a series of management and organizational innovations whose full implementation would prove as difficult as the technical innovations to have preceded them.

Rodolfo (Rody) Salas—ICCG's new senior vice president and the primary architect of the recent changes—had articulated five "organizational guideposts" for ICCG:

- Focus on the customer.
- Clarify the direction of the business.
- Simplify the business.
- Measure the critical aspects of the business which determine success.
- Involve and develop our people.

Salas was confident that within the framework of these guideposts, the radical restructuring and repositioning of ICCG's business would indeed help Allen-Bradley to reach higher in the 1990s than ever before. At the same time, however, the sweeping changes would present ICCG with a new set of challenges.

Company Background

The history of Allen-Bradley offered little foreshadowing of the massive changes that were to sweep through the company—and ICCG in particular—in the 1980s and 1990s. The company traced its origin to 1893 when 15-year-old Lynde Bradley developed a homemade motor controller in his family's cellar workshop in Milwaukee. In 1903, with the financial backing of his friend Stanton Allen, Bradley began the Compression Rheostat Company, renamed Allen-Bradley in 1909. Lynde's brother joined the company soon thereafter, and the two brothers ran the business together for the remainder of their lives.

Although the company grew steadily and came to occupy a central position in the city of Milwaukee, Allen-Bradley remained until the 1970s a conservative privately-held manufacturer of electromechanical equipment that, despite a number of foreign ventures, supplied its products to a primarily domestic market.

The typical Allen-Bradley product of the 1970s was, in concept if not in appearance, not far removed from the products on which the company had been founded: The business continued to be organized around an array of electromechanical products, or "boxes," that were used to control primary machinery on other companies' factory floors. The company, whose culture had for many years been steeped in the tradition of European artisanship, was renowned for being cautious and paternalistic. The organization of the company was bureaucratic and hierarchical, and a job at Allen-Bradley held the implicit promise of lifetime security. With sales topping a billion dollars and over 13,000 employees, the Allen-Bradley of the 1970s developed a reputation as the "Cadillac" of the industrial controller business.

The First Repositioning

In the late 1970s, as American manufacturing edged toward a crisis that most did not foresee, J. Tracy O'Rourke—who would later serve as President and CEO—went before the board and proposed what would come to be known as the first repositioning of Allen-Bradley. Although the company had become a leading provider of the control hardware used to mechanize plants and factories and was enjoying the strongest profits in its history, O'Rourke argued that the company needed to expand into international markets and turn its focus toward solid-state products that could be used in an increasingly automated factory environment. The result was a rapid move to become a provider of electronic programmable logic controllers (PLCs), a product which used microprocessor technology in order to control the functioning of machinery on the factory floor.

The shift toward PLCs proved a boon to the young Industrial Computer and Communication Group. PLCs had been developed in the late 1960s by an Ann Arbor, Michigan, based company that had been acquired by Allen-Bradley in 1969. In 1970, Allen-Bradley bought a Highland Heights facility called the Numerical Control Systems Division from the Bunker-Ramo Corporation, renamed it the Systems Division, and integrated it with the recently-acquired Ann Arbor company. While PLCs had been a marginal part of Allen-Bradley's business during the 1970s, the timely decision to focus on programmable controllers made the Systems Division an increasingly important part of the Allen-Bradley organization. The Systems Division became the Systems Group and finally the Industrial Computer and Communication Group. As this occurred, the Ohio-based facility went through a series of major hiring phases. While marked by the same hierarchical structure evidenced elsewhere in the company, the resulting organization was significantly younger and more freewheeling in style than the rest of Allen-Bradley. By 1990, ICCG had approximately two thousand employees. Nearly half of these worked in Highland Heights, while the rest worked either in Ann Arbor or in the manufacturing facilities in Twinsburg, Ohio, and Dublin, Georgia.

Structure of ICCG

Until the spring of 1990, ICCG's formal organizational structure was highly conventional. The group, overseen by a senior vice president, had three main product divisions and a fourth product unit. (Exhibit 10.1 shows the organization of both Allen-Bradley and ICCG at this time.) The most significant part of the business was the Programmable Controller Division, often called simply PC, which had served as the breeding ground for other elements—

Industrial Computer, Communication, and the smaller Engineered Systems unit—that had been "spun off" into relative autonomy within the group. While PC contributed 80% of ICCG's revenues and nearly all of its profits, the financial contribution of the other divisions often appeared marginal.

Although manufacturing was centralized at the group level and all sales were by a single companywide sales force, the various divisions of ICCG maintained independent market strategies. Each division was run essentially as a separate business that offered a particular range of products and did so with its own engineering and marketing departments. The same sort of decentralization and diversity also occurred within divisions: functions such as engineering and marketing, for example, tended to have quite different procedures and vocabularies.

Computer Integration and the Second Repositioning

During the 1980s, the concept of Computer Integrated Manufacturing (CIM) became an overall vision both for the products Allen-Bradley would create and how the company would manufacture these products. When asked to define the notion of CIM, O'Rourke—who the *Wall Street Journal* was later to call the "guru" of CIM—was fond of describing his vision of a "single closed loop." According to O'Rourke:

> Computer Integrated Manufacturing integrates the factors of production to organize every event that occurs in a manufacturing business from receipt of a customer's order to delivery of the product. The ultimate goal is to integrate the production processes, the material, sales, marketing, purchasing, administration and engineering information flows in to a closed-loop, controlled, system. . . . CIM is a whole new philosophy of business.

While pitched as a new philosophy, the impetus for CIM as a manufacturing strategy was, even by O'Rourke's own accounts, almost wholly economic. Global competition was increasing in the industrial control industry, and it was no longer safe to assume that domestic customers would buy expensive American products when the same products could be bought from foreign suppliers at a fraction of the price. While foreign firms could compete on the basis of cheap labor, O'Rourke saw the CIM innovation as Allen-Bradley's key to long-term competitive advantage in an increasingly global industry.

As Allen-Bradley migrated toward a CIM environment, so did many of its customers. By the mid-1980s, CIM was seen as a cornerstone in a second, perhaps more radical, repositioning at Allen-Bradley: in an environment that

Exhibit 1   Allen-Bradley Organization Chart (abridged)

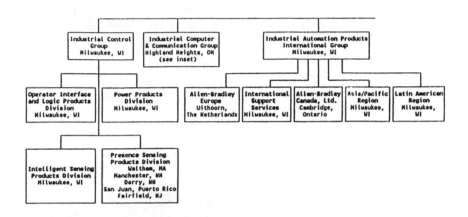

Inset 1a   ICCG Organization (Pre-1990)

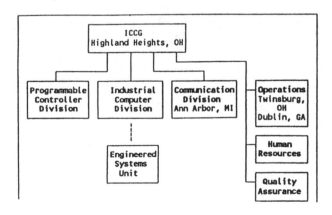

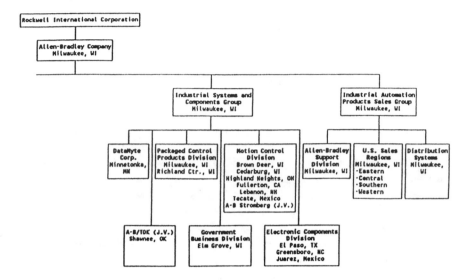

increasingly required the integration of heterogeneous systems, Allen-Bradley would both become a leading user of CIM technology and would move from being a supplier of "boxes" to being a global supplier of computer-integrated "solutions." Such a repositioning, it was reckoned, would require not only a new way of thinking about Allen-Bradley's products, but a new way of thinking about the functioning of the organization in general.

The Twinsburg Facility

Allen-Bradley's decision to adopt CIM as a "business philosophy" led to the establishment of a CIM facility at ICCG's Twinsburg, Ohio, plant. The Twinsburg plant, which assembled printed circuit boards for the different engineering divisions of ICCG, was a low-volume, high-mix facility: Average lot size was small (seventeen) and engineering changes were frequent due to the rapidly evolving technology. By 1986, when ICCG decided to adopt the advanced production technique of surface mount technology—a technique which effectively doubled the "real estate" on a given circuit board by allowing components to be placed on both sides of the board—an improvement in the flow of information in the manufacturing function was becoming crucial. Existing information flows could just barely accommodate the processes of the old technology; with denser board designs and shrinking time horizons for the introduction of new products, there would be even less room for the delays and imprecisions inherent in the traditional manufacturing environment.

With the trend to smaller lot sizes and the introduction of surface mount technology, CIM was seen as crucial to the continued success of the Twinsburg facility. According to Vice President of Operations, Al Hails, the smooth functioning of the new manufacturing environment was largely a matter of information:

> The idea is to get the right information to the right place at the right time, using common data. The flip side of this is to collect the information at all the distributed points of activity and put it back together in a database that can be accessed by anyone on the other side.

Getting the "right information to the right place at the right time" could mean many different things, as there were lots of "other sides" that could make use of the information generated in a flexible CIM environment. Information needed to be exchanged between the engineering and manufacturing functions, but information also needed to be better controlled and distributed within the manufacturing area itself. Finally, there needed to be a way to bring the information generated on the factory floor into the information systems of the business at large.

Integrating Engineering and Manufacturing

The lack of a streamlined information flow between engineering and manufacturing was a constant headache at ICCG. The manufacturing area was accustomed to exchanging huge quantities of paper with the engineering departments of each product division, a process that generated both errors and large wastes of time. It was doubted whether the transition to surface mount technology could be supported by such a system.

Each of the four different design/engineering areas had its own protocols for how it would generate the designs that it would "throw over the wall" to the manufacturing area. Vital exchanges of information between engineering and manufacturing were done manually, and because each design area had been able to choose its own species of Computer Aided Design (CAD), it was left to manufacturing to make sense of whatever landed in its territory. According to Greg Mesko, a manager on the manufacturing side at Twinsburg, this state of affairs was not that unusual in a company like Allen-Bradley. "I think what we had was typical of every company that had implemented CAD," said Mesko. "What happened was that every engineering group had a different personality for how it generated drawings, and there were no standards internally." Redundant information was being kept on both sides of the wall, and the laborious and inaccurate process of re-entering data by hand was accepted simply as the way things were done. The problem was exacerbated by the close collaboration that was required between engineering and manufacturing even after the initial design phase: Engineering Change Notices (ECNs) occurred as frequently as every two hours, and information continued to pass back and forth between the two areas throughout the product's life.

The initiative to integrate the processes on either side of the fence came from people within the two areas rather than from above. Rody Salas would later stress that this sort of approach was part of the new way ICCG was to work: The CIM vision was articulated at the top yet implemented from the bottom, with empowered employees given the opportunity to architect specific tasks of integration. Mesko was friends with Jeff Kent, a manager in engineering, and the two regularly convened in the mid-1980s to complain about the poor interface between their organizations. Approvingly described by one ICCG employee as "buddies who drink beer and play golf together," Kent and Mesko decided to do something about the communications bottleneck between their respective areas by setting out to design an end-to-end information flow that would bring the various functions together, while providing the needed levels of flexibility and security.

It was not easy to sell the merits of a streamlined and integrated design process to many of the engineers at ICCG. While the existing system cried out for change, an entire design culture at ICCG had grown up around it. Kent noted:

> Changing the mind-set of the people was the biggest challenge. . . . The whole culture [of the design engineers] was built upon drafting and doing drawings, not upon databases and information. They had this whole draftsman mentality and liked to see things on paper.

To create a paperless and standardized environment, ICCG instituted a system whereby a single relational database held universally-available CIM files for both design and manufacturing. No longer would a design engineer create a drawing and simply send it over to the manufacturing arena for "translation." Instead, designers became responsible for maintaining a database file that held all the data manufacturing would need; as design revisions occurred, it was necessary to update the database file to ensure the integrity of this data. The files provided full electrical and mechanical descriptions of all component parts using a common part numbering system and supplied all the data necessary to assemble and test the designs.

At first, design engineers resisted the changes, as they found ways of reinventing the old system and circumventing the database. Eventually, however, they were able to see the benefits of "closing the loop" with manufacturing and developed an allegiance to the new system. ICCG figured that, in the quality test area alone, the new process saved 50 hours in data entry and 40 in debugging per board design, and found that it dramatically reduced the number of undetected errors that propagated through the system.

The implementation of Computer Aided Process Planning—which was to the manufacturing side what the single design database was to engineering—allowed people in manufacturing to access the relational database in order to generate the programs needed to direct actual factory processes. In turn, data generated on the plant floor could be gathered and used wherever in the business it was needed. For example, data collected in the manufacturing environment could be used by people in quality or for the purpose of tracking inventories and resources. To help with the various integration tasks, two people from MIS were transferred to Twinsburg to help manufacturing with the process of computer integration.

Due to the relative youth of ICCG's main information systems, the task of integration was not as traumatic as it could have been. Mike Krueger, a manager in MIS who worked along with Kent and Mesko, noted that ICCG had the luxury of living in an environment where the current large-scale information systems were no more than 10 or 15 years old. While Kent and Mesko agreed that the youth of these systems had certainly helped, they felt that the success of ICCG's integration project was due primarily to a spirit of cooperation and teamwork. People in different areas were able to agree on a common goal, and thought it better for their career development to cooperate with one another than to compete. A prime motivation, said Mesko, was "simply seeing things work." There had been no one from above dictating what a "true" CIM implementation would finally look like, a state of affairs that confused people looking in on the process from the outside. Mesko and Kent joked that people always would ask who their CIM czar was. Their reply was that ICCG didn't really have one or need one.

Pyramid Integrator

As ICCG was integrating its internal functions, other people in the group were beginning to explore the development of CIM tools for ICCG's customers. Allen-Bradley had realized that its customers wanted to unite the plant-floor with the rest of their companies, and that they were turning to systems integrators, software companies and consultants in order to tackle many of the same integration difficulties that ICCG had faced in Twinsburg. Allen-Bradley perceived a critical opportunity to enter an emerging market for CIM "solutions," although it was evident that no single company would be able to provide all the capabilities required for such a large integration task.

For Allen-Bradley to provide what its customers were beginning to demand, it was necessary for ICCG to join forces with a company whose expertise complemented its own. In 1987, ICCG entered a joint venture with Digital Equipment Corporation (DEC) to bring out a product that—through the combined resources of DEC and Allen-Bradley—could provide the first step in a customer's CIM solution. Named the Pyramid Integrator, the product would not only serve to capture and integrate the wealth of data generated on the plant floor but would also serve as an intelligent gateway into the other areas of the business.

In October 1987, a cross-functional Control and Information Integration (CII) team was put together to begin working on the project. Don Davis— then ICCG's senior vice president and later the president of Allen-Bradley— wanted a product announcement by October 1988, but there were absolutely no hard-and-fast rules as to how the partnership with DEC would work or what it would produce. Pat Babington, a manager on this team, marveled at how freewheeling the project often seemed to those involved. She recalled:

There was no master plan—just a good concept and strong support. There were no preconceived notions on how to market it, what it would be called, or even on what it would be. . . . It was all operating on a handshake and good faith.

A joint venture of such a scope—Allen-Bradley had almost 100 people formally involved in the partnership, with many more on the periphery—opened the company to a sizable amount of risk and legal sensitivity, but top management was supportive and kept a very "hands-off" attitude. For many months, team members from Allen-Bradley and DEC lived, as Babington said, "in each others' back pockets." People from the two companies would shuttle back and forth between Cleveland and Boston several times a month, working more like members of the same firm than like representatives of two different firms.

On October 4, 1988, Allen-Bradley announced its alliance with DEC and introduced the Pyramid Integrator. Within the Pyramid Integrator chassis was a Digital MicroVAX computer, which was manufactured and sold by Allen-Bradley exclusively. The product was introduced as a platform which would support future Allen-Bradley products from all its divisions and would serve as the first major element in what became known as the company's Pyramid Systems Architecture, the blueprint for the standards and interfaces required to manage the flow of data through information and control systems.

While the creation of the Pyramid Integrator was a landmark technical development, Babington knew that the project ultimately meant much more to upper management:

We knew we were a pilot in more than just a technical sense, but in an organizational sense too. We needed to learn how to team both internally and with outside organizations. People like Don Davis made this clear and also made it clear that there would be great benefits for the team if we could make it work.

Clearly, the technical capabilities of the Pyramid Integrator were innovative and impressive. Just as impressive, however, was the impact it would have, and already had, upon the way people worked together. At a media event a few weeks after its announcement, Don Davis expressed his opinion that the Pyramid Integrator was more than just a streamlining of existing technical processes; it was also a "people integrator." He said:

In addition [to facilitating the flow of information both within manufacturing and the company at large], the Pyramid Integrator is also a people integrator. It can integrate the people within an individual business so that they can work better together using shared information. And, as we have seen, it has been the means of integrating separate businesses into cooperative partnerships. We've learned to cooperate with people in different businesses, across company lines, and that has been a valuable experience for us.

Adapting the Organization

For ICCG, Pyramid Integrator was a whole new way to think about the industrial controller business, and Davis's words plainly stated that the future of ICCG was to lie in the direction that the Pyramid Integrator project had pointed. Davis's tenure as ICCG's senior vice president had served to reintroduce the customer as the group's focus, and the ethic of customer focus demanded the breakdown of both internal and external boundaries in order to allow people to work together in new ways. In 1987, Davis hired Rody Salas away from IBM to serve as vice president of ICCG's Industrial Computer Division (ICD). In July 1989, when Davis became president of Allen-Bradley, Salas was chosen to replace him as senior vice president.

Consistent with Davis's initiatives and with his own organizational guideposts, Salas initiated four broad management programs at ICCG: Priorities, Teaming, Metrics, and People Development. By the end of 1989, the guideposts and programs were evident in changes in both ICD and the organization as a whole.

Priorities and Teaming

Throughout the 1980s, informal "teaming" had become increasingly common at ICCG. CIM required a team mentality, and the Pyramid Integrator project had introduced many ICCG employees to the idea of teaming as a way to conduct business. Furthermore, the entrepreneurial environment at Highland Heights tended to encourage the development of a network of informal relationships that cut across functional boundaries. One person commented that these ad hoc cross-functional relationships would often leave new employees wondering where they fit into the organization. Although there was in theory a clear formal structure, seasoned employees knew how to bypass this structure when it became an obstacle to getting work done.

As teamwork became an increasingly important part of ICCG, it became important to give some structure to a process that—aside from Pyramid Integrator—had typically occurred on an ad hoc basis. In Ann Arbor, the Communications Division, under the direction of Vice President Bill Little, began in 1989 to experiment with more formalized team structures. It was in Salas's Industrial Computer Division, however, that the need for change was becoming most evident. Functions such as engineering and marketing were interacting both poorly and inefficiently, and Salas responded by hiring Assad Ansari—who had previously worked with Little—as ICD's Director of Information Engineering.

Assessing ICD in 1989, Salas and Ansari faced a situation where the need for focus was becoming critical. Nearly 70 engineering projects were occurring concurrently, and as many as 18 people would regularly convene in a conference room to put in their "two cents" on a given project. While the area was a hub of activity, it was in fact neither particularly productive or efficient. According to Ansari, "If you were an engineer, you didn't know what project you would work on next. It was hard just to keep track of what was going on."

The first response was to draw up a list of all 70 engineering projects in order of their importance to the company. Those at the top of the list survived, the rest—with few exceptions—were unceremoniously shelved. This "prioritization" brought schedules under control and increased both the productivity and the contentment of the engineers.

After a set of thorough skip-level reviews with ICD employees, Salas and Ansari decided to develop a formal process for guiding the development of individual projects. Under their plan, a cross-functional project team would assume most of the responsibility for overseeing the development of new products. These teams—consisting of representatives from marketing, engineering, manufacturing, scheduling, and quality assurance—would essentially own product development from "womb to tomb." Formed and dissolved as the project warranted, the teams would handle all the aspects of day-to-day project management and would be responsible for their performance in terms of costs, profitability, time-to-market, and quality.

Related project teams would be supervised by business teams charged with the responsibility for allocating resources and for making decisions concerning strategies and priorities. While business teams would play an important role in approving the goals and activities of project teams, they would do so while keeping interference with these teams to a minimum.

When the team system was introduced as a pilot in ICD, many employees were skeptical. Ansari recalled:

> Some people took it as a management edict. Then after three or four meetings, they liked it better since no one was second-guessing them. We consciously stayed out of their way.

Ansari stressed that the move to a team structure provided structure rather than took it away "Whether people admit it or not, people really do like structure in their life," he claimed, "and this is a situation where there was a certain amount of structure." While team members were responsible for making their own schedules, they had a new sense of focus and purpose that steered them without intervention from above. People put in reasonable hours, working overtime when their project demanded. In general, there was little of the burnout that came from working on several critical projects at once.

The T60 Industrial Workstation, the fruit of ICD's pilot in formal-teaming, was the first product to be developed using the new business team/project team approach. In all aspects, the development of the T60—a personal computer workstation for factory floor applications—met or exceeded expectations: time to market was less than 12 months, final cost was within 2% of estimated cost, and both the team and the product were featured prominently in an article in *Control Engineering.*

Quality and Customer Satisfaction

The idea of quality was nothing new at Allen-Bradley, and was now being rethought through the lens of customer focus. The artisanal tradition upon which the company was founded made quality a significant part of the original Allen-Bradley culture, and the company proudly displayed the word "quality" beneath its name in its corporate logo.

Roger Hartel, Vice President of Quality Assurance, believed that ICCG had remained abreast of the leading-edge techniques in total quality management advanced in the 1980s. Nevertheless, he saw two important new directions for quality assurance in the group. First, Hartel wanted the "white collar" regions of ICCG to examine processes much in the way processes were examined in the manufacturing area. Toward these ends, a Business Process Management program was initiated in February 1990 to examine and improve the quality of management processes at ICCG.

Second, Hartel also believed that quality considerations needed to be made more explicit in ICCG's relationships with suppliers and customers. Under the theory, "you are what you eat," ICCG needed to work with its suppliers to achieve tighter quality controls. Likewise, Hartel fervently believed in the importance of measures of customer satisfaction. Because its goods were sold primarily through distributors, ICCG had tended to be somewhat isolated from many of its customers. Yet with an increasing emphasis on meeting the specific needs of end-users, Allen-Bradley had a growing need to break down this isolation with customer surveys and direct interaction.

On the suggestion of Quality Assurance manager Jim Weber, ICCG put together a cross-functional team called the Total Customer Satisfaction Taskforce, popularly known as "Ghostbusters." Ghostbusters consisted of approximately 10 core people from across the entire organization who were empowered to "bust" the almost imperceptible practices that negatively impacted customer satisfaction and to resolve such problems without elevating them to senior management. In its first few months of existence, Ghostbusters put together an impressive list of accomplishments, including a more readable label font, minimization of loose parts in packaging, and coordination of price changes across divisions.

Metrics

Measurement systems of all kinds had undergone fundamental changes at ICCG. Under Salas's direction, ICCG instituted a new metrics program that emphasized nonfinancial measures in addition to traditional accounting measures. According to Ted Crandall, Vice President of Finance and Business Planning, it had been the quality movement of the 1980s—both at Allen-Bradley and elsewhere—that had implicitly driven the evolution toward non-financial measures. There was a new sense that financial performance was only the end result of a wide array of operational factors, and that attempts to control only financial measures would tend to overlook important determinants of the group's performance.

The prevailing practice was for upper management to review financial performance on a monthly basis. Under the new metrics program, implemented in the fall of 1989, upper management would also gather separately to examine a wide array of nonfinancial measurements. It was easy for executives to arrive at a general agreement upon four broad categories for these measurements: manufacturing, quality, human resources, and customer service. Determining the measurements to be included within each category, however, was slightly more difficult. Clearly, any given measure had to be relevant to the goals of the category, but it was equally important that it be easily measurable and controllable: it was difficult to measure customer service or satisfaction, for example, unless one could find a way of turning a qualitative measure into a quantitative one. Eventually, executives agreed upon a core list of approximately twenty measures. (See Exhibit 10.2.)

Once per month, Salas met with all his direct reports and some of their key staff to review the status all of the measures included in the new program. Actual measurements were compared with a targeted value, and the person responsible for the measurement would generally give a "top five" list of the five factors that inhibited the measurement from a better showing. For example, the measurement for warranty failures might be accompanied by a "top five" list of the five particular products that were causing the most problems. For each component of the top five list, the person had to specify an action plan, a date by which the action would be achieved, and the person who would be responsible for overseeing the remedy. To the outsider, goals for metrics seemed impressively high: Under ICCG's policy of continuous improvement, quality measures were charged with the goal of a 20:1 improvement every 5 years.

Crandall saw the new metrics system as fulfilling an important function at ICCG. He commented:

EXHIBIT 10.2 Metrics Adopted Fall 1989

Quality
  Warranty returns (parts per million)
  Finished good audit results (ppm)
  % lots rejected at incoming
  Scrap and rework cost % total material cost
  Repair: % audit test yield
Customer Service and Support
  Compliance to want date
  Compliance to schedule date
  Shipping/pricing errors
  Training: Number of student weeks
  Response to customer calls
  Repair: Average turnaround time
Manufacturing
  % attainment of MPS
  Direct labor productivity
  Utilization loss due to change notices
  Cumulative lead time
  Number of vendors
  Repair productivity
Human Resources
  % requisitions beyond target date
  % turnover
  Number of special awards

Establishing these metrics and raising their visibility to the senior management level communicates to the entire organization what is important to senior management. And by the simple act of measuring, you affect people's behavior. These metrics will be the dimensions along which people will optimize, so we have to be especially sure that these are the right dimensions.

To ensure that people would optimize along the right dimensions, ICCG's metrics were allowed to evolve along with the organization and its knowledge about itself. According to Crandall, 1990 was seeing a major reevaluation of all the performance measures for manufacturing, and there was a constant effort to make sure the right variable was being tracked.

Like Crandall, Rody Salas also felt that the metrics program was more than just a way of keeping track of ICCG's business; it was a fundamental means of focusing and understanding its activities. "If you can't measure it," he said, "you probably can't understand it. In areas where we haven't succeeded, we're probably not measuring the right thing." Salas believed the new metrics program fostered a sense of openness and honesty, and while he believed the motivation for cheating or gaming on the measures was low, he wryly commented that the wise manager lived by the motto "Don't expect, inspect."

Rethinking the Organization

By the end of 1989, ICCG had done much to bring the second repositioning of the firm from concept to reality. Teaming was spreading throughout the organization, the group was forging creative alliances on a global scale, and Pyramid Integrator and the Pyramid System Architecture were making it easier for customers to customize their own CIM needs. Despite the healthy appearance, however, Rody Salas—now settled into his role as senior vice president—saw the group heading for a crisis much like the one that had earlier beset ICD. "Decisions," recalled Salas, "were getting harder and harder to make." For every business or product decision facing ICCG, there were too many people, too much bureaucracy, and too many issues; Salas saw a desperate need to energize and empower the organization.

Consolidation and Reorganization

Salas was impressed with the changes that had occurred in the previous five years at ICCG. But as the 1980s drew to a close, it became apparent that something fundamental had yet to change: "With all the changes, one thing that hadn't changed was the organization itself," he noted. "And the organization was suddenly under tremendous stress." Developments at ICCG had led to a situation where overlapping functions, interdepartmental politics, and drawn-out decision making threatened to become the rule rather than the exception, a situation Salas attributed to the fact that recent changes had taken place against an organizational background in which nothing had really changed at all. ICCG was—despite the increasing importance of horizontal, cross-functional, and interorganizational relationships—still essentially a collection of autonomous divisions whose relationships both with customers and with one another had never really been examined or changed.

Phil Bessler, the new vice president of ICD, felt that the divisional structure of the company left him besieged by contradictions. His job was to optimize financial return for ICD, but often the right thing for ICD was hardly in the interests of ICCG as a whole. For example, ICD could optimize its own profits by investing in its line of man-machine interface products, but such a use of resources was foolish if ICCG's interests could be served best by concentrating on customer integration solutions instead. On the other hand, if ICD chose to do what seemed best for ICCG, they would be undermining their own financial performance as a division.

Bessler's dilemma was not unique. Salas believed that the problems being encountered at ICCG could be traced back to the fact that all the components of the organization had been "created around technologies" rather than created around the needs of the business. Each division had a small technological fiefdom and thought it was out to be a world leader in a particular line of products. But technology, Salas felt, was no longer the differentiator in the factory automation business; technology now disseminated instantly through the industry, and the new differentiator would prove to be how well a company could respond to the special needs of its customers. As the industry changed, the costs of having a divisional structure organized around an aging principle of technology-orientation were becoming evident. Often the products and missions of different divisions overlapped or blatantly contradicted one another, a situation which bred confusion in the sales force. Money was wasted as three separate profit centers introduced conflicting products with no clear strategy across divisions.

Salas's plan was radical: All boundaries between divisions would be effectively struck down, and the group would be restructured according to the needs of the customer and the business. Bessler explained the process as being akin to "throwing all the components of ICCG into a single pot and thinking about how the elements could best be recombined." By analyzing the performance of the group's various product lines, it was determined that ICCG's "core businesses" lay in two basic product lines in the PC division, while everything else played an essentially supporting role that added value to these core products for the customer.

Having identified these two core businesses, Salas oversaw the design of a new concentric model for the organization of the group. At the center would be Control Systems, the group's core business. A second ring, entitled Communication and Information Systems, would focus on tying these core products together through the use of information technology and would differentiate Allen-Bradley products to the customer. A third layer, Application Systems, would add value by packaging and integrating systems into end-user solutions. Functions such as operations, human resources, finance planning, and marketing were in an "orbit" around these three rings, along with the suppliers and customers with whom ICCG did business. Profit and loss responsibilities for the old divisions would be eliminated. Although each would maintain a set of financial objectives, the boundaries that had formerly existed between divisions—and between the firm and the outside world—were henceforth to be thought of as provisionary and permeable. (See Exhibit 10.3.)

In some ways, the new organization of ICCG formalized the ethic of customer focus that had begun with the announcement of the second repositioning several years earlier. The core PC business was at the center of the new organizational chart, and the customer was at the chart's periphery, outside the third ring. As one moved toward the center, one moved closer to the "heart" of the firm; as one moved away from the center one reached the increasingly permeable boundary between the firm and the outside world. At

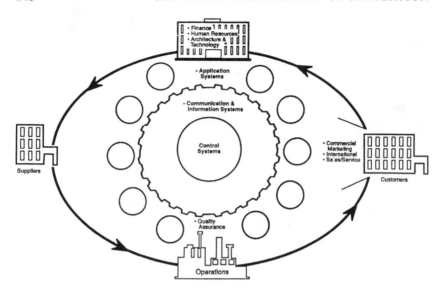

Exhibit 10.3. ICCG Organization After May 1990

the public announcement of ICCG's consolidation into a single business on May 23, 1990, Salas said:

> This consolidation will improve our customer focus and enhance our ability to develop and deliver superior integrated control and information systems. We will be able to work together better, make decisions faster and bring higher quality products to market earlier because we are now organized to reflect how our customers are applying our technology.

The world beyond ICCG's third ring contained not only customers, but also other firms, including Allen-Bradley's competitors. The new organization was designed to allow ICCG to interact more freely and more successfully with these firms: The new model, for example, permitted Salas to see at a glance which kinds of partnerships made sense for ICCG and which did not. Companies for whom Salas could envision a concentric model similar to that of ICCG could be ruled out immediately; companies with different models—ranging from third-party software vendors to large computer companies such as DEC—could be seen as opportunities for strategic alliances on the firm's periphery. In consolidating the three divisions, ICCG also consolidated the divisions' three distinct marketing departments into a single Commercial Marketing area. Now a single organization (with the exception of a number of employees who remained behind to do primary marketing for

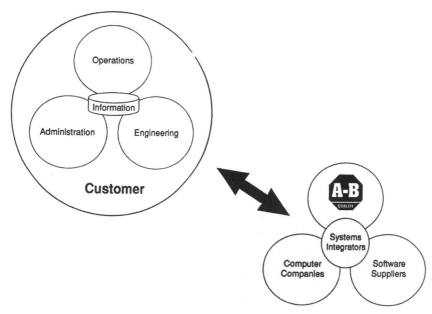

Exhibit 10.4. External Teaming for Customer Solutions

products), the marketing function could better pursue innovative alliances with other businesses, such as software companies or computer companies, all in the interest of providing customers with equally innovative automation solutions. (See Exhibit 10.4.)

While all of its products belonged to the category of high technology, A-B's new orientation had little to do explicitly with technology. Salas summarized A-B's new mission as "managing processes and systems that deliver value to the customer."

Groupwide Prioritization and Councils

During late 1989, Salas also led ICCG through a groupwide prioritization akin to what he and Ansari had implemented in ICD. The group had been trying to satisfy so many different interests that it often ended up satisfying no one: Sales and marketing would say yes to everything, and projects piled up on top of one another until postponements and frustration became inevitable. Salas compiled a list of all the concurrent projects in ICCG and, within 9 months, the group reached consensus on a new list one-third the size. The result, he predicted, would be a threefold increase in the number of products brought to market over the next 18 months.

In Salas's view, less was more. After focusing on the customer and clarifying the nature of the business, the next most important thing was to make things as simple as possible:

> What we're saying is focus, focus, focus. . . . It's all the idea of doing the fewest number of things and doing them all exceptionally well.

One example of this ethic of focus and simplicity was evident in ICCG's relations with its suppliers. While ICCG had traditionally been served by a wide range of suppliers, the group now aimed to develop intense partnership-like relationships with only a select number of these firms. Along these lines, ICCG had reduced its number of suppliers by 45%, and had set the goal of trimming 30% of the remainder.

To enable the proper focus at the executive level, ICCG also initiated a set of four executive councils, also known as executive teams. Each of these teams—Priorities, Customer Value-Added, Pyramid Systems Architecture, and Quality, Cost, and Time-to-Market—was headed by a vice president and was charged with the examination of a crucial aspect of ICCG's business.

Groupwide Teaming

By the middle of 1990, the functioning of business teams and project teams had been formalized and instituted groupwide. With a teaming system in place across the entire organization, authority and accountability would be driven down to the lowest levels possible within the group.

The structure and functioning of the new teams closely followed the model that had been used in ICD. Initiatives could be generated anywhere in the organization, but a team could be formed only with the explicit charter of an executive sponsor, normally one of Salas's direct reports. Once formed, business teams were overseen directly by the team's executive sponsor. Project teams, however, were managed by supervisory business teams that only rarely elevated project-related issues to the executive level. While business teams were responsible for defining success parameters and identifying strategic business issues, most of the responsibility for the management of ICCG's projects now rested entirely within the project teams. (See Exhibit 10.5.)

Although responsibility had been pushed far down in the organization, ICCG employed a formal review process—known as general manager (GM) milestone reviews—in order to oversee the various stages of product development. At five such reviews during the life cycle of a project, teams met with Rody Salas and his direct reports to give a presentation concerning their status. A successful GM milestone review served as a seal of approval that allowed the team to advance to the next stage of their project. Likewise, if

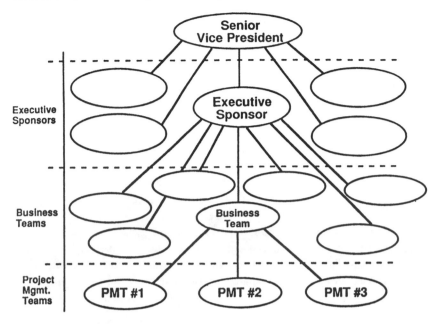

Exhibit 10.5. ICCG Teaming Structure

the project was encountering obstacles or was failing to meet certain objectives of cost or scheduling, the milestone review process could serve as a forum for the negotiation of new terms.

In general, leadership of project teams rotated according to where the project was in the milestone process. Marketing assumed the lead role for the business proposal and project definition segment, up through the first GM milestone review. Engineering then guided the team through the design and development phases, followed by manufacturing's lead during pilot activity and full production. Marketing took over again for field performance reviews and the final GM evaluation, which occurred six months after the first shipment.

Looking Ahead

While the comprehensive reorganization of ICCG's divisional structure appeared to put the crowning touches on the second repositioning that had been announced four years earlier, it also raised a new set of issues. The consolidation of the business and the introduction of the concentric ring model were—after many years of piecemeal change—signs that there was no going back for the newly reorganized group. As ICCG settled in for the long term,

Salas identified three major challenges that ICCG would have to face in order to capitalize most fully on the bold measures that had been taken. First, ICCG needed to learn how best to manage the intersection of its management structure with a team structure that had absorbed many of management's old responsibilities. Second, ICCG faced the challenge of developing a human resources system that would be compatible with the rest of the organization. Third, the group needed to find ways to extend the principles of teamwork and cooperation beyond the "four walls" of ICCG, both to the rest of Allen-Bradley and to the group's suppliers and customers as well.

Salas believed it was very important to arrive at the right set of interfaces between management and teams. While much of the day-to-day running of the company could now be handled at the team level, Salas and his direct reports maintained four crucial "windows" into the organization through financial reviews, metrics, milestone reviews, and executive councils. Ninety-five percent of ICCG's employees, however, did not participate in such meetings, and Salas felt that the prime challenge was to ensure that teams were properly tied in to the management of the organization. Salas posed the question:

> If I'm a third-level manager or director with a team under me, then where do my powers begin and end? What responsibility and accountability should management retain and what should be delegated to teams?

While Salas believed that the proper control systems existed, he noticed that in practice the responses of managers tended to vary. Some managers were not comfortable with letting go of their traditional means of control, while others adapted quickly to embrace the new system.

The reactions of lower-level employees varied as well. While at first there had been a rush to get on as many teams as possible—Jeff Kent joked that the principle seemed to be "Whoever dies with the most teams wins"—some team members were unsure of how to behave in the new environment, while others were flourishing and emerging as future candidates for positions in upper management.

Keith Hamilton, Director of Human Resources, anticipated the need for some considerable changes. In the past years, human resources had realized the need to match Allen-Bradley's new approaches to technology with new approaches to people. Hamilton recalled:

> At Twinsburg, we woke up one day with a terrible feeling that our manufacturing processes were so far ahead of our people processes. People would ask what the link between our new manufacturing processes and our people processes was, and we didn't really have an answer.

For some time, human resources had been working to answer this question. Hamilton's area was training people to "understand the transition from functional to project-oriented management," and to give lower-level employees a new sense of empowerment and contribution through awards and recognition programs. For supervisors, Hamilton believed that focus needed to be moved away from strict control to issues of teaming, training, coaching, and boundary-management. At all levels, cross-training was becoming prevalent as employees began to require an increasingly wide view of the business.

The working environment at ICCG was now so dynamic that it no longer made any sense to distribute comprehensive employee handbooks. Instead, ICCG now provided only broad policy manuals and relied upon a set of basic principles to guide employee behavior. These four "behavior principles"— customer focus, sense of urgency, ownership, and teamwork—were now displayed everywhere in ICCG: on plaques, posters, even on T-shirts. In November 1989, the group had instituted an informal recognition program by which employees exhibiting behavior relating to one of the principles could be nominated for a T-shirt award. By the end of 1990, over 650 employees had received blue and white Allen-Bradley T-shirts, which on one side proclaimed "I did it just right!" and on the other listed the four guiding principles that would allow Allen-Bradley to "reach higher in the nineties." Salas felt that programs such as the T-shirt award served the dual role of both communication and motivation at practically no cost to the company: "There are ways you can create a motivational environment without having to spend a nickel," he claimed. "People work for pride. When you give them the opportunity to take initiative and you listen to them, they can be as high as a kite."

As informal award programs proliferated, however, questions of formal recognition could be seen waiting in the wings. The sticky issues of compensation and performance appraisal were getting increasingly hard to ignore, both in human resources and elsewhere. Salas and Hamilton both felt that their current performance appraisal systems were not oriented to the new way the organization was working. It was clear that ICCG's appraisal system needed to be made consistent with policies of customer-orientation, continuous improvement, and teamwork, but there were lingering questions about how precisely this might be achieved. A first step toward this goal had been taken when human resources put together a cross-functional team charged with the design of a new performance evaluation system. An engineer who sat on the team would have direct input into the design of a new system, something Hamilton felt would never have been possible even a few years before.

Both Salas and Hamilton felt that traditional compensation programs were "just not going to cut it," but they were as yet unsure of what a new system would require. How was one to go about measuring contribution to a team?

What sort of new compensation practices would be required in an increasingly flat organization? Salas was eager for ICCG to confront these issues, but felt there might be a long way to go until they were resolved.

The final challenge for ICCG, according to Salas, would be cooperation and teamwork outside the group's walls. Since customers were looking for solutions that involved multiple products—both from Allen-Bradley and from other firms—ICCG needed to develop close working relationships with other organizations, some of which had traditionally been considered competitors. According to Salas, accomplishing this would not necessarily be easy: "Egos," he said, "must learn to get out of the way." Salas reckoned that it would take some time for this new collaborative spirit to become the norm, just as it would take time for ICCG itself to master its own transition.

11 LAKEVILLE CHEMICAL PLANT

Charles Heckscher

The best thing in this plant is the absence of bureaucracy. I can go talk to upper management when I need to—there are no back door situations.

A maintenance worker

It frustrates me that people still show irresponsibility here. This plant has got to be run on trust.

A manager

There's much better relationships here than in other plants—better rapport between process and maintenance people, maintenance and engineering, foremen and managers—just about every cross-link you can think of.

A maintenance supervisor

A worker can talk to his manager—and if anything's going to undermine unions, that's it.

A local union officer

I have always maintained that to keep a well-paid work force together in a union, we have to provide programs that improve their daily lives. . . . We use this experience to show people that the union can offer something to them besides another nickel.

National union officers

AUTHOR'S NOTE: This case was prepared by Assistant Professor Charles Heckscher as the basis for class discussion rather than to illustrate either effective or ineffective handling of an administrative situation. Harvard Business School case No. 9-487-053 (12/87). Copyright © 1986 by the President and Fellows of Harvard College. No part of this publication may be reproduced, stored in a retrieval system, or transmitted in any form or by any means—electronic, mechanical, photocopying, recording, or otherwise—without the permission of Harvard Business School. Distributed by HBS Case Services, Harvard Business School, Boston, MA 02163.

We feel this system has proved itself to be extremely effective.

The plant superintendent

We've created a high degree of expectation. Now we're faced with the frustration of people whose expectations are too high.

A labor relations manager

People are willing to take more leadership, responsibility in general and there are more opportunities for this [than in comparable plants.]

A union official

It's OK to be smart around here; if you are you get recognition, not flack.

A process worker[1]

These statements represent different perspectives on a chemical refinery in Lakeville, Canada. It was an unusual plant in many respects. First, it was based on self-managing teams of workers who were capable of running the entire plant by themselves; that alone put it in a group of only a few dozen companies in North America. Second, it was one of the earliest of such efforts to be started: as of late 1986 it had been in full operation for seven years. Finally, the Petrochemical Workers' union, which represented the workforce, was a full and very visible partner with management from very early in the design phase and throughout the plant's history.

Structure

The Lakeville plant was owned by a large international petrochemical corporation. Its two major products were isopropyl alcohol, used in the manufacture of rubbing alcohol, solvents, and antifreeze; and polypropylene pellets, used for a large variety of items from rope to steering wheels to chair shells. The Lakeville complex cost $200 million to build and had an estimated 1984 replacement cost of $700 million. It included two plants, one for each of the chemical products; a feed preparation unit which supplied purified propylene for both; and a warehouse operation handling shipping and storage. The production process was highly automated and continuous, operating without break 365 days a year, and also quite complex. In particular, polypropylene was manufactured in many different grades, required very exacting quality control, and involved high pressures and temperatures with the consequent risk of explosion.

About 200 people worked at the plant, of whom about 140 were members of the Petrochemical Workers' Local 100. The process workers averaged about 30 years of age and had a minimum of 12 years of education; since there had been no layoffs and no firings in the life of the plant, most had been there for close to 8 years. Their work, like that in any chemical plant, involved considerable responsibility and variety. Because of the size of the complex, people often worked alone and had to establish their own schedules for monitoring the equipment. During "normal" periods, the mix of chemicals had to be watched and finely adjusted, which required a sophisticated understanding of the effects of variations of pressure and temperature on the chemical balance. These periods were interspersed with crises in which intense group problem solving were required to avoid shutdowns of the process. Such crises, combined with the potentially disastrous consequences of mistakes and the wearing effects of shift scheduling, also carried the potential for significant stress.

The central element of the organization structure at Lakeville was the operating team. Any of the six process teams, with about 20 members each, was capable of running the plant; a separate craft team performed specialized maintenance and repair functions. Each team included a union steward and two "coordinators," appointed by management with input from the team members. The coordinator role varied from group to group, but generally centered on sustaining the necessary level of technical competence. In the normal course of events the teams were fully responsible for all aspects of their functioning, including selection of new members (from a short list supplied by Personnel), scheduling, authorization of overtime, discipline, and training.

The pay system for process operators was based on the number of skills they had mastered—a "pay-for-knowledge" system. The top rate, around $19.00 an hour, was attained when a worker could perform 6 of the 10 basic jobs required in the two production processes and the feed preparation unit. Teams were responsible for certifying their members' achievement of each level. Since it usually took 6 years to learn all these skills, by 1986 over 90% of the workforce had reached the top rate. By contrast, in a conventional plant only one or two "lead operators" would be paid at this level.

In addition to learning six production skills, each process worker was also trained in another job in a support area; this was known as the "second skill." Some learned maintenance jobs, such as electrician, pipefitter, or instrument/analyzer mechanic; others worked in the laboratory or the warehouse. The process workers spent about 20% of their work time in their second skill jobs rather than with their operating teams.

The general operation of the plant above the team level was coordinated by several overlapping structures. The *Union/Management Committee* had authority over any issue that touched on the collective bargaining domain, or that the two parties had agreed should be part of the joint decision-making process. Generally, however, this committee intervened only in especially controversial issues. Most problems were discussed first and most extensively by the *Team Norm Review Board* (TNRB), composed of representatives from each of the seven teams, as well as from management and the union. This body lacked formal decision-making power, but had the potential for effective influence because of its broad scope of representation. It generally took up concerns that emerged from the teams but went beyond the scope of any one of them. From time to time the TNRB would establish *task forces* of employees from all parts of the organization to consider major issues, such as revisions in the pay progression system. Finally, there were a number of committees that met only as required, such as one involved in the selection of team coordinators. Altogether more than 25 major committees had been formed in the life of the plant, and over 90% of the Local 100 members had served on at least one of them.

Coexisting with these unusual structures were more common organizational control systems. The management hierarchy was similar to other plants, though simpler than usual: Whereas traditionally there would be four operating and three support departments, the Lakeville plant was defined as a single department. The union local was governed by a five-person executive board. In terms of ultimate authority, management and the union retained almost all of their traditional rights: Task forces, for example, issued recommendations rather than decisions. On occasion management did reject task force proposals, overruled disciplinary decisions of the groups—sometimes because these were seen as too harsh—or vetoed scheduling changes.

A four-step grievance procedure was also available for cases of unresolvable conflict. The first step was discussion by the team members, and the second was the Team Norm Review Board. The approach avoided legalism: The union steward did not formally represent the grievant; discussions focused on problem solving rather than rule definition; and on occasion special task-finding task forces were established. In the first 7 years there were approximately 11 formal grievances, none of which went to the final step of outside arbitration. The national union representative said, "It is the best system for resolving problems that I've seen in any plant."

The written guidelines for the plant formed a similar mixture of elements. A collective bargaining contract was negotiated yearly to set wage rates and basic benefits. Unlike other contracts in the industry, however, it was extremely short—10 pages compared to the common norm of over 60. Among the things left out were management and union rights clauses. Also omitted were all the details of implementation: the pay progression system, vacation and overtime scheduling, confidentiality, hours of work, the grievance procedure, and so on. Plantwide policies on these matters were incorporated instead in the *Good Work Practices Handbook* (or Guidebook) issued by the Union/Management Committee. The GWPH differed from a normal contract in two important ways: It was written in nontechnical language, and it could be continuously renegotiated. Its preface stated:

One of the key premises of our organization design is that the Chemical Plant is a "learning organization." . . . This *Good Work Practices Guidebook* is, therefore, also intended to permit evolutionary process of continuous examination, evaluation and redesign by employees without the traditional constraints imposed by a Collective Agreement.

Each of the teams developed its own set of norms. A major function of the Team Norm Review Board was to ensure that there were no damaging inconsistencies across groups. The norms were informally phrased and always open for revision, but they played a key role in regulating the decisions of the teams. Some of them were:

- Support Team decisions even if not in total agreement.
- Clarify all Team rumors immediately.
- Keep confidential personal problems as long as they don't affect other Teams.
- The Teams will perform a checkout of persons in their weak areas.
- Overtime meals will be supplied if needed.
- Teams should be instrumental in choosing new Team Members.
- Personal records open to respective individual.
- Company provides Teams with up-to-date information.

Framing all these documents was a one-page statement of philosophy which became, especially during the early years, a touchstone in discussions of change. The concepts outlined in the philosophy included participation, personal growth, autonomy, variety, career development, and the minimization of status differentials. (See Exhibit 11.1) The first plant manager said, "The philosophy statement is the conscience for all design issues. For every major issue we come back to it, are we consistent or are we not."

The distinctions among all these structures and documents, and the exact procedures to be followed in using them, remained somewhat fluid, with the decision-making process frequently being redefined for each major issue. Often several layers were involved. Overtime scheduling, for example, was primarily the responsibility of the teams, which could authorize call-ins and

EXHIBIT 11.1 Lakeville Chemical Plant: Philosophy Related to Work Design

The primary objective of [this plant] is to obtain an optimum return on investment in capital and human resources, operating in a safe environment as a responsible member of the community, while being responsive to its employees' needs. It is believed that this objective can best be achieved by establishing and sustaining an organization and management system consistent with the following philosophy.

I. Social and Technical Interactions

The Company recognizes that, in order to achieve its primary objective, it is necessary to give appropriate consideration to design and management of both the social and technical aspects associated with its operation. The former is related to employees and encompasses such areas as organizational structure, levels of responsibility and authority, supervisory roles, communication networks, interpersonal relationships, reward systems, etc., while the latter deals with the physical equipment—its capacity, layout, degree of automation, etc. Although our operations involve a high degree of sophisticated technology which can be exploited to improve efficiencies, it is only through the committed actions of our people that the full benefits can be realized. The social and technical systems are interrelated and must be jointly taken into account to achieve overall organization.

II. Key Considerations for the Social System

A. Communications. Our operation is a tightly integrated system, functioning on a 24-hour, 7-days-a-week basis, with associated support activities carried out on a weekday schedule. Involved are people at various levels and widely dispersed in locations both inside and outside the plant. The nature of our industry is such that delay in recognizing errors or need for operational changes, and taking corrective action, is likely to result in substantial costs. Considerable consideration must, therefore, be given to the design and maintenance of a communication network that avoids lapses of attention and errors in observing, diagnosing, and communicating or acting upon information. Accordingly, information should be directed to the individual capable of acting most promptly and for that individual to have the authority to take action and to be internally motivated to do so.

B. Individual Commitment. An essential ingredient for the success of our operation is a high level of individual employee commitment. Such commitment, however, can only be expected to develop if, in addition to provisions of satisfactory working conditions and terms of employment related to remuneration and benefits, other needs such as the following are met:

1. The need for the content of the work to be reasonably demanding of the individual in terms other than those of sheer endurance, and for it to provide some variety.
2. The need for an individual to know what his job is, how he is performing it, and how it relates to the objectives of the Company.
3. The need to be able to learn on the job and go on learning.
4. The need for some area of decisionmaking where the individual can exercise his discretion.
5. The need for the individual to know that he can rely on others in time of need and that his contribution is recognized.
6. The need to feel that the job leads to some sort of desirable future.

The relative significance of these needs varies from individual to individual and it is not possible to provide for their fulfillment in the same way for all people. It is also recognized that different jobs will provide varying degrees of opportunity for the fulfillment of particular needs. Allowance must, therefore, be made to accommodate individual differences.

EXHIBIT 11.1 Continued

III. Implementation and Maintenance of the Philosophy

In developing a social system within our plant, the following are regarded as key criteria to be incorporated:

1. Policies and practices should reflect the belief that
   a. our employees are responsible and trustworthy.
   b. individuals are capable of making proper decisions related to their sphere of responsibility, given the necessary information and training.
   c. groups of individuals can work together effectively as members of a team with minimal supervision, collaborating on such matters as problem solving (operational and personal), training, "hands-on" operations, maintenance, etc.
2. Employees should be permitted to grow, advance and contribute to their fullest potential and capability.
3. Compensation should be on the basis of knowledge and applicable skills, rather than the task actually being performed.
4. Communications should be open and meaningful. Direct communication across departmental boundaries between specific individuals concerned, without passing through intermediaries, is most effective.
5. Information flow should be for the purpose of ensuring that the most expeditious action is taken on the basis of that information, and should, therefore, be directed to those in a position to most quickly act upon it. Dissemination of such information to others should be only for purposes of appropriate audit and not for the purposes of decisionmaking and exercise of control.
6. "Whole jobs" should be designed so that individuals are involved from start (premises, conception, economics, etc.) to end (evaluation of results).
7. Systems should be designed to provide direct, immediate feedback to the individual of the results of his actions in meaningful terms, to the fullest extent possible.
8. Work should be designed to permit the workers a maximum amount of self-control and discretion. They would be given authorities commensurate with position and held personally accountable.
9. A system should be developed which permits any employee to undertake any task required for the efficient operation of this plant, provided he has the skills to do the work effectively and safely. Artificial, traditional departmental, or functional demarcation barriers should be eliminated and work allocated on the basis of achieving most effective overall results. The training and remuneration program must be designed accordingly.
10. Jobs should be designed and work schedules developed to minimize time spent on "shift."
11. A system and climate must be established for early identification of problem areas with problem solving occurring in a collaborative fashion.
12. It is necessary to have a climate which encourages initiative, experimentation, and generation of new ideas. Error situation should be reviewed from a "what can we learn" standpoint and not from a punitive one.
13. Status differentials should be minimized. It is recognized that bringing about change in an ongoing operation is an extremely difficult task which must be approached realistically and patiently, because we are dealing with deep-rooted attitudes and practices. The most promising opportunities lie in "grass-roots" circumstances. Building a new facility adjacent to an existing one does not necessarily require that

(continued)

EXHIBIT 11.1 Continued

the practices of the older operation be extended to the new installation. Indeed, the new installation provides an opportunity to introduce changes to the older organization.

There are many factors which place restraints on the extent to which the above criteria can be embodied in our management systems. Our task will be to properly examine all our practices and determine strategies for overcoming these obstacles.

Key Criteria to Be Incorporated Into the Organization

1. a. Employees are responsible and trustworthy.
   b. Employees are capable of making proper decisions given the necessary training and information.
   c. Groups of individuals can work together effectively as members of a team.
2. Advancement and growth to individual's fullest potential and capability.
3. Compensation on the basis of demonstrated knowledge and skill.
4. Direct, open and meaningful communications amongst individuals.
5. Information flow directed to those in position to most quickly act upon it.
6. "Whole jobs" to be designed to provide maximum individual involvement.
7. System that provides direct and immediate feedback in meaningful terms.
8. Maximum amount of self-regulation and discretion.
9. Artificial, traditional, or functional barriers to be eliminated.
10. Work schedules that minimize time spent on shift.
11. Early identification of problems and collaboration on solutions.
12. Errors reviewed from "what we can learn" point of view.
13. Status differentials to be minimized.

---

holdovers; but the coordinator, a management appointee, was to be involved in the decision or, if unavailable, informed of the arrangements. Guidelines for these decisions had been evolved from discussions by the teams, which had centered on one key norm: "The opportunity for equalized overtime should be present." The Team Norm Review Board had brought the team norms together and had appointed a task force to ensure that implementation was consistent and equitable. The resulting guidelines were ratified by the Union/Management Committee and incorporated in the *Good Work Practices Handbook.* An example was:

> When offering OT opportunities, . . . the OT opportunity will be offered to the employee who is qualified in the unit and has the lowest *total* number of O/T hours *actually worked plus* OT hours *refused.*

The informal atmosphere of the plant was extremely open. Any worker could walk into any management office at any time for discussion or consultation; this was not a mere promise, but a constant fact of the organization's operation. Few distinctions of dress or privilege marked the different levels of employees.

Certain aspects of the physical design and technology of the plant had been modified to support the guiding philosophy. The computerized information system, central to the management of the continuous flow process, was designed to help educate the operators about the effects of their decisions rather than minimizing their discretion. Workers had full access to financial and production information for the plant, including data on costs, sales, and productivity, and they could assess the exact economic implications of adjusting many of the operating variables. The design was unusual also in having one control center for both production processes, and in locating the quality control laboratory more centrally than in comparable plants; both these aspects enabled the teams to perform a wider variety of functions.

History

During the early 1970s, the parent company of the Lakeville plant began studies of its way of managing its workforce. These studies revealed a strong undercurrent of dissatisfaction and a sense among workers that their capacities were being limited by needless rules and restrictions. The Lakeville plant was designated by corporate management as an experimental site from the beginning of its planning process in 1975 and given unusual leeway to modify traditional elements. An outside consultant on "Sociotechnical Systems" helped to develop the philosophy statement and to examine the relation between technology and employee requirements.

The union was not involved in this first phase of developing the general concepts and approach, and indeed there was considerable disagreement about the wisdom of bringing it in. After much discussion, however, a consensus developed that excluding the union would create a serious risk of destructive confrontation. The Petrochemical Workers were therefore invited to join in planning the concrete design of the organization, including job structures, rewards, training, and controls. The union accepted on condition that it be an equal and visible partner in the process. Within a fairly short time, according to the participants, the joint design team was operating on a cooperative basis with no consistent distinction between management and union representatives. The development of detailed plans and the negotiation of the short contract, which was the first of its kind, were completed during 1977 and 1978.

Careful attention was paid to the selection and training of the initial employees. Applications for team coordinator were solicited by the unusual step of open advertising within the company. The 108 team members were selected from a pool of 2,600 applicants according to criteria that had been worked out in a recruitment workshop. All managers and staff attended a 5-day session to discuss the meaning of the organization principles, while team members attended 7½ days of training to develop team norms and personal skills in group dynamics.

The first 2 years of operation, from 1978 to 1980, were often rocky. In retrospect, managers believed they raised initial expectations too high, underestimated the complexities of start-up, and provided too little technical training. These difficulties were compounded by the fact that about three-quarters of the process workers were young and inexperienced in the indus-try—a deliberate choice of the design team in order to minimize carryover from traditional systems. Both team members and managers also had diffi-culty in working out the new relationships required by the organizational design. An internal facilitator who later worked in the plant commented:

> We were sending a lot of mixed messages to coordinators: build a strong team; maintain control but delegate; be responsible and accountable but work yourself out of a job; be a facilitator but be a lead hand; listen to others but do as I say.

In any case, production in the first 2 years rose very slowly. During the first year several union members felt that management had acted unilaterally and unfairly on some issues. This became focused at the end of the first year in a major union-management conflict: The union demanded contractual right of due process; when management refused, the union took a strike vote, receiving 100% support. The company agreed to a formal grievance proce-dure the day before the potential strike.

By 1980, however, many of the initial problems had been worked out. With the help of an internal facilitator brought on after the first year, progress was made in increasing the shared understanding of the system. Technical prob-lems were gradually solved. Operating measures began a dramatic climb which continued at least until 1986.

The system's ability to adapt and change was frequently tested. By 1986 the plant had had three superintendents and five local presidents. From the beginning, moreover, there were major disagreements and proposals for change.

The Shift Schedule

In the original design the process teams were to operate on traditional rotating 8-hour shifts, which would have resulted in their spending one-third of their time on each of the three shifts. During the start-up phase, however, team members began to explore the possibility of reorganizing the schedule by taking advantage of second skills. They developed a complex proposal that involved four and a half teams working a 12-hour rotating shift, with one and a half teams working 8-hour day shifts in their second skill areas. This plan allowed process operators to spend a startling two-thirds of their time on days, and also permitted more frequent breaks for long weekends or more extended periods.

The plan was, however, initially rejected by management, and it was also opposed by the national union representative. Both felt that 12-hour shifts would increase stress and reduce safety, and they feared the effects of the precedent on other plants. The proposal was nevertheless kept alive in team discussions and the TNRB until an effective consensus was built. The new shift schedule was incorporated into the *Good Work Practices Handbook* late in 1979 and into the contract the next year. Within a short time there was widespread agreement on the beneficial effects of the system.

Coordinators

The original design included a "coordinator" in each work team. Though this role was rather undefined, it was envisaged that the coordinator would be not a traditional supervisor, but rather a facilitator and resource to the teams.

During the initial production difficulties management introduced a second appointed coordinator in each team to help speed up the development of technical skills. From the start the move produced great controversy. Many workers felt that it violated the fundamental principles of self-management embodied in the plant design. Others, however, favored the change—some because it increased their chances of promotion, and some because it reduced their responsibility for difficult decisions, including peer discipline. Furthermore, it turned out to be difficult to reverse the decision, even if there had been agreement to do so, because there was no place to move the second coordinators: The parent corporation was undergoing a downsizing. Though the issue never came to the bargaining table, the union's position was that it refused to accept coordinators back in the bargaining unit if it meant the layoff of current workers.

These problems led to the formation of several task forces. The plant manager issued a "challenge" to those who opposed the second coordinator, offering to go back to one if the teams could show that they could perform the functions of the second. In 1983, the TNRB recommended, and the superintendent approved, that the existing level of two coordinators be maintained, but that the teams gain a stronger voice in their selection.

The exact role of the coordinators continued to be variable and vague. By 1986 it was widely felt that at least some teams could operate without two coordinators; but other teams relied more heavily on them to carry out administrative responsibilities.

Process Operator Progression

The complexity of the plant's start-up phase meant that some skills could be developed much more rapidly than others. This led to inequities in the pay-for-knowledge progression system: Some workers were "stuck" in areas that were still trying to stabilize the production process, while others were learning new skills and moving up the ladder. Management, moreover, felt that some people were moving too quickly, leading to operating inefficiencies. These problems led, in early 1981, to a move to totally redesign the process progression system.

The discussions began in team meetings, then moved to discussions between teams and among union stewards. When a consensus emerged that the problem required plantwide attention, the union insisted that it be handled by the Union/Management Committee rather than the Team Norm Review Board. A task force was formed, including top managers and union executives.

The union immediately held a general membership meeting to clarify the mandate of the task force. An unexpected outcome of this meeting was that a new task force member was chosen by the workers to represent those with prior experience in the industry—a category which was not represented among the union leadership, but which had special concerns about the progression issue.

The task force took 3 months to develop its recommendations. The union membership then spent 2 days reviewing and clarifying the proposal with their elected leaders, which led to some modifications. Finally, the executive board decided to hold a membership vote to ratify the change: the turnout was 100%, with an approval vote of about 90%. Subsequently a specialized, streamlined grievance procedure—distinct from the usual system—was set up to handle inevitable disputes and confusion which resulted from the change.[2]

Craft Team Progression

The skilled craft workers, who formed a seventh team separate from the operating groups, often felt that they were "left out" in the design. In addition to their regular duties, they had to train process operators in second skills, a role which, they argued, went far beyond craft jobs in other plants. Yet despite this perception of increased responsibility, they were paid at the industrywide level, and significantly less than operators who had made the top rate. As more and more reached this top level, craft workers became the lowest-paid group in the refinery. Management, while acknowledging the problem, did not feel it demanded urgent attention.

During 1984 and 1985 the craft workers and the union used several tactics to draw attention to the issue. Craft members refused overtime call-ins, while process operators temporarily "forgot" their craft skills. The union also put forward new contract demands which management was unwilling to meet. Finally the company agreed to set up a joint task force; at that point all the pressure tactics, including the new contract demands, ceased.

The union was less insistent in this case than in the operating progression revision on maintaining a direct role for the elected officials in the decision process. Although an executive board member was initially on the task force, he withdrew once its terms of reference had been developed. The approval of the system redesign, after 3 months of work, was handled essentially by the craft team rather than higher management, the union, or the membership as a whole. The final proposal, in late 1986, involved the ability of crafts workers to achieve higher grades by cross-training in other maintenance skills and gaining additional expertise in their primary skill.

Many other important changes went through similar processes of discussion and participation in the plant's first 7 years. A plan to introduce a new computerized control system in the warehouse, for example, was reviewed and significantly modified by a task force to improve the clarity and efficiency of the control mechanisms. In the period after 1980 productivity increases made possible a reduction in team sizes from 20 to 19; management and the union agreed to seek this goal by attrition, and the teams were continuously involved in evening out their memberships and replanning their distribution of work. As demand continued to increase, however, overtime requirements became so heavy that by 1986 team size was again a concern.

In general 1986 was a quiet year, marked principally by two events. The first was the "pizza incident." In the Lakeville plant, unlike a traditional plant, individuals were allowed to order their own overtime meals. When meal costs began to rise, management looked more closely and found, among other questionable items, a $30 pizza order for one person. They sent out a stern warning to all teams and added the requirement that meal orders be checked first with the coordinator. Feelings among the union membership were strong but mixed: They generally agreed that trust had been abused and that some discipline was necessary, but they resented management's "blanket statements" and punishment of everyone for the faults of a few. Managers were well aware of the criticisms but generally felt it was necessary to assert some control.

The second event was an unusually difficult contract negotiation. The problems were not, on the whole, in local issues, but in proposed changes in the industry pattern by the national union—especially establishing limits on contracting-out. For the second time since the plant's opening, the local took a strike vote, again receiving over 90% support. Even during the negotiations, however, relations in the plant remained calm and open; several workers commented on the lack of tension compared to other plants in similar situations. And the conflict evaporated when a pattern-setting settlement was reached between the national union and another company.

Management's Perspective

Many managers had specific complaints about the design of the Lakeville plant. One common note was the number of meetings: "This place just runs on meetings." Some, especially in the middle levels, felt that aspects of the operation could be tightened up: They felt that the second skill work, for example, was often inefficient, and that rotation of jobs entailed unnecessary start-up and ongoing costs. They also noted that the discipline system sometimes allowed troublemakers to slide along, with no one taking responsibility for bringing them into line. In general, managers felt that their jobs were somewhat more difficult than in a traditional system, because the boundaries of their authority and responsibility were less clear.

These concerns were, however, a minor theme in a general mood of satisfaction. It appeared that while the systems were not perfect, they worked quite well overall. In terms of discipline, for example, most teams were able to work out approaches which suited them. Some groups left discipline primarily to the coordinators; others were quite effective on their own. "Once," commented a coordinator, "when we were having a problem with absenteeism, the team asked me not to come to a meeting. I don't know what happened, but things got much better after that." Managers also pointed out that the pervasive commitment to the values of the plant kept the general level of problems quite low, with much "disciplining" being very informal and preventive in nature.

Some benefits of the system could be clearly documented. A careful, 6-month long evaluation of the plant was undertaken in 1984, studying all aspects of its operation in comparison with several refineries with similar products and technology. The results were so positive that when the corporation opened a major new refinery in 1984, it adopted the Lakeville design almost intact— though without union involvement in the process. At the time of this study the plant was operating well above its design capacity. Most measures of efficiency and quality, moreover, continued to improve significantly for several years afterward.

A major economic advantage could be traced to the second skill concept: Because members of the process teams had developed maintenance and repair skills, they were often able to act quickly to prevent shutdowns of production when it would have taken too long to call in a specialist. They were also able, when shutdowns did occur, to help the craft team members to get the system back up more quickly; and they performed some routine maintenance during the course of their work. Since shutdowns entailed major costs and disruption of schedules, these benefits were extremely important.

The excellent quality performance of the plant could likewise be traced in part to the second skill system: Some process operators worked part time in the laboratory, which encouraged much greater than usual interaction between quality control and production. Finally, the plant was also strong on many other dimensions: Safety, energy efficiency, grievance levels, and waste were all significantly better than the norm. The plant superintendent attributed a considerable portion of this success to the cooperative relations with the union and the high commitment and dedication of the workforce.

As of 1986 the plant superintendent expressed only three important concerns, none of which were critical in the short run. The first was the problem of "topping off": He feared that when everyone reached the top rate, which would happen within a year or two, there would be little opportunity for further advancement over the balance of their careers. The second was the risk of losing momentum and commitment. He and the union's local president both claimed to see some loss of interest in the values of participation and teamwork as fewer major problems came under discussion, and both spoke of the need for renewed training. The superintendent said, "The plant is less turbulent and emotional than it was, it's a lot calmer. But some of the idealism is gone, too."

The third concern was more concrete. There was growing dissatisfaction with the warehousing operation, which was run by process operators as a second skill job. Compared with process work, warehouse work could be relatively low-skilled and routine. This meant, from management's perspective, that they were paying an above industry-average wage rate for the work; and for many workers, that they were doing uninteresting and physically tiring labor. Many people felt that a dedicated warehouse crew would be better. The trouble, however, was that it would be difficult to reassign the warehouse people because there were not enough other second skill jobs for them to go to. In addition, many people pointed out that such a move would run strongly counter to the original philosophy statement by creating a separate class of low-paid, dead-end nonrotating jobs.

The Union Perspective

The Lakeville structure presented difficult challenges for the union. As one steward put it, "Here we are just one party in a galaxy of parties—the union, management, and seven teams." Coordinating this complex set of relationships was more difficult than the traditional role, in which the union is essentially the only channel of worker voice. "You can't stop people from trying to make individual bargains," continued the steward. "You almost want to go back to the old days, when the union cracked the whip and said, 'You will not,' in order to keep our strength and unity."

The breadth of direct participation, and some of the particular agreements necessary to sustain the system, were seen as dangerous by some in the labor movement. Representatives of Local 100 were often heavily criticized, and on occasion heckled and shouted down, when they described their system to other union leaders. These objected most strenuously to the progression system, in which skill acquisition replaced seniority as the principal criterion for advancement, and they were very uneasy with the short contract and the consequent vagueness of union rights.

The national leadership of the Petrochemical Workers, however, was prepared for the challenge. The union had a history of support for worker participation efforts, and it encouraged an unusual degree of internal innovation and participation. It was almost unique among industrial unions in being governed by a board of rank-and-file members rather than full-time elected officials. The leadership quickly grasped the opportunity to be involved in the Lakeville design and maintained a high profile for the union throughout.

The new system required many changes in the structure and strategy of the local. At the start of the process Local 100 was separated from the local at the neighboring oil refinery in order to facilitate these changes; it began by including elements of the plant's philosophy statement in its constitution. Local 100 differed from others in the industry on a number of dimensions:

- *Decentralization:* Though the executive board retained full responsibility for collective bargaining and major issues which touched on the contract, it allowed the teams to deal directly with an unusual range of issues. Management, for instance, offered two options when supervisors went on vacation: either to take on the normal supervisory functions as a team, without extra pay, or to promote someone temporarily to the position. The union, after some debate, allowed each team to make the decision on its own.

Stewards spent very little time in processing grievances. Instead they were responsible for keeping the membership aware of the strategic concerns of the union, and maintaining communication with the executive board. National representatives were strongly impressed by the knowledge and problem-solving ability of Local 100 stewards.

- *Openness:* In general, the union was not insistent about maintaining a unified position in relation to management. It was willing to deal openly with internal disagreements and to build toward consensus. Leaders of other locals expressed astonishment at the breadth and intensity of discussion in membership meetings.

The leadership was also willing to open decision making, even on crucial contract issues, beyond the executive board when necessary. In the discussion of the process progression system, as mentioned before, a new delegate who was not a regular local official was taken onto the task force to voice concerns which were not well represented. "I know it's heresy," said one executive board member, "but sometimes the interests of the local don't coincide with the interests of the members."[3]

• *Accountability:* Several union officers expressed a sense that they were accountable "minute by minute" to the membership. One chief steward who was seen as insufficiently responsive was quickly forced out of office.

• *Leadership:* The difficulty of "cracking the whip" over the membership meant that difficult skills were required from the union leadership. The local president said, "The difficulty is that you have to look at both sides. You have to look at the person with the problem, and you have to look at the people who don't have the problem. A national officer added:

> In a traditional [union] organization it's nice and simple—the boss is obviously wrong. So the executive hammers the boss and defends the union's position. . . . But here, how do you deal with it when it's your own members who are opposing something the union wants? We find ourselves almost playing a mediation role."[4]

Several in the union described their role in the Lakeville plant as "the conscience of the company. We make people conscious of the principles," said one steward. "The company probably regrets that they wrote down so much at the beginning, in terms of the philosophy statement and goals. Now when they do something which violates them, like rejecting a task force recommendation, we can hold them to it." Others focused on the union's role in dealing with general problems beyond the team level: "We try to make the teams aware of the bigger picture."

• *Education:* The union went to unusual lengths to educate members and officers about the development of the participative system. Stewards often held impromptu meetings with members on shifts, as the variation in the workload permitted. At the start, the local executive worked with the membership to develop "an alternative vision" of the philosophy statement, in which it emphasized the importance of developing the self-management capacity of the groups. In 1981 a special weekend school attended by about 60 members was held to take stock of the union's experience with the Lakeville structure and to plan the next steps.

The union was careful, however, to maintain its formal role as the sole worker representative. In the original conception the Team Norm Review Board was to be the primary governing body, with direct authority over many operational issues. Union members of the design team, however, felt that this would "usurp the rightful role of the union." They insisted that the TNRB have only the power of recommending to the Union/Management Committee. Management resisted strongly at first but conceded the point to avoid an impasse. For the same reason the union demanded that the discussion of the process operator progression system be governed by the joint committee. The relation between the TNRB and the Union/Management Committee continued to be a focus of discussion for many years after the start-up.

In general, the fears expressed by some labor officials had not been realized at Lakeville. On several occasions members showed the capacity for traditional militance and unified action—in rallying behind the leadership's strike call over the need for a due-process system, in supporting the craft team members in their demands for a review of the progression system, and in refusing to handle output from a plant under strike by another local. There had been no major splits within the membership, and no grievances over the handling of peer discipline. No local president had been defeated for election in the history of the plant.

The local leadership expressed three major concerns in 1986. Most generally, they felt that many managers had still not fully accepted the concept, and that there were too many occasions in which worker proposals were rejected without adequate discussion. Such problems had developed, for instance, when teams allowed more people to take simultaneous vacations than management thought was acceptable.

Second, the leaders felt that the maintenance of the second coordinator was a fundamental violation of the participative philosophy. Yet at the time there were no joint discussions under way: the union refused to take up the issue without a guarantee from management that any layoffs would come first from coordinators rather than the bargaining unit.

Finally, they felt that some form of gains-sharing would be essential to maintaining motivation and equity once nearly everyone had reached the top rate. The Lakeville management was open to the idea, but it ran counter to corporate wage policy. It seemed unlikely that such a variation would be permitted by the parent corporation in the near future.

The local leadership, like most of their membership, continued to express strong support for "the concept" of the plant. They did, however, feel concern that commitment to the concept might be eroded by the failure to make further progress in developing full autonomy for the teams. "The problem now," said a steward, "is that people want to do more but they're not allowed to."

Diffusion

Efforts were under way by both the union and management to extend the lessons of Lakeville beyond the plant. The union was exploring worker participation efforts with other employers, and it had already instituted with several of them a "continuing dialogue" approach to bargaining—shortening

EXHIBIT 11.2   Lakeville Chemical Plant: Petrochemical Workers Union Policy
on Quality of Working Life

WHEREAS the Petrochemical Workers Union and its predecessors have led many programs in improving working conditions; and

WHEREAS programs like our shorter work week, automatic progression, and workplace democracy have benefitted our membership, and where it is part of the Union's responsibility to continue making improvements in working conditions; and

WHEREAS it is necessary to provide leadership in the labor movement to improve the quality of working life and in turn increase our ability to influence other sectors of society as well, be it

RESOLVED that the Petrochemical Workers Union "Program on Improvements in Working Conditions" be based on the following:

1. Recognition that there are only TWO parties to a collective agreement, the Employer and the Union. That the Union, through the democratic process, is the legitimate representative of the employees of the employer and without a Union there can be only one party with any ability to effect change, the employer. In that case, change can only be accomplished through management judgment and without any real opportunity for input from the workers. The workers' ability to question management's judgment is seriously curtailed by the individual worker's fears of speaking up and the subordinate status of an employee. Without the protection of a collective agreement, the workers' job security can be threatened.
2. Recognition that workers are capable of making decisions given the proper training and authority. In general, workers are honest and trustworthy.
3. In existing Bargaining Units, all changes must be done within the framework of the collective agreement. Any changes desired by the parties which would take it outside of the collective agreement should be negotiated and the required changes to the agreement be ratified by the membership and approved by the National Director.
4. The program should have a built-in monitoring system. One method is a steering committee consisting of senior management and senior union people to continually review and monitor a program.
5. The necessary costs of any program must be advanced by the employer. These costs might include training, paid time off for meetings, renting of outside facilities, etc. One cost may very well be an initial reduction in productivity. We require agreement that productivity will not be the sole measuring standard of the success of a program. If management's sole motive for entering a program is improved productivity then it is doomed to failure.
6. A program must have the demonstrated support of top senior management. This support must be made known to everyone involved.
7. Sacred Cows must be identified early by both parties to determine if what is left is sufficient to allow the development of a program. Two typical sacred cows are job- or tasks-sharing (especially in the trades area), and management rights clauses.
8. The relationship now existing between the Union and employer should be examined. Has the Company resisted any fundamental changes in bargaining? Are the joint safety and health committees working successfully? Where automatic progressions are in effect, has there been problems from undue management interference? What is the grievance record on promotions outside the line of seniority? Are people in

(continued)

EXHIBIT 11.2 Continued

    Industrial Relations decision makers, or are they only resource people to production managers?

  9. There must be a stated willingness on the part of the management to share with us in the decision-making process. This includes greater decision-making authority on the part of the workers as well as a greater input into decisions that may be vested with more senior management people. To accomplish this, it must provide for a high degree of knowledge sharing.

 10. The program development and operation should, as far as humanly possible, be accomplished between management and the Union. The use of outside "advisors" and "experts" should be kept to a minimum.

SOURCE: Submitted by the Executive Board

the fixed contract, and opening many issues to ongoing discussion. Within the Lakeville parent corporation, most plants opened after 1978 contained at least some significant elements of the participative approach; and the new chemical refinery built in 1984, as mentioned earlier, was modeled closely on the Lakeville design.

Yet there were obstacles as well. The management changes had all been made at the plant level; there was no corporate policy favoring designs like that at Lakeville. Indeed, at points corporate decisions had conflicted with the Lakeville concept. They sometimes had the negative effect of preventing consideration of approaches which might develop further participation, such as gains-sharing or other variations on the pay system. On occasion, moreover, the plant manager had had to "fend off" inappropriate interventions from higher levels. In the early 1980s, the corporation mandated a productivity program which included detailed training and mechanisms for employee participation; the Lakeville management had a difficult time winning the right to meet the program objectives in their own way. Some Lakeville managers felt further that the skills they developed in the plant, and the accomplishments they could point to, would not be rewarded if they moved to other sites in the corporation.

Such pressure from beyond the plant was, moreover, increasing for several reasons: Deregulation of the oil part of the business in Canada was leading to an increased corporate focus on cost control and productivity; a general downsizing was in process; and an overall "cultural change" process with an emphasis on these themes was beginning to reach the plant level. The problem of integrating these environmental changes into the Lakeville concept had yet to be faced.

Notes

1. I am grateful to Tom Rankin for his help in understanding the Lakeville plant. His dissertation, *Unions and the Emerging Paradigm of Organization,* is the source of much of the information in this case. The eighth, ninth, and the first part of the fifth of these quotes are from Rankin, op. cit., pp. 159 and 177.

2. Rankin, *Unions,* pp. 170-173.

3. Rankin, *Unions,* p. 129.

4. Rankin, *Unions,* pp. 193-194.

INDEX

ABOUT THE AUTHORS

Lynda M. Applegate is Associate Professor at the Harvard Business School. Her research and recent publications focus on the role of information technology in enabling and supporting corporatewide organization change initiatives and new organization forms. In 1992, she was awarded Harvard Business School's prestigious Berol Faculty Fellowship for research excellence. Since arriving at Harvard, she has taught courses on management information systems, organization design, management control, human resource management, and managerial economics. She also teaches regularly in the Harvard Business School executive education program and is an active international consultant. Prior to joining the faculty at the Harvard Business School, she held a number of management positions and she has held previous faculty appointments at the University of Michigan, the University of Washington, and the University of Arizona. She is an Associate Editor for *Management Information Systems Quarterly*, *Journal of Organizational Computing*, and *Group Decision Making and Negotiation* and is on the editorial board of *Organization Science*.

James D. Berkley worked as a Research Associate in organizational behavior at the Harvard Business School between 1990 and 1994. His primary research interests concern contemporary intellectual paradigms and their interrelation with technological and social change. Along with Nitin Nohria and Robert G. Eccles, he is a coauthor of *Beyond the Hype: Rediscovering the Essence of Management*. He studied literature and philosophy at Williams College, where he received his B.A. in 1990, and is currently working toward a Ph.D. in the humanities.

Anne Donnellon is Associate Professor in the Management Division of Babson College in Wellesley, MA, and a Research Associate at Harvard Law School Program on Negotiation. Her research focuses on the process and performance of decision-making groups. Donnellon is writing a book on cross-functional teams, which identifies the linkages between organizational factors and team dynamics to explain the contractions and challenges entailed by this organizational form. She has a Ph.D. in Organizational Behavior from Pennsylvania State University, an M.A. in linguistics from Columbia University, and a B.A. in English from the University of Cincinnati. She was previously on the faculty of Harvard University Graduate School of Business.

Russell A. Eisenstat is an Independent Consultant specializing in the management of large-scale organizational change and innovation, strategic human resource management, and improving corporate staff group effectiveness. His prior work experience includes 6 years on the faculty of the Harvard Business School. His most recent book, *The Critical Path to Corporate Renewal*, written with Michael Beer and Bert Spector, received the Johnson, Smith & Knisely Award for New Perspectives on Executive Leadership. Eisenstat earned a Ph.D. in organizational psychology from Yale University and has a B.A. from Harvard College.

Frederick M. Gordon studied philosophy at Harvard, and received his Ph.D. in philosophy at University of California, San Diego, working with Herbert Marcuse and Stanley Moore. For the past 15 years, he has been interested in democratic workplaces and why they succeed and fail: working with Demos Research at the Harvard Graduate School of Education empirically tracking the history of union-management democratization efforts; with the Industrial Cooperative Association studying the history of worker-owned businesses; with the Institute for Work Democracy developing models of democratic work organizations; and in an effort to test these models, in a collaborative project with the Center for the Study of Effective Organizations testing the effect of alternative compensation systems on productivity and social relations in laboratory simulations.

Charles Heckscher is Chair of the Labor Education Department and Professor of Human Resources Management at Rutgers University. He has been involved in the theory and practice of participatory organization change from many directions, including working for labor unions, consulting for participatory redesign projects, and writing on employment representation.

Janice A. Klein is Visiting Associate Professor at M.I.T.'s Sloan School of Management, where she teaches both operations management and human resource management courses. Her research focuses on workplace management, job design, and the changing role of lower levels of management with the introduction of new technology and employee empowerment programs.

From 1983 to 1991, Klein was a member of the Production and Operations Management Faculty at the Harvard Business School, where she taught in both the first and second years of the MBA program as well as the Program for Management Development (PMD) and Manufacturing in Corporate Strategy (MCS). Her textbook, *Revitalizing Manufacturing: Text and Cases*, is a compilation of the material she developed for her second-year course, entitled the Management of Operations, which focused on the implementation of new manufacturing systems and technologies.

Klein is a graduate of General Electric Company's Manufacturing Management Program (MMP). During her years at GE (1972-1981), she held various manufacturing and human resource management positions. She received her B.S. in Industrial Engineering from Iowa State University, M.B.A. from Boston University, and Ph.D. in industrial relations from M.I.T.'s Sloan School of Management.

Benn R. Konsynski is the George S. Craft Distinguished Professor of Business Administration and Area Coordinator for Decision and Information Analysis at Emory Business School in Atlanta. He is also Hewlett Fellow at the Carter Presidential Center. He was previously on the faculty at Harvard Business School and the University of Arizona. He holds a Ph.D. in computer science from Purdue University. He specializes in issues of electronic commerce—including electronic data interchange, interorganizational systems, and the electronic marketplace. He serves in board of director and senior management advisory responsibilities at several corporations.

David Krackhardt is Associate Professor of Public Policy and Organizations at the Heinz School of Public Policy and Management, Carnegie Mellon University. Prior to this appointment, he was a Marvin Bower Fellow at Harvard Business School. He received his undergraduate training at M.I.T. and his Ph.D. in organizational behavior at University of California, Irvine. His primary research area is that of understanding how social networks affect social systems, especially organizations. His current research efforts include several new projects, such as developing appropriate methods of data analysis, developing theory and methods for assessing structural properties of an organization as a whole, uncovering the biases in cognitive representations of social structure, and the effects of informal structures on organizational diffusion. He recently completed a review of how theories in social network analysis can be applied to the field of organizational behavior. Formerly an editorial board member for *Administrative Science Quarterly* for 9 years, he now sits on the editorial board of the *Academy of Management Journal*.

Nitin Nohria (Ph.D., Massachusetts Institute of Technology) is Associate Professor of Business Administration at the Harvard Business School. In collaboration with Robert G. Eccles, he has recently written *Beyond the Hype: Rediscovering the Essence of Management*, which examines the role of rhetoric, action, and identity in the management of organizations. He has also coedited *Networks and Organizations: Structure, Form, and Action*, a volume of original articles that explore the usefulness of a network perspective in studying organizations. He currently is investigating the dynamics of organizational change through a series of projects that include studies of the spread and impact of strategic alliances and the quality movement in the 1980s.

Thomas J. Rice is President and Chief Executive of Interaction Associates, an international consulting and training firm. His consulting focuses on workplace innovations, leadership-followership dynamics, and collaborative organization systems. Before joining Interaction Associates, he was a member of the sociology faculty at Georgetown University and a Research Associate at Harvard University. He has served as External Examiner in Social Science at the National University of Ireland and consulted and conducted workshops in over 200 organizations (in the United States, Canada, Mexico, Ireland, Britain, and Hungary). He is the recipient of numerous grants and national awards for teaching and consulting innovations. His current research interest is "the relationship between collaboration, leadership commitment to learning, and productivity." He has presented and published over 30 articles on problem solving, public policy, and strategies for organizational restructuring and transformation.

Maureen Scully is Assistant Professor of Management in the Industrial Relations Group at the Sloan School of Management, M.I.T. She received her Ph.D. in Organizational Behavior from the Stanford Graduate School of Business and spent a year studying business ethics as a Fellow in Harvard University's Program in Ethics and the Professions. Her research interests focus on employees' perceptions of distributive justice, changes in reward systems from both the top down and the bottom up in organizations, and alternatives to merit-based rewards.

John J. Sviokla is Associate Professor and Baxter Fellow in Information Technology at the Harvard Business School, where he teaches first-year marketing. He received his B.A. from Harvard College and his M.B.A. and D.B.A. from Harvard University with a major in management information Systems. His current work focuses on how managers can effectively harness the power of advanced information technology (IT) to create more value for their customers and extract that value in superior financial performance. His most recent books and articles have focused on how to drive sales increases, higher price, or superior quality through a judicious combination of IT and organizational innovation. He has served as an invited speaker and presented papers at international conferences on information systems research and is a member of the National Academy of Management and the Institute for Management Science.

Sviokla is an active consultant and teaches regularly in corporate executive programs. At Harvard, he has taught courses on management information systems, knowledge-based systems, managerial economics, and research topics in the doctoral program. He also teaches in the Harvard Business School executive education programs.